Thucydides

Thucydides

AN INTRODUCTION FOR THE
COMMON READER

Perez Zagorin

PRINCETON UNIVERSITY PRESS

PRINCETON AND OXFORD

Copyright © 2005 by Princeton University Press
Published by Princeton University Press, 41 William Street, Princeton, New Jersey 08540
In the United Kingdom: Princeton University Press, 3 Market Place, Woodstock,
Oxfordshire OX20 1SY
All Rights Reserved
ISBN: 0-691-12351-9

Library of Congress Cataloging-in-Publication Data

Zagorin, Perez.
Thucydides : an introduction for the common reader / Perez Zagorin.
p. cm.
Includes bibliographical references and index.
ISBN 0-691-12351-9 (cl. : alk. paper)
1. Thucydides. History of the Peloponnesian War.   2. Greece—History—Peloponnesian
War, 431–404 B.C.—Historiography.   I. Title.

DF229.T6Z34 2005
938'.05'072—dc22
2004058635

British Library Cataloging-in-Publication Data is available

This book has been composed in Sabon

Printed on acid-free paper. ∞

pup.princeton.edu

Printed in the United States of America

10 9 8 7 6 5 4 3 2 1

This book is dedicated to my son Adam Zagorin,
an acute observer of the connection
between money, politics, and power in
contemporary America

War is the father of all and king of all, and some he shows as gods, others as men; some he makes slaves and others free.

—Heraclitus, *The Cosmic Fragments*, 53

Contents

Acknowledgments

WHILE WRITING this book I have benefited greatly from the wealth of erudition and acumen that classical scholars and historians of ancient Greece have lavished upon Thucydides. I am especially indebted to the historical commentary on Thucydides by A. W. Gomme, Anthony Andrewes, and K. W. Dover (1945–1981), which covers all eight books of the *History*, and to the more recent commentary by Simon Hornblower (1991–1996), which takes the *History* to book 5.24, with a further volume still to follow.

My thanks are also due to the two anonymous readers for the Princeton University Press for their valuable suggestions and comments. I must likewise thank Brigitta van Rheinberg, my very able editor at the Princeton University Press, for her enthusiastic and helpful response to this book. Finally, I wish to express my appreciation to my son Adam for his encouragement while this work was in progress.

Abbreviations

CAH   *The Cambridge Ancient History*, 2nd ed., vol. 5, *The Fifth Century* B.C., ed. D. M. Lewis, John Boardman, J. K. Davies, and M. Ostwald (Cambridge: Cambridge University Press, 1992).

CT   Simon Hornblower, *A Commentary on Thucydides*, 2 vols. (Oxford: Clarendon Press, 1991–1996).

Hammond   N.G.L. Hammond, *A History of Greece to 322* B.C., 2nd ed. (Oxford: Clarendon Press, 1967).

HCT   *A Historical Commentary on Thucydides*, 5 vols. (Oxford: Clarendon Press, 1945–1981); vols. 1–3, ed. A. W. Gomme; vols. 4–5, ed. A. W. Gomme, A. Andrewes, and K. J. Dover.

OCD   *The Oxford Classical Dictionary*, 3rd ed., ed. Simon Hornblower and Anthony Spawforth (Oxford: Oxford Univeristy Press, 1996).

Thucydides

Introduction

OF ALL THE HISTORIANS of war past or present, the ancient Greek Thucydides, author of the *History of The Peloponnesian War*, is the most celebrated and admired. His book, written in the fifth century BCE, is one of the supreme classic works of Greek and Western civilization that continues to speak to us from across the vast gulf of the past. Over the centuries a universal judgment has come to esteem it as one of the greatest of all histories. The famous nineteenth-century English historian Lord Macaulay, whose *History of England* itself became a classic, declared, "I have no hesitation in pronouncing Thucydides the greatest historian who ever lived."[1] The account Thucydides wrote of the twenty-seven-year war of 431–404 between Athens and Sparta is taken up with the details and actions of warfare on land and sea, but also with much, much more. It is equally a story of diplomacy and relations among the Greek city-states, of political values, ideas, and argument, of the success and failure of military plans and strategy, of renowned and striking personalities, and most fundamentally, of the human and communal experience of war and its effects. Its time is the later fifth century, an era in which Sparta, one of the two great powers of Greece, was a formidable militaristic society organized for war, and Athens an intensely vital democracy that ruled over a large empire of subject city-states and stood at the height of its unequalled achievements as a creative center of culture, intellect, literature, and art.

In many ways Thucydides is one of our contemporaries. Despite the twenty-five hundred years that separate him from the present, and notwithstanding the vast differences in the beliefs, values, and general conditions of life between his society and ours in the twenty-first century, numerous aspects of his thinking and of the world he depicts in his book will seem recognizable and familiar to us today. Those who possess any knowledge or memory of the blood-soaked history of the twentieth century—its terrible international conflicts and the huge slaughter of human life caused by its two world wars, the revolutions that brought communism and fascism to power and the horrors of persecution and terror

1

that followed, and the violence and catastrophic collapse of moral standards manifest in the bombing and destruction of cities and killing of civilian populations by all the combatants in their conduct of war—will see resemblances in some of the scenes Thucydides describes. And they will likewise see nothing strange in the historian's observations on the aspirations of men and states to power and domination as permanent and recurrent elements of human nature in politics and international relations.

Because of the Peloponnesian War's wide extent and the large number of states involved, which included not only the Greek city-states but also the mighty Persian empire, Thucydides considered it to be a world war and the greatest conflict that had so far taken place in history. It is not surprising that in later times scholars and others have often looked at the Peloponnesian War as a paradigm of later wars and to Thucydides' work for its lessons and parallels. In 1918, at the conclusion of the First World War, the Briton Gilbert Murray, one the most famous Hellenists in Europe and renowned as a translator of some of the masterworks of Greek literature, published a lecture, *Our Great War and the Great War of the Ancient Greeks*, which was based on Thucydides. Crediting the Greek historian with the faculty of seeing "both present and past . . . with the same unclouded eye," it noted a number of similarities between the war of 1914–1918 and the Peloponnesian War. It closed with the fervent hope that after the vast suffering and destruction of the war just ended, mankind would take the opportunity of building out of the ruins a better, more cooperative life between nations.[2] This hope, of course, was destined to be unfulfilled, as Thucydides himself would have guessed, and two decades later the Second World War began.

Likewise in 1947, following this second great war, General George C. Marshall, U.S. Secretary of State and author of the Marshall Plan, which led to the reconstruction and revival of a severely war-damaged Western Europe, spoke of the Peloponnesian War's importance for understanding the contemporary world. Addressing an audience at Princeton University, he suggested that no one could think with full wisdom and conviction about some of the basic international issues of the present "who has not reviewed in his mind the period of the Peloponnesian War and the Fall of Athens." This theme was echoed during the Cold War by an American foreign policy expert who wrote in 1952 that "since

World War II Thucydides has come still closer to us so that he now speaks to our ear."[3] A volume of essays in the 1990s by ancient historians and political scientists dealing with international power politics centers on Thucydides and the light his work casts on current problems of foreign and military policy.[4] Many students and theorists of international relations agree in regarding Thucydides as one of the founders and greatest thinkers in their discipline.

I cite these examples not in order to stress the contemporary relevance of Thucydides' *History*, which is of course an arguable question, but to indicate how widely his work has been seen as a major source of political insight.

In the introduction to his course of lectures at the University of Basle on Greek cultural history, later published posthumously as his distinguished book *The Greeks and Greek Civilization*, Jacob Burckhardt, a leading European historian of the nineteenth century, said of himself, "the lecturer is and will remain a learner and fellow student, and it must also be pointed out that he is not a classical scholar."[5] It is in the same spirit that I have written this short book on Thucydides and his *History*. As a historian, my professional field of study is not ancient Greece, and my research and books deal chiefly with the thought, politics, religion, and culture of early modern Britain and Europe in the sixteenth and seventeenth centuries. As a student, however, I took classes in Greek and Latin and developed a lifelong interest in the history of Greece and Rome. I first read Thucydides when I was in my twenties. During the years since, I have often returned to him as one of the towering and most compelling figures of Western historiography. A recent rereading, in particular, has been for me an intense experience that I should like to share.

Even in this present age of computers, almost instant communication, and continually advancing technology, when the past seems to recede from us more swiftly than ever before, ancient Greek literature, culture, and philosophy continue to be recognized and studied as a great legacy to all subsequent generations and a unique formative element in the creation and evolution of our Western civilization. Because of Thucydides' high stature as a historian and thinker, present-day humanists and teachers of the humanities generally agree that his *History* is just as essential a part of a true liberal education as are Homer's *Iliad*, Sophocles'

Oedipus Rex and *Antigone*, and some of the *Dialogues* of Plato and writings of Aristotle. College students are sometimes lucky enough to encounter Thucydides in survey courses in the humanities or the history of Western civilization in which they may learn a little about him from a textbook or be required to read a few selections from his *History*. This kind of exposure, however, is usually too limited to give them much of a conception of his work and achievement. My purpose in writing this book, therefore, is to promote a wider interest in Thucydides and especially to assist common readers, whether students or intellectually curious people who have heard of the Greek historian and wish to know more, to understand and appreciate his work. It is not, needless to say, a substitute for reading him, but rather an introduction and invitation that I hope will encourage them and whet their desire to read and experience him themselves.

In his lectures on Greek history, Burckhardt also told his listeners that "it is perfectly in order to make use of excellent translations."[6] The literary, philosophical, historical, and other writings that have come down to us from classical antiquity continue to live today not only because of the indispensable labors of generations of scholars, but because they exist and can be read and taught in modern translations. To understand and appreciate Thucydides' *History*, it is not necessary to know Greek. I hope this statement will not be misunderstood. Something is always lost in translation, and only proficient readers of the original text can perceive the nature, peculiarities, and flavor of Thucydides' style and the nuances of meaning in his use of language. Those who do not read Greek, however, should have no difficulty in following the course of events and extraordinary speeches the *History* records or in comprehending its author's remarkable thoughts. I have always read Thucydides in translation and have made continual use of translations in writing this book, although I have also sometimes compared passages I have discussed with the Greek original.

There are at present a number of good English translations in various editions which can be recommended to the reader. Those by Richard Crawley (1874) and Benjamin Jowett (1881) were done in the Victorian era and have been often reprinted. Crawley's translation is now available in a new revised edition, *The Landmark Thucydides* (1996), edited by Robert L. Strassler, which contains an introduction by Victor Davis Hanson, a well-known specialist on Greek military history, and includes many notes and maps as well as informative appendices by a number of scholars. An abridged edition of Jowett's translation, published in the Great Historians series by the Washington Square Press in 1963, is preceded by an excellent introduction by a leading ancient historian, P. A. Brunt, which has been reprinted in Brunt's *Studies in Greek History and Thought* (1993). Charles Foster Smith's translation (1923) is presented in parallel pages with the Greek text of Thucydides in the Loeb Classical Library edition published by the Harvard University Press. The most widely read translation today is the one by Rex Warner, British poet, novelist, and classical scholar, which was first published in 1954 in the Penguin Classics series and has gone through many later editions. It includes an introduction by M. I. Finley, another distinguished historian of the ancient world.

Since this book is an introduction to Thucydides, not to the Peloponnesian War, I should also tell the reader that the fullest modern account of the war from its origins to its end is Donald Kagan's outstanding four-volume work (1969–87) a clearly written, deeply informed scholarly narrative that serves as an indispensable supplement to Thucydides' *History*. In 2003, Kagan also published a new, one-volume account, *The Peloponnesian War*, based on his earlier study.

I have intended this book to be brief in keeping with its purpose. Its plan is as follows. The first four chapters discuss some of the background to Thucydides' *History*; its subject, method, and structure; its explanation of the causes of the Peloponnesian War; and the historian's view of the Athenian leader Pericles. The next three chapters present an overview or survey of Thucydides' account of the war to the point in 411 where he ceased writing, and also continue the story to the end of the war in 404. The main focus in these chapters is on a number of revealing and significant events as related by Thucydides, such as the revolution in Corcyra, the Melian Dialogue, and the Sicilian expedition. The eighth and concluding chapter deals with Thucydides as a thinker and philosophic historian. My emphasis throughout has been on the mind of Thucydides and his treatment of the subject and for this reason I have quoted him liberally. I have included a number of notes in every chapter in order to document certain points and to suggest further references to the reader. To assist the reader, I have also added a short list of some recommended works at the end of the volume.

Thucydides' *History* enjoys a lasting fame and is in no need of further tributes. Its masterly narrative and analysis of the conflict between Athens and Sparta in a high age of Greek civilization has much to teach us. I shall be very satisfied if this book helps to increase the number of his readers and to provide them with some insight into his work.

Thucydides' *History* and Its Background

> My history is an everlasting possession, not a prize
> composition that is heard and forgotten. (1.22)

THE PROUD and unparalleled claim that Thucydides made at the beginning of his *History of the Peloponnesian War* has been borne out by time. Of all the world's historians—whether ancient, medieval, or modern—he has been the most extensively read and studied. From the early nineteenth century onward, the amount of scholarship devoted to him and his epoch-making history has steadily increased and by now far exceeds that dealing with any other historian. What is the explanation of this remarkable fact about a writer born in classical Greece whose work belongs to the very beginning of Western historiography? A part of the answer is that Thucydides' narrative of the great war of 431–404 BCE between Athens, Sparta, and their allies, although he left it unfinished, is the only continuous contemporary historical account of it that exists. The Greek authors who continued his history or wrote on the same subject later lacked Thucydides' authority and were intellectually not on the same level.[1] He is therefore the chief source for this vital central period of Greek history, which began when Athens as an imperial city-state under democratic government stood at the height of its power and glory.[2] But this in itself hardly suffices to explain why so many scholars of varied interests have continued to focus their attention on Thucydides. The principal reason for his unique position in Western historiography is the austere and powerful philosophical intellect he brought to the writing of history and the resulting originality, intensity, and sweep of the vision that informs his work. While one may not be particularly interested in the Peloponnesian War and its details, it is impossible not to be interested in the mind of Thucydides and the kind of history it created. George Grote, one of the foremost nineteenth-century historians of ancient Greece and Athenian democracy, very justly said of him that "his purposes and conceptions . . . are exalted and philosophical to a degree almost wonderful, when we consider that he had no pre-existing models before him from which to derive them. And the eight books of his work . . . are not unworthy of these large promises, either in spirit or in execution."[3] The story Thucydides tells in his *History* is about the triumphs, pathos, and tragedies of war; it might be subtitled "The Greatness and Decline of Athens as a Superpower." It contains gripping depictions of combat and the vicissitudes of war, and penetrating, somber insights on politics, the use of power, interstate relations, and the human condition, which are conveyed both in his narrative and searching analyses of events and by means of the extraordinary speeches and debates he records. These distinctive features together with his striking comments on historical method have exerted a continuing fascination (the word is not too strong) upon generations of scholars and readers. They have caused Thucydides to be commonly regarded as not only the greatest of ancient historians but also as one of the greatest historians of all time, so that his history has become one of the classic and canonical works of Western culture.

For almost two centuries classical scholars, philologists, editors, textual commentators, and historians of ancient Greece have subjected the work of Thucydides to the closest scrutiny. In what was considered for many years the basic Thucydidean question, they have devoted intense effort to the problem of determining the successive stages and probable dates of the *History*'s composition and its revisions without, however, reaching any agreement on the subject. They have painstakingly analyzed its language and its difficulties of style and striven to clarify obscure passages in the text. They have likewise sought to identify errors, omissions, partiality, and even deliberate misrepresentations in Thucydides' treatment of the events leading to and occurring during the war. This great mass of literature is generally technical and addressed very largely to specialists. Most of the problems with which it deals need not concern the common reader, although several of them will be touched upon in this book.

Only a few facts are known about Thucydides' life, nearly all of which derive from his own statements in his *History*. Born around 460, he was an Athenian citizen who loved his city although not its democratic polity. The son of a wealthy and aristocratic family, he was related to several other of the most eminent Athenian families and owned inherited mining properties in Thrace in northeastern Greece. He belonged, therefore, to the same class of rich, well-born men as those who are shown in Plato's *Dialogues* gathered around Socrates in philosophical discussion. His high social position was a great advantage in giving him access to well-placed sources who could provide him with information for his history. The latter states that he began to write it at the outset of the war in 431 (1.1). He took part in the war himself after being chosen in 424 as one of the ten annually elected Athenian generals. Unhappily, he was unsuccessful in his military operations and was voted into exile because of his failure. Virtually nothing is known about his remaining years. He spent most of them in exile and probably did a lot of traveling to collect information for his history, although he would have been able to return to Athens at the conclusion of the war. He died around 400 or a few years later, leaving his work unfinished. It stops abruptly in mid-411, seven years before the Peloponnesian War came to an end with Athens's total defeat.[4]

The Greeks of Thucydides' time and the preceding age lived mostly in independent city-states scattered all over mainland Greece, the islands of the Aegean Sea, the Ionian coast of Asia Minor and its offshore islands, and southern Italy and Sicily. Some of these cities originated as colonies founded by their older mother cities in Greece itself. Every city-state or *polis* included its surrounding rural territory and inhabitants, and all strove to remain independent and autonomous. Often enough one city was in rivalry or at war with another. Loss of independence by external domination or conquest was for any city the ultimate calamity and seen by its citizens as a fall into slavery. Thucydides shows that this was one of the major issues in the Peloponnesian War.

In the sixth and fifth centuries, many Greek city-states were subject to bitter class conflicts, and most of them were either oligarchies dominated by a well-to-do minority that monopolized political power and rights, or democracies in which the *demos* or "people," the whole body of adult male citizens, including the poor and propertyless, possessed supreme power. A few cities were ruled by tyrants, the term the Greeks used for men who wielded absolute power acquired illegitimately. In northern Greece lay the monarchy of the Macedonians, a people whom the other Greeks of the city-states regarded as semibarbarous. To the east, extending all the way from the coast of Asia Minor to central Asia and over Mesopotamia, the Levant, and down into Egypt, was the Persian monarchy, a huge empire whose monarch the Greeks simply called the King or Great King. Throughout Greece and the entire ancient world east and west, the institution of human slavery was universal.

In the later sixth century Athens and its rural territory of Attica was ruled by the tyranny of Peisistratus and his sons, but following its overthrow in 510, the reformer Cleisthenes initiated political changes that made the city into a democracy. Democratic institutions expanded during the fifth century, in the course of which Athens developed into a genuinely popular state which put down deep roots. In the later fifth century the population of Attica may have been between 150,000 and 250,000, of which the number of Athenian citizens amounted to 30,000 or more. The government of Athens was based on a sovereign assembly (*ekklesia*) in which all citizens had the right to participate personally and which made its decisions by majority vote. Women, the large numbers of slaves, who were owned both by private individuals and the state, and resident foreigners, of whom there were many in Athens, were excluded from the rights of citizenship. The nine highest magistrates or archons, the council of five hundred (*boule*) that exercised daily executive authority, the ten generals (*strategoi*) in command of the city's naval and military forces, numerous officials, and juries in the law courts were chosen annually either by election or by lot. All were accountable to the citizen body. Citizens received payment for involvement in various governmental functions like membership on the large juries of the Athenian courts, and after 403 were also paid for attending meetings of the assembly. Athenian democracy insured that men of little or no property, who formed the majority of the citizens, were fully entitled to make their will felt in state decisions and take part in public affairs. Its polity stood for the ideal of liberty (*eleutheria*) in the double sense of both the enjoyment of political rights by the mass of the people and of individuals being free to live as they pleased as long as they were law-abiding. One of its essential principles was the rule of law and equality before the law (*isonomia*).[5]

In contrast to Athens, Sparta was a strict oligarchy. Its citizens, the Spartiates, were a small exclusive warrior caste ruling over a large indigenous peasant population of Messenians and Laconians whom they had conquered and reduced to serfdom in the eighth century. These enslaved people, known as helots, were forced to serve and cultivate the estates of their Spartan masters, who were forbidden to engage in agricultural labor or economic activity. Beside citizens and helots, the city also included perioeci or "out-dwellers," who lived in their own village communities. These were formally free, but had no political rights and occupied themselves in trade and manufacture. Spartan social organization and culture were unique in Greece. Separated from their mothers at the age of seven, boys were reared apart for fourteen years in a system of severe training designed to make them disciplined, courageous, and skillful fighters in war, capable of the hardest physical endurance, and ready to sacrifice themselves for their city and people. Although allowed to marry earlier, they were not free to establish households until they reached the age of thirty, and continued to be part of a masculine warrior society not only in their regular drills and physical exercises, but through their common messes or eating clubs, at which they were obliged to dine daily until they were sixty. Spartan women, whose main function was to breed soldiers, also received physical training and were believed to be less subject to their husbands than any women in Greece. Spartan society lived in constant vigilance against the danger of a helot revolt. It did not welcome foreigners and its government was secretive. Its principal political institutions were a citizen assembly and an authoritative council of elders, an executive of five annually elected magistrates called ephors, and two hereditary kings who led its armies in war.[6]

In the course of the late sixth and the fifth century, Athens and Sparta rose to ascendancy over the other Greek cities as the two predominant powers in Greece. In this process, Sparta preceded Athens, whose main development occurred in the aftermath and largely as a consequence of the Persian War of 490–479. In 490, Darius, king of Persia, who already ruled over the Ionian Greek cities of Asia Minor and had recently crushed their rebellion, sought to expand his empire to mainland Greece. This first attempt at conquest failed when a coalition of Greeks defeated the Persians at the battle of Marathon. Ten years later Darius's son and successor Xerxes made a second attempt, leading a great invading army into Greece, but again the Persians were forced to turn back after their defeats in 480 in the naval battle of Salamis and in 479 on land at Plataea and Mycale. Not all of the Greeks were willing to join in the resistance to the Persians. Of the cities who decided to do so against seemingly overwhelming odds, Athens and Sparta played the leading role and gained the greatest fame as champions of the Greek cause. The Greeks' success in their struggle against Persia had a profound effect in shaping their identity. Their victories against an Asian monarchy so much mightier than themselves became lastingly enshrined in their historical memory as monumental events bearing witness to superlative Greek courage, heroism, and sacrifice in defense of Greece's freedom and independence.

Sparta had started to build up a system of unequal alliances in which it was dominant a few decades before the Persian War. This system, which eventually became the Peloponnesian League, consisted of a number of cities in the Peloponnese and some others located elsewhere. Sparta's aim in creating the League was to provide a protective shield around itself and its homeland territory in the Peloponnese. The Peloponnesian League's members—among whom were Tegea, Corinth, Megara, Thebes, and Aegina—were not allied to one another but only to Sparta, to which each was separately bound by treaty. By the terms of the latter, every ally obliged itself under oath to have the same friends and enemies as the Spartans, to help them against a helot revolt, and to follow wherever they might lead. In return, Sparta's obligation was to aid any of its allies who were attacked by a third party. Sparta led the Peloponnesian League as a hegemonic power. It summoned and presided over its meetings and commanded its army in any joint action. At meetings of the alliance each member had one vote and decisions for common action required the approval of the majority.[7]

While Sparta became Greece's greatest land power, Athens turned its energies to the sea. Prior to the Persian invasion of 480, the Athenians followed the advice of their leading statesman Themistocles to build up their fleet. They continued this policy in the subsequent period and thus emerged in the subsequent years as the supreme naval power in Greece with the biggest fleet of warships and merchant vessels, a vigorous economy, and an expanding trade throughout the Greek world. Sparta eventually withdrew from the conflict with Persia, which went on intermittently for a number of years. Athens meanwhile took the lead in company with some of the other Greek cities of the Aegean islands, the western coast of Asia Minor, and the area of the Hellespont (the modern Dardanelles), in forming an anti-Persian defensive alliance in 477. This body of allies, the Delian League, held its meetings in the sanctuary of the god Apollo's temple on the island of Delos, where its common treasury was also kept. With Athens as their head, the cities belonging to the alliance—which included Samos, Lesbos, Chios, and others with naval forces—agreed to contribute either ships or money for their joint defense and action against Persia. During the following decades, the Delian League ceased to be an alliance of equals and fell increasingly under Athenian domination. By the mid-fifth century it had developed into an Athenian naval empire in which the allies had been transformed into Athens's subjects to a greater or lesser degree. At the outset or in the early years of the war, the empire numbered about three hundred subject states. Imperial Athens did not permit any of its allied cities to quit the alliance. It exacted tribute from them, compelled cities to join, forcibly repressed allies who tried to revolt, and imposed settlements of Athenian citizens upon them. In 454 it transferred the League's treasury from Delos to itself, a clear sign of its hegemonial position.[8] The 450s also saw Athens strengthen itself militarily and strategically by the construction of its Long Walls, the great fortification that assured the protection of the road connecting the city with its vital port at Piraeus. It was at this period also, from around 460, that Pericles, a man of aristocratic birth and outstanding political gifts, attained to the unrivaled position which he held till his death, as the preeminent leader of the Athenian democracy. This brilliant statesman, a central figure in Thucydides' *History*, is depicted by him in a very favorable light.

It may seem like a paradox or contradiction that Athens, a steadily evolving democracy which embodied a conception of political and individual freedom, should become at the same time an oppressive imperial state that dominated and exploited its allies. The Athenian democracy, however, benefited materially from its empire in numerous ways. Imperial rule brought wealth, business, profit, and slaves to Athens. It drew streams of suitors and litigants to the city and provided increasing employment and opportunities for its people in many lines of work, including ship construction, maritime and other commerce, and manufactures. It also provided allotments of land to those of Athens's people who went out as colonists to subject cities. The rowers who were needed for the great Athenian fleet received a daily wage for their labor. The accumulation of allied tribute that flowed into Athens helped pay for the costs of its government, festivals, public works, and beautification. The Parthenon, the magnificent temple on the Acropolis dedicated to Athens's patron goddess Athena, was built between 447 and 432 from the proceeds of empire. Athenian policy also as a rule favored the overthrow of oligarchies in its allied cities and support of the democratic faction. The citizens of Athens had no compunction in imposing their dominion on their imperial subjects. They had no wider allegiance than to their own city, which was their chief concern, and as Thucydides' *History* shows, they were intent only upon its and their interests.[9]

Thucydides usually refers to the Spartans as Lacedaemonians because both Sparta and the territory in which it was situated in the southern Peloponnese were known in ancient times as Lacedaemon. I shall refer to them mainly as Spartans. The historian makes a point of contrasting the Spartans and the Athenians, not only as the enemies they became, but also in their different traits as peoples. The Spartans were highly conservative and wedded to their traditions, stolid and slow to act, and famously terse and economical in their speech. The Athenians were quick, adventurous, articulate, imaginative, inventive, and daring. In due course, the Peloponnesian League under Spartan leadership came into conflict with Athens's expansionist ambitions aimed at conquests in mainland Greece. For over a decade after 460, sporadic warfare took place between the two power blocs of Athens and Sparta, a period that modern historians have termed the First Peloponnesian War. Neither side was able to win this conflict, which ended in 445 with the agreement of the parties to a Thirty Year Peace maintaining the status quo. Sparta retained its dominant status on the Greek mainland, while Athens remained in control of the sea and its empire. The peace treaty continued in effect until it was broken in 431 by the onset of the Peloponnesian War. In the first book of his history, Thucydides relates how and why the Thirty Year Peace failed to last and war began in a Greece divided between Athens and Sparta and their allies.[10]

One of the main puzzles about Thucydides is how he came to produce a history so innovative that it had no real forerunner. He was the creator of political history, which did not exist before him, and his analyses of events and use of speeches were unique.

Among the Greeks, history in the sense of the systematic investigation of the past was a new literary form in the fifth century. Of Thucydides' predecessors one of the best known was Hecataeus of the Ionian city of Miletus, who lived around 500 and wrote about geography and genealogies in which he traced the history of families back to mythical times. Another, whose life spanned the fifth century, was Hellanicus of Lesbos, a mythographer and ethnographer. One of his compositions, the first of its kind, was a local history of Attica, in which Athens was situated, that included lists of mythical kings and Athenian magistrates. Thucydides criticized the accuracy of its chronology (1.97), so had obviously read this work. Only fragments of the writings of these two historians or proto-historians have survived.

They and other early Greek recorders of the past whose names are known to us are entirely overshadowed by Herodotus (c. 485–425), far the most important of Thucydides' predecessors and his elder by about twenty-five years. He was born in the Ionian city of Halicarnassus (Bodrum in modern Turkey), and called "the father of history" by the Roman writer Cicero. His *History of the Persian War* is considered with very good reason the first great work of Western historiography.[11] Conceived on a very broad scale, it is a wonderful pioneering achievement. Herodotus, a humane and tolerant man of keen curiosity about other peoples, traveled widely in Egypt, Scythia, and the Near East. He also lived for a considerable time in Athens, whose democracy he admired, and spent his last years in the city of Thurii, an Athenian colony in southern Italy. The purpose of his history, as he stated it at the opening, was to preserve the memory of the great deeds of the Greeks and barbarians and to explain the reasons for the feud between them. This was an allusion to the wars waged between East and West or Europe and Asia, such as that between the Greeks and the Trojans, which culminated in the Persian War of 490–479. He called what he had written a presentation of his inquiries or researches, *histories* in Greek; hence the title of *History (historia)* later given to his work. Its division into nine books, each named for one of the Muses, was an addition made after his time by ancient editors.

Herodotus's personality and exceptional intelligence, his sense of wonder and the wide humanity that pervade his work, are among the main reasons for its appeal. He was a historian and an

15

ethnographer of broad horizons, much interested in the customs, religion, and geography of the strange lands and peoples he visited. He was especially impressed by the Egyptians, whom he considered as probably the most ancient of nations and to whom he devotes all of his second book. The account he gives of them was based on what he saw himself and on his conversations with many priests during his stay in Egypt. He relates the history of the Lydian monarchy of Asia Minor and Croesus, its king, whom the Persians overthrew in the middle of the sixth century, and the rise of the Persian monarchy through several kings to become the ruler of a vast empire that included the Greek cities of coastal Asia Minor. For the materials of his work in addition to his own observations, he relied on oral testimony, previous writers like Hecataeus, myths, social memory, and tradition. He talked to many people and asked many questions. In dealing with these sources of information, his attitude was neither consistently critical nor generally credulous but somewhere in between. He believed some of them but not others. To his readers he declares that he considers it his duty "to report all that is said, but I am not obliged to believe it all alike—a remark which may be understood to apply to my whole History" (7.152). When he records conflicting statements, he refrains from judging between them. "Which [of them] is true," he says in one place, "I shall not trouble to decide" (1.5). His work is full of the most varied facts, speeches, stories, and digressions for whose truth it is impossible to vouch. Although his narrative, which has been compared to the looping and eddying of a river,[12] is very diffuse in the great number of subjects it covers or touches on, it is united by its overall theme of the conquests and expansion of the Persian monarchy leading to its attempt to subjugate Greece. The fifth and sixth books of the *History* include the revolt of the Ionian Greek cities against Persia in 499, its suppression, and its sequel in the Persian invasion of Greece and defeat in 490. The final three books contain the climactic narrative of the renewed Persian effort by King Xerxes in 480 to conquer Greece and its failure. Herodotus viewed the Persian War as a momentous battle for Greek freedom against an Asian despotism. Partial to Athens, he held that "the Athenians were the saviors of Greece," since it was they, he believed, "who, when they had determined to maintain the freedom of Greece, roused up that portion of the Greek nation which had not gone over to the [Persians], and so, next to the gods, repulsed the invader" (7.139).

Herodotus excelled as a teller of tales, some of which are pregnant with moral meaning and pointers to future developments. In one of his most famous stories he relates how Croesus, the Lydian king, boasted to his visitor, the Athenian sage Solon, that his great wealth and good fortune had made him the most happy of men. Solon in reply admonished the monarch that no one could be called happy until his end was known, "for oftentimes God gives men a gleam of happiness, and then plunges them into ruin," so that "in every matter we must mark well the end" (1.30–33). This warning was borne out by Croesus's subsequent tragic loss of his son, the conquest of his kingdom, and his own capture by Cyrus, the king of Persia (1.34, 44, 86).

In connection with the Persian invasion of Greece, Herodotus tells of King Xerxes' conversation with the Spartan exile Demaratus, to whom he had given hospitality and friendship, and whom he asked whether the Greeks would resist his great invading army. Demaratus answered that his countrymen the Lacedaemonians, who were the bravest of all, would fight, because, though free men, "they are not in all respects free; Law is the master whom they own, and this master they fear more than your subjects fear you. Whatever it commands they do; and its commandment is always the same; it forbids them to flee in battle, whatever the number of their foes, and requires them to stand firm, and either to conquer or to die" (7.104). Another of the stories that none of Herodotus's readers is likely to forget is his description of Xerxes seated on a white marble throne on a hill outside Abydos, from which, as he looked down upon the strait of Hellespont, the gateway from Asia to Europe, he saw his fleet of ships covering the waters and his huge army filling all the shore and plain. At this grand sight he congratulated himself at first, the historian reports, but then broke into tears, explaining that he wept because "there came upon me a sudden pity, when I thought of the shortness of man's life, and considered that of all this host . . . not one will be alive when a hundred years are gone" (7.44–46). Equally memorable in his account of the Persian invasion is the episode which relates that when a great storm destroyed the bridge Xerxes had ordered built across the Hellespont, "he was full of wrath, and straightway gave orders that the Hellespont should receive

300 lashes and that a pair of fetters should be cast into it. It is certain," the historian adds, "that the king commanded those who scourged the waters, to utter, as they lashed them, these barbarian and wicked words, 'Thou bitter water, thy lord lays on thee this punishment because thou hast wronged him without a cause. . . . Verily, King Xerxes will cross thee, whether thou wilt or no. Well dost thou deserve that no man should honor thee with sacrifice, for thou art in truth a treacherous and unsavory river' " (7.35).

Because of the Persian monarch's arrogance and desire for aggrandizement, Herodotus had no doubt that the gods would punish him. Running through his work is a religious piety, a belief in the principle of retribution that evil deeds will be repaid, and a faith in oracles, signs, and supernatural causation.[13] When great wrongs are done, he said, "the gods will visit [the wrongdoers] with great punishments" (2.120). He was convinced "that whatever is human is insecure" (1.86), that "happiness never continues long in one stay" (1.5), and that events were ruled by fate determined by the will of the gods. *Hubris*, behavior that intentionally humiliates or dishonors others in order to demonstrate one's own superiority, he was certain would inevitably meet with nemesis from the divine powers, as was shown by Xerxes' defeat.[14] When the Persians were retreating, he records the following declaration about the Greek victory, which the Athenian leader Themistocles delivered to a war council: "Be sure we have not done this by our own might. It is the work of gods and heroes, who were jealous that one man should be king at once of Europe and Asia . . . a man unholy and presumptuous . . . who even caused the sea to be scourged with rods and commanded fetters to be thrown into it" (8.109).

Thucydides' work is very unlike that of Herodotus, whose history he knew and used, and several of whose statements he corrects without ever mentioning the earlier historian's name. Not only was his *History* much more integrated, but he was also more rigorous, had much stricter standards of evidence, and was far more concerned with truth and accuracy. Unlike the poets and chroniclers to whom he refers disparagingly, he expressly excluded the "mythical" or fabulous from his narrative (1.21).[15] Very likely he placed Herodotus among the class of writers who he said take little trouble in the search for truth and "readily . . . accept whatever comes first to hand" (1.20). Thucydides' exceptional intellectuality, the use he made of the speeches in his history, and the penetrating political analyses they contain, have no parallel in the work of the older historian. He also differed from him in his apparent lack of belief in the gods or the intervention of supernatural forces, even though he did recognize the important role that chance could play in human affairs.[16] Unlike Herodotus, he doesn't take pleasure in telling good stories, but relates the incidents of the years of war in ways that are often deeply moving. It was probably Herodotus's work that he had in mind in the famous comparison he drew between "a prize composition that is heard and forgotten" and his own *History of the Peloponnesian War* as "a possession for all time" (1.22).[17]

The originality of Thucydides' work is connected with the extraordinary ferment of thought and the varied intellectual influences to which he was exposed in his formative years in Athens. While it is difficult to trace these influences directly, it can hardly be doubted that the changing intellectual climate of Athens in the period between the end of the Persian and the commencement and continuance of the Peloponnesian War left its mark upon him. Thucydides would have been only in his late twenties when he began to write his *History* at the start of the war. As he talked to witnesses and studied the events of the years that followed, he must have grown in thought and come into contact with many different ideas and perspectives. During his lifetime the city of Athens became the foremost cultural center of Greece and witnessed an enormous outburst of creativity in many fields—science, philosophy, literature, and the arts. The Athenian writers of the period included the creators of tragic drama, Aeschylus (d. 456), Sophocles (d. 406), and Euripides (d. 406), the latter two being Thucydides' older contemporaries. He could have seen and read their plays, which, in reworking mythical themes and legends and dealing with historical subjects, presented tragic conflicts, clashes of values and ideas, and penetrating human portraits. There are in particular striking affinities between him and Euripides, the youngest of the three great tragic dramatists, which suggest an indebtedness to the playwright, an innovative poet and artist whose plays were distinctive in their new psychological realism, their exploration of the irrational forces in human nature, their concern with contemporary issues, and their bold iconoclasm. The growth of rationalism in philosophy and social thought was among the most

19

significant developments of the time. The presence of leading thinkers and teachers who came from elsewhere in the Greek world to reside in Athens contributed to the intensity of philosophical activity. Alongside speculation about cosmology and the nature of the physical world by philosophers like Anaxagoras and Democritus (one of the founders of Greek atomic theory), a new interest in man and the nature of justice and the good emerged in the mid-fifth century. Socrates (469—399), an Athenian citizen and the teacher of Plato, was the foremost of the philosophers who exemplified this shift of attention from nature to man. The theme of justice—its nature and obligations—is prominent in Thucydides' *History* in a number of its speeches.

The Hippocratic school of medicine likewise flourished in these years, producing a corpus of medical writings of which some rejected popular superstitions in favor of a naturalistic attitude toward the understanding and treatment of disease. Certain treatises by the physicians of this school stressed the necessity of the careful recording of symptoms and the search for their underlying causes. The influence of Hippocratic medicine upon Thucydides is probably seen most clearly in his vivid portrayal of the dreadful plague that struck Athens in the second year of the war (2.47–54). While certainly not devoid of sympathy for its victims, it is a largely a careful and objective account. It depicts in detail the disease's symptoms and stages, the effect of crowding in promoting its spread, and the high mortality, physical suffering, and psychological and social demoralization it caused owing to "the violence of the calamity" (2.50–52). Having himself contracted the plague but survived it (2.48), Thucydides was in an excellent position to observe it closely at firsthand.

One of the most significant factors in Thucydides' intellectual formation was his exposure to the unconventional and radical conceptions of the Sophists, which centered on man and his life in society. The German philosopher Hegel was apparently the first to speak of the Sophistic movement of the later fifth century as the Greek Enlightenment, thus comparing it to the eighteenth-century Age of Enlightenment in Europe, which brought the solvent of secular reason to the examination of religion, politics, and morality.[18] The Sophist were active as philosophers and professional teachers of rhetoric and other subjects in Athens during and after Thucydides' time. Among them were such noted figures as

Protagoras of Abdera, Hippias of Elis, and Gorgias of Leontini, the last of whom exerted a major influence upon oratorical style and argument when he came to Athens on an embassy in 427. All of these and other Sophist thinkers and teachers appear as characters in some of Plato's *Dialogues*. They stood essentially for an unrestricted rationalism that strongly affected the temper of the age by subjecting traditional morality and law to a skeptical analysis and criticism. The Sophists denied the existence of any absolute truths. Some held that justice was nothing more than a convention or the right of the strong to dominate the weak. Protagoras, the most celebrated of them, was among other things an agnostic who maintained that it was impossible to know whether or not the gods existed. He was also the author of the well-known saying attributed to him by Plato that "man is the measure of all things, of things that are, that they are, and things that are not, that they are not,"[19] a relativistic concept which suggests that all sensory appearances and beliefs are true for the persons whose appearances and beliefs they are. The Sophists, who charged for their instruction, claimed to be able to teach men virtue or *arete*. By this they generally meant that they could show their pupils how to achieve worldly success in the pursuit of one's interests. Their ideas had a corrosive effect upon inherited beliefs and moral principles. One of their key doctrines was the difference between nature (*phusis*) and custom or convention (*nomos*), a distinction intended to demonstrate that moral and political values believed to be universally valid and rooted in nature were merely variable customs dependent on agreement.

As rhetoricians, the Sophists introduced new techniques of argument to equip their pupils to speak effectively in public assemblies and the law courts. Successful persuasion was their aim, and their methods included *antilogy*, which taught a speaker how to argue either side of a question; appeals to ideas of expediency and interest in presenting a case; reliance on arguments of probability or likelihood in the weighing of issues of policy; and considerations based on the innate propensities and psychological driving forces of human nature. As various scholars have pointed out, instances of the ideas the Sophists stood for and of the types of arguments they taught appear frequently in the speeches in Thucydides. Antithesis, the presentation of the opposing sides of an argument, is a very prominent feature; so are arguments founded on probability and on expediency and calculations of advantage. Presumably he would have heard reasoning of this kind in the speeches delivered in the Athenian popular assembly, which he must have attended before the Peloponnesian War and during his years in Athens prior to his exile in 424. He says very little about himself in his history, nothing concerning his education or reading, and makes no mention of the Sophists or any philosophers. We may be pretty certain, nevertheless, that the teachings of the Sophists left a substantial impression upon his thinking and contributed to the character of his history.[20]

The Subject, Method, and Structure
of Thucydides' *History*

> Thucydides, an Athenian, wrote the history of
> the war in which the Peloponnesians and the
> Athenians fought against one another. He began
> to write when they first took up arms, believing
> that it would be great and memorable above any
> previous war. For he argued that both states were
> then at the full height of their military power,
> and he saw the rest of the Hellenes either siding
> or intending to side with one or the other of
> them. No movement ever stirred Hellas more
> deeply than this; it was shared by many of the
> Barbarians, and might be said even to affect the
> world at large. The character of the events which
> preceded, whether immediately or in more remote
> antiquity, owing to the lapse of time cannot be
> made out with certainty. But, judging from
> the evidence which I am able to trust after most
> careful inquiry, I should imagine that former
> ages were not great either in their wars
> or in anything else. (1.1)

THUCYDIDES did not give his work a title or call it a history. This term is a later addition and is used in modern translations. He referred to it simply as a writing, probably because the Greek word for inquiry, *historia*, which Herodotus had used, had not yet become a common term for an inquiry into or a narration of some part of the human past.[1] In the following centuries, Greek, Roman, and subsequent historians appropriated the word "history" for this type of writing, and it became established with this meaning in the various European languages. Similarly, it was not the historian, but later editors who divided his *History* into eight books of numbered parts.

The first thing Thucydides tells his readers about the work he has written is that its subject is a war, the one between the Athenians and Peloponnesians. This statement implies the inclusion of politics, since he takes for granted that the latter are inseparable from war and necessary to its understanding. He is thus the first historian to write a political history centered on a war. The great Prussian military theorist Carl von Clausewitz famously stated in the early nineteenth century that war is a political instrument and a continuation of politics by other means. Thucydides would have agreed with this view and treats the Peloponnesian War as the consequence of a political conflict between Athens and Sparta. For many centuries after his time, politics and war remained the main subject of written histories. Thucydides has sometimes been wrongly criticized for narrowness in focusing on war. A well-known study of Western historiography chided him for ignoring the greatest theme that lay before his eyes: the civilization of Athens in his own and Pericles' time. It also erroneously accused him of believing that war was the only proper subject of history.[2] Nowhere, however, does he make any statement of that sort. The reason he gives for writing about the Peloponnesian War—that it was greater than any previous war, affecting not only the entire Greek world (Hellas), but even the barbarians and beyond—is, one might suppose, a sufficient justification for his choosing it as a subject. Nor is it true that his history is inherently narrow. War, as he very rightly saw, is one of the most testing and extreme experiences human beings and political communities can undergo. It can be decisive in determining the destiny of states, and he shows that when men embark upon it they try to direct it with intelligence and foresight but often fail. Bringing vividly before the reader's eyes its cruelty, horror, suffering, destructiveness, and unforeseen consequences, his narrative drives home the profound lesson that

> in peace and prosperity states and individuals are actuated by higher motives, because they do not fall under the dominion of imperious necessities; but war which takes away the comfortable provision of daily life is a hard master [violent teacher, *biaios didaskalos*] and tends to assimilate men's characters to their conditions. (3.82)

Although Thucydides' *History* is much more concentrated and selective in its treatment than is the work of Herodotus on the Persian War, it nonetheless possesses great breadth in describing the politics, diplomacy, and extended military operations of the combatants, and offers a richness of political reflection that challenges and expands the reader's mind.

Thucydides chose a contemporary subject and says he started to write at the beginning of the war (1.1). Of ancient historians Greek or Roman he is one of the very few who attempted a history of events belonging entirely to their own time, since he lived through the full duration of the conflict between Athens and Sparta. We might pause for a moment to ask whether it is really possible to write a contemporary history. Most historians today would probably answer in the negative. They would be likely to say that it is impossible due to the fact that the evidence necessary for such an undertaking would be very insufficient if not mostly unavailable. That is why worthy contemporary histories of the First or Second World Wars of the twentieth century, for example, could not have been written while they were in progress. Although journalists might have tried to produce such accounts, these would have fallen well short of being adequate histories. Not until scholars had gained reasonably full access to the collections of sources and documents pertaining to the origins, course, conduct, and conclusion of these wars, and been able to make use of additional materials such as the private papers, memoirs, and biographies of the leading figures, politicians, military men, and others who played a role in affairs, would they have considered it possible to write the history of either of these wars. Some might want to add that it is necessary for a period of time to elapse after great events like a war or a revolution before historians who study them can hope to achieve anything like a balanced view and sense of historical perspective regarding their subject.

Thucydides nevertheless proved to be very successful in writing a contemporary history. Of the way he went about it he says very little, although it must have cost him an immense effort to gather the enormous amount of information he incorporated in his *History*, covering as it does such a wide expanse in space and time. For a great many centuries and up to the present day, historians have relied almost entirely on books and other written records of various kinds as sources. These are the documents that they use and subject to critical examination in their investigation and reconstruction of the past. Most of the evidence on which Thucydides based his narrative, however, did not come from books or other written sources. It consisted chiefly of what he saw himself (*autopsy*) and of the oral reports and testimony he obtained from the many witnesses he questioned but whom he does not identify. He would have had to visit many places to collect evidence, and he obtained his knowledge not only from Athenian but from Spartan informants, since he says that "because of his exile" he associated "with the Peloponnesians quite as much as with the Athenians" (5.26). One would suppose that he made notes of all the materials he accumulated. For certain facts he was able to draw on the work of Hellanicus, Herodotus, and other previous historians. Sometimes he derived his knowledge from monuments and inscriptions (e.g., 5.56), and it would likewise have been from an inscription that he quotes the words of an official document, the treaty of peace made in 421 between Athens and Sparta, which temporarily ended the war and failed to last (5.18–19).[3] On occasion he turned for evidence to the Greek poets, quoting, for example, the Homeric hymn to Apollo in order to explain a festival the Athenians held at Delos in 426 (3.104). In the first book of the *History* he presents a concise account of the earlier state of Greece (1.2–19), a description modern scholars call the Archaeologia, to which I shall presently return. To produce it he relied partly on the evidence of material remains to draw some of his conclusions about the Greek past. In explaining what this past was like, he also repeatedly engages in a process of rational reconstruction and deduction to fill in gaps in the evidence and discern causal sequences. Thus he infers that the older towns of mainland Greece and the islands were built inland to protect them from the piracy prevalent at that period, while in later times when navigation became general and wealth accumulated, cities were built on the seashore (1.7).[4] He often uses the word *tekmerion*, which can mean both "evidence" and "inference from evidence," as well as the phrase *tekmerion de*, "evidence for" or "proof of" something. When he declares in the Archaeologia that the term "Hellenes" as the common name for the Greeks was late in appearing, he cites Homer as the "best evidence" of this fact (1.3).[5]

Unlike modern historians, Thucydides does not discuss his sources. He also avoids dealing with historical controversies and differences of opinion, and only infrequently offers any arguments to support his judgments and interpretations of events. Modern scholars generally make use of footnotes not only to cite sources and references but to comment on opposing views. In Thucydides' time, however, books took the form of rolls made from papyrus or leather and were also quite commonly read aloud.[6] There was thus no place in them for footnotes, a device then unknown and one that would not have been consistent with the literary character of a work of history.

Thucydides writes in an authoritative, even magisterial, manner and assumes and expects that the reader will accept what he says. His modern editor Gomme did not exaggerate in stating that "Thucydides has imposed his will, as no other historian has ever done."[7] Although some of his statements can be checked from other sources and occasional inaccuracies have been identified by modern scholars and editors, most of what he relates stands on its own without any independent evidence to corroborate it. In his narrative he provides countless factual particulars on all kinds of subjects. They include the proper names and patronymics of individuals, their places of origin, the names of towns and locations of action, numbers of ships in a fleet or battle, military dispositions, details of combat and sieges, numbers of troops and of men killed or taken prisoner, and so on. He likewise supplies a great amount of historical and topographical data and other information about the different peoples, Greek and barbarian, who became involved in the war. When telling, for example, how Sitalces the Odrysian, son of the king of Thrace and an ally of Athens, raised troops among his Thracian subjects, he mentions the various tribes, the places where they lived, how they were armed, and some of their customs. He adds details as well on the extent of the empire of the Odrysae, observing that if measured by its coastline, "the voyage round can be made by a merchant vessel, if the wind is favorable the whole way, at the quickest in four days and as many nights," while an expeditious traveler going by land who takes the shortest route could accomplish the journey in eleven days (2.96–97). Similarly, in one of the highpoints of the *History*, the account in books 6 and 7 of Athens's Sicilian expedition in 415, the narrative is noteworthy for the quantity of information it provides on the island's geography, inhabitants, and cities. On the whole, although the innumerable particulars that Thucydides put into his pages may seem dry at times, they do not encumber the work, but contribute significantly to its richness and variety. They also testify to the scope, rigor, and minuteness of the researches he

27

undertook in order to produce his *History*, to which they give an enormously strong foundation. Even though the reader cannot test most of these facts, their effect is to create a firm confidence in the historian's credibility and to confirm the reader's overwhelming impression of the reality, veracity, and authenticity of his description of events.

The only instance in which Thucydides presents an extended argument of evidence to support a judgment is when he defends the claim he makes in book 1 at the very beginning of the *History* that the Peloponnesian War was much greater than any previous war. To prove this proposition, he proceeds at once to insert the historical sketch referred to as the Archaeologia (1.2–19), which contains the results, he says, of his "inquiry into the early state of Hellas" (1.20). As a historical survey, this brief account is a small masterpiece, equally remarkable for the linkages it establishes between particular facts and generalizations, its depiction of a lengthy process of historical evolution and progress concluding with the historian's own day, and its use of critical intelligence to achieve a conception of a past that lay beyond the memory and knowledge of any living witnesses. In it Thucydides first shows "the feebleness of antiquity," as proved by the fact "that there appears to have been no common action by the Hellenes before the Trojan War" (1.3). He points to the poverty and small population of Greece in early times as "the real reason why the achievements of former ages were insignificant" (1.11). He then notes the first appearance of sea power with King Minos of Crete, who expelled piracy from the islands he colonized, and later the Greek expedition against Troy, which the wealthy King Agamemnon was able to assemble because as a naval potentate he was the most powerful ruler of his time. Nevertheless, Thucydides asserts that even the celebrated Trojan War "falls short of its fame and the prevailing traditions to which the poets have given authority" (1.11). He next goes on to trace the growth of settlement, the gradual increase and accumulation of wealth, the development of navies many generations later than the Trojan War although their size was still inconsiderable, and the development and progress of Athens and various other city-states. Coming down finally to the period of the Persian War, he relates how the Greeks, led by Sparta and Athens, repelled the Persian invaders, only to become divided thereafter as the allies of either the one or the other of the two cities, who were now the foremost powers in Greece. From the Persian to the Peloponnesian War, he declares, the Lacedaemonians and Athenians "were perpetually fighting or making peace, either with one another or with their own revolted allies: thus they gained military efficiency, and learned experience in the school of danger." Describing the differing methods of the two hegemonic states, he observes that "the Lacedaemonians did not make tributaries of those who acknowledged their leadership, but took care that they should be governed by oligarchies in the exclusive interest of Sparta," while the Athenians, on the other hand, "deprived the subject cities of their ships and made all of them pay a fixed tribute, except Chios and Lesbos." Finally, to underscore how formidable Athens had become, he states that its single power "at the beginning of this war was greater than that of Athens and Sparta together at their greatest, while the confederacy [between them] remained intact" (1.18–19).[8]

Upon winding up this survey of earlier Greek history, he cautions against being misled by the exaggerated fancies of poets and romantic tales of chroniclers who write to please the ear rather than to tell the truth and whose information "cannot be tested." In the case of such remote times one must be satisfied with conclusions "resting upon the clearest evidence which can be had." On this basis he affirms that while men will always judge a war in which they take part as the greatest of the time, "still the Peloponnesian War, if estimated by the actual facts, will certainly prove to have been the greatest ever known" (1. 21). A bit further, as another proof of the war's greatness, he adds that it was a protracted struggle "attended by calamities such as Hellas had never known. Never were so many cities captured and depopulated—some by barbarians, others by Hellenes themselves fighting against one another. Never were exile and slaughter more frequent, whether in the war or brought about by civil strife." Along with these ravages committed by men he also lists the signs that nature itself was disturbed and collaborated, as it were, with the unprecedented horrors and scale of the war: "earthquakes unparalleled in their extent and fury . . . eclipses of the sun more numerous than are recorded to have happened in any former age . . . great droughts causing famines, and . . . the plague which did immense harm and destroyed numbers of the people" (1.23). By the time he concludes this discussion, the reader is likely to be satisfied that the historian has made a convincing case for his judgment that the Peloponnesian War exceeded all previous conflicts in its magnitude.

Thucydides' most important statement concerning his historical method follows immediately after the Archaeologia and pertains to the speeches and events included in his work. Concerning the speeches made either before or during the war, he tells the reader that

> it was hard for me, and for others who reported them to me, to recollect the exact words. I have therefore put into the mouth of each speaker the sentiments most[9] proper to the occasion [*ta deonta malista*], expressed as I thought he would be likely to express them, while at the same time I endeavored, as nearly as I could, to give the general purport [*xumpasa gnome*] of what was actually said [*alethos lechthenton*]. (1.22)

In Crawley's translation, the last sentence in this passage reads as follows:

> [M]y habit has been to make the speakers say what was in my opinion demanded by the occasion, of course adhering as closely as possible to the general sense of what they really said.

As to the events of the war, Thucydides continued,

> I have not ventured to speak from any chance information, nor according to any notion of my own; I have described nothing but what I either saw myself, or learned from others of whom I made the most careful and particular inquiry. The task was a laborious one, because eye witnesses of the same occurrences gave different accounts of them, as they remembered or were interested in the actions of one side or the other. And very likely the absence of anything mythical [*to muthodes*] in my narrative may be disappointing to the ear.[10] But if he who desires to have before his eyes a true picture of the events which have happened, and of like events which may be expected to happen, given the human condition,[11] shall pronounce what I have written to be useful, I shall be satisfied. (1.22)

These remarks distinguish two separate categories, one consisting of speeches and thoughts (*logoi*), the other of events, deeds, or actions (*erga*), and explain that he dealt with them differently. Let us look first at the speeches.

The *History* contains more than forty speeches in direct discourse occupying between a fifth and a quarter of the work. Twenty-seven of them are political speeches, and one is a political dialogue; of the remainder, fourteen are addresses by generals to their troops.[12] The political speeches as a whole are of inestimable significance in the narrative. They represent the play of human intelligence in providing the rationale for proposed courses of action and hence forecast and illuminate the events of the war. They include competing and profound political analyses and pose issues of power and morality that occur perennially in the relations between states. Some speeches come in pairs when two speakers on the same occasion present dramatic confrontations of opposing views. One speech, the funeral oration or *epitaphios* that Pericles delivered in 431 to honor the Athenian dead killed in the first year of the war, contains an imperishable encomium on Athens's democracy and civilization which is among the most celebrated utterances in the annals of Western oratory. It is no wonder, therefore, that scholars have devoted a great deal of attention to the question of the authenticity of Thucydides' speeches. Opinion is broadly divided between those who regard them as largely fictional inventions of the historian and others who consider them as approximations in some degree to what the speakers actually said.

In thinking about this problem, it is well to keep in mind that no historian ancient or modern ever attached a higher importance than did Thucydides to the necessity of truth and accuracy or exactness in the writing of history.[13] According to Dionysius of Halicarnassus, a Greek literary critic and historian of the first century BCE who wrote a number of observations on Thucydides that were not always favorable by any means, "philosophers and rhetoricians . . . bear witness . . . that he has been most careful of the truth. . . . He adds nothing to the facts that should not be added, and takes nothing therefrom."[14] Nearly all later scholars are in accord with the opinion of antiquity concerning his allegiance to historical truth. A leading modern authority states a common view in speaking of his "singular truthfulness," noting that "he saw more truly, inquired more responsibly, and reported more faithfully than any other ancient historian."[15] It would be strange, therefore, and seems quite improbable, that he would report in the speaker's words any speeches of which he had no knowledge or invent false speeches that were never delivered. Some of the speeches he includes, like the three delivered by Pericles before his death in 429, he could have heard himself in Athens. Even in

31

the case of these or any other speeches he might have heard in Athens or elsewhere, however, he confesses that it was beyond his power to recall their exact words. From his description in 1.22 of the procedure he followed, we may gather that the basic limiting conditions he set himself in reporting speeches were (1) fidelity to the general sense or point of what was actually said, which he had to make sure to convey, and (2) expressing what was most appropriate to say in light of the particular circumstances and in a way that the speaker was likely to do. There is some ambiguity, though, in this second condition, because it fails to indicate how much latitude the historian would allow himself in deciding what was appropriate and likely for the speaker to say in conveying the gist of his point of view. As he could not reproduce the speakers' words, however, he would have had to rewrite their speeches in his own language in order to serve their aim by expressing his conception of what was most appropriate to the occasion. This would help to explain the similarity in the character of the speeches throughout the *History* as evidenced by their consistent intellectualism, pregnant generalizations, and acute political reasoning in exposing the issues at stake.

Some historians have cited the similarity of the speeches as one of the reasons for doubting their authenticity and as proof that that they are simply the historian's own free creation. They likewise hold that the language and thought of many of the speeches are too abstract for their audiences to have understood them. It has also been pointed out, as an indication of Thucydides' manipulation of the speeches, that in certain instances the speakers answer arguments contained in previous speeches which they couldn't have heard or known. Thus, Pericles' first speech in the *History*, an address to the Athenian assembly in 432 prior to the war (1.140–44), appears to reply to some of the statements in the speech made earlier in the same year by the Corinthian envoys at the congress of the Peloponnesian League held in Sparta (1.120–24).[16] Some scholars have doubted or denied that Thucydides could have known what the Athenian envoys and the representatives of Melos said to each other in the Melian dialogue of 416, one of the most famous political exchanges in the *History* and a classic expression of the supremacy of power politics in international relations (5.85–113).[17]

Whatever Thucydides may have done to produce the speeches, the opinions voiced in them were not of course his own personal views but those he considered appropriate to the speakers in the particular context in which they spoke. We might wonder why he wasn't content simply to summarize the various speeches using only indirect discourse in the third person, which would have succeeded in conveying the substance or general meaning of what the speakers said but without putting words in their mouths. In various instances he did rely on indirect discourse to summarize a speech. Thus he reports entirely in the third person the important oration that Pericles delivered at the outset of the war in order to encourage the Athenians by pointing out to them the factors favoring their victory (2.13). Another example is the speech in book 8 by the Athenian general Phrynicus persuading his fellow commanders to withdraw their ships from Miletus, which is likewise summarized in the third person (8.27). With regard to a number of the speeches, however, we have to assume that the historian deemed them so vital and illuminating, and perhaps also had adequate information concerning their content, that he decided to present them in direct quotation and at length. The appearance of speeches in Homer and Herodotus must have encouraged him to introduce speeches in his own work, and he may never have even considered not doing so. We may be pretty sure, moreover, that he would not have acknowledged any contradiction between his practice of direct presentation of speeches and his professed commitment to truth and accuracy, especially since he candidly explains his procedure to the reader and claims to reproduce the speakers' general sense even if not his exact words. Most of the speeches that Herodotus reported verbatim in his *History of the Persian War* were quite obviously fictitious.[18] Thucydides, who insisted on rigorous accuracy, would not have imitated his example. We are thus led to conclude that although the speeches were written by himself in his own style, they are a record of addresses that were actually delivered and conveyed at least the general opinion the speakers held, though not necessarily the particular arguments they advanced to support their position. On this point we may also mention the opinion of K. J. Dover, one of Thucydides' eminent editors: "The available evidence does not compel us to say that that there is any argument or sentiment in any Thucydidean speech which cannot have been voiced in some form or other by the original speaker on the original occasion."[19]

We should notice too how closely some of the speeches seem to fit the speakers' characters. This is the case, for example, of the ones King Archidamus of Sparta and the ephor Sthenelaidas delivered in 432 to the Spartan assembly on the question of whether Sparta should comply with the urgings of its allies in the Peloponnesian League to go to war against Athens.[20] The old, experienced Archidamus, who opposed the immediate commencement of war, spoke not only of the discipline and honor of the Spartans but defended the ancestral policy of slowness and procrastination. "If you begin the war in haste," he said, "you will end it at your leisure, because you took up arms without sufficient preparation. . . . [W]hen many lives and much wealth, many cities and a great name are at stake, we must not be hasty, or make up our minds in a few short hours; we must take time" (1.84, 85). The ephor Sthenelaidas, who spoke very briefly and favored war, began with the curt remark, one typical of the Spartan attitude, that he could not understand the "the long speeches of the Athenians" (1.86). In the case of an outstanding speech like Pericles' funeral oration, its elevation of thought in its eulogy of Athens and the spirit of its citizens is highly appropriate to the great patrician leader of the Athenian democracy and could well have reflected actual features of his oratorical style, which Thucydides presumably knew well. The speeches of the rich young Athenian aristocrat Alcibiades in the later part of the *History* effectively delineate a character in which pride, egotism, and personal ambition predominate.

Concerning Thucydides' second category, that of events and actions, we may take him at his word that he strove to describe them as accurately as he could, relying both on his own observation and on the careful sifting of the evidence he collected from others of whom he made particular inquiries. He had to be selective in his narrative, of course, as every historian must be, and in order to do this he was continually obliged to make judgments of relevance and relative importance. He does not claim that he made no errors or omitted nothing that should have been included. Modern historians have pointed to various mistakes, omissions, and neglected subjects in his *History*, not least, for example, his inadequate account of Athens's relations with Persia.[21] When he is uncertain of his facts, he says so. In describing the big battle of Mantinea in 418 between the Lacedaemonians and Argos and its allies, he declares that he cannot give the exact numbers on either side because Spartan secrecy did not allow the strength of its army to be known while "the numbers on the other side were thought to be exaggerated by the vanity natural to men when speaking of their own forces" (5.68). What Thucydides wishes us to understand, however, is that he went to great trouble in trying to establish the truth and to state what really happened, and that he expressly excluded the mythical or fabulous from his account.

It is essential not to overlook the last thing Thucydides tells us in 1.22 in explanation of his historical method. This is that he has written his book to be of use to those people who want to have a true picture not only of events that have happened but of analogous events that may be expected to occur in the future, given the human condition. I shall return to this subject in a later chapter.[22] For the present it is sufficient to note that implied in this statement is the conviction that the study of history can be useful because some future events may resemble past ones owing to certain permanent elements of human nature.

One of the first problems Thucydides faced in writing his history was to decide how to date the events he described. Time as the medium of ceaseless change is the fundamental dimension in which human life is lived, and a chronology is essential to history in order to mark the place of events in the flow of time. Since the Greeks had no single or common calendar, it was left to Thucydides to determine what system of chronology he would use. At the beginning of book 2 he recorded the commencement of the war as a result of the violation of the Thirty Year Peace in its fifteenth year when Sparta's ally Thebes attacked the city of Plataea, the ally of Athens. This took place, he states, "when Chryseis the high-priestess at Argos was in the forty-eighth year of her priesthood, Aenesias being Ephor at Sparta, and at Athens Pythodorus having two months of his archonship to run" (2.2). Dating events in this fashion was obviously complicated and inconvenient, so it is understandable that he adopted a different type of chronology, as he informs the reader:

> And now the war between the Athenians and the Peloponnesians and the allies of both actually began. Henceforward the struggle was uninterrupted, and they communicated with one another only by heralds. The narrative is arranged according to summers and winters and follows the order of events. (2.1)

In book 5, at the end of the first ten years of the war, he explains this system further by pointing out that he preferred to reckon "the actual periods of time" rather than to rely upon the lists of archons or other officials "whose names may be used in different cities to mark the dates of past events." Some version of the latter way of recording dates was general in the cities of ancient Greece.[23] But because among other defects this method left it uncertain whether an event occurred in the beginning, middle, or at another time in a magistrate's term of office, Thucydides says he considered it better "to measure by summers and winters," counting each season as one-half of the year (5.20). Hence he organized his account in the form of annals, noting in each numbered year of the war the seasonal succession of summers and winters. Sometimes he also mentions the part of the season in which an event occurred. This system of dating constituted a firm chronological basis for the *History*, and each time his narrative arrives at the end of a year he records the fact, usually in a formula like the following: "Such were the events of the winter. And so ended the second year in the Peloponnesian War, of which Thucydides wrote the history" (2.70; cf. 2.103; 3.25, 116; 4.51, etc.).[24]

Thucydides did not finish his *History*, which ended abruptly in the year 411. The structure or sequential segments and contents of his narrative can be conveniently divided into five major parts as follows:

(1) Part 1, which encompasses all of the first book, the longest of the work, is an introduction describing his historical method and the antecedents and causes of the war and its preliminary incidents. It includes the Archaeologia, a sketch of earlier Greek history intended, as previously pointed out, to justify the claim that the Peloponnesian War was the greatest of all wars. It likewise contains a brief account in 1.89–117 of the half-century from the Persian to the Peloponnesian War, which modern scholars call the Pentecontaetia or the Fifty Years. The latter's purpose, as Thucydides said in introducing it, was to show "how the Athenians attained the position in which they rose to greatness" (1.89).

(2) Part 2 extends from the beginning of the second book to 5.25 and covers the period to 421, the first ten years of the war, which modern scholars have named the Ten Year or Archidamian War, after the Spartan commander King Archidamus. One of its major episodes is the revolution and massacre in 427 in Corcyra, Athens's ally, which is described in book 3 and upon which Thucydides offers a number of significant personal observations

(3.70–84). Anothers prominent episode is the important defeat of Sparta at Pylos in 425 and its consequences (4.3–23, 26–41). This second part concludes with the Fifty Year Peace of 421 between Athens and the Peloponnesians that seemingly terminated the war, leaving the Athenian empire intact.

(3) Part 3, comprising the fifth book from 5.26 to 5.116, deals with the six-year period from 421 to 415 and describes the instabilities and breakdown of the Fifty Year Peace of 421. It contains one of the outstanding parts of the *History*, the Melian dialogue between the representatives of Athens and Melos, which shows how the Melians' refusal to heed the Athenian arguments and submit to Athens's rule led to their conquest, the slaughter of all their men of military age, and the enslavement of their women and children (5.85–116).

(4) Part 4, consisting of the sixth and seventh books, occupies the years 416–413. Its main subject is the Athenian decision to conquer Sicily and its sequel. It describes Athens's great Sicilian expedition and the politics that led to it, naval and military operations in Sicily, the Athenians' disastrous failure to capture the city of Syracuse, and the expedition's total defeat and annihilation. Many readers consider the narrative of the Sicilian expedition as the high point of the entire work.

(5) Finally, part 5, the unfinished eighth book, carries the history to 411. It includes the difficulties and danger created for the Athenians by the Spartans' permanent occupation of Decelea in Attica, which lay close to Athens; Sparta's alliance with the Persians against Athens; and the revolution in Athens that overthrew its democractic government. The narrative simply breaks off after 8.109.

This is a very concise overview of the *History*'s contents and narrative sequence. But how did Thucydides write his *History*? When and in what order did he draft its various parts, and what revisions did he make while he was writing? These questions about the stages and strata of the composition of his work do not permit of a definitive answer, as is shown by the failure of generations of scholars who have examined the subject to reach any generally accepted conclusions on this controversial and much discussed problem. The extent of disagreement among leading authorities may be seen in the contrast between the judgment of John H. Finley Jr. that the *History* was largely composed at one time after the end of the war in 404, and of F. E. Adcock, who regards it as most probable that Thucydides "composed his history *pari passu* with events and with his observation of them."[25]

Although he stated in 1.1 that he began to write at the outset of the war, this gives us no clue to the procedure he followed or the order of the *History*'s composition. He could have made notes on some events and then written them up much later and he could have set down an account of other events shortly after they occurred. As further information came to him or his thinking about certain events possibly changed, he would also have made revisions in parts of the work that he had written previously. Internal evidence indicates that some of the earlier passages in the *History* were not written until after the end of the war. A speech by Pericles in book 2, for example, which belongs to the year 430, foresees the fall of the Athenian empire (2.64), and in the historian's notice of Pericles' death in 429, two and a half years after the war began, he alludes to the error of the future Sicilian expedition, which set out in 415, and to Athens's final defeat (2.65). He makes a similar allusion to Athens's future under the year 415 in speaking of Alcibiades, a supporter of the Sicilian expedition, as a man whose "wild courses [in the end] went far to ruin the Athenian state" (6.15).

It is possible that Thucydides originally wrote the history of the first ten years of the war as a separate narrative extending from the beginning of book 2 to 5.25, which covers the decade from the start of the war to the peace of 421. At the date the peace was made, he could not have known for certain that it wouldn't last; yet he no sooner mentions the peace treaty (5.25) then he also looks forward to the breaking of the treaty and the resumption of hostilities six years later. He thus links his narrative of the first ten years of the war with some remarks that immediately follow in 5.26 comprising what scholars have called the Second Preface. Here he announces that he has continued his history up to the destruction of the Athenian empire and proceeds to argue that the war lasted for a full twenty-seven years, it being a mistake to exclude the years of the peace since the entire period constituted one war. He also adds a personal note which includes the statement that "I lived through the whole of it, and was of mature years and judgment, and I took great pains to make out the exact truth" (5.26). All of this Second Preface must have been written following the end of the war as a bridge between the earlier and the subsequent narrative. His insistence in 5.26, moreover, that the Ten Year War was not a separate event but part of a single war lasting twenty-seven years seems to suggest that his claim in the first book with its accompanying proof in the Archaeologia about the unparalleled magnitude of the Peloponnesian War must also have been written after the conclusion of the war, when its full length and scale had unfolded themselves.

Thucydides was working on his *History* after the war ended, but left it unfinished when he died at an unknown date around 400 or possibly later.[26] Scholars have speculated that it may have been published posthumously by an unknown editor who had charge of the text. There is also a tradition that its publication was due to Xenophon, a younger contemporary of Thucydides who continued his work. It is not necessary to discuss its order of composition further, since the problem is of far greater importance to the specialist than to the ordinary reader. What should be emphasized, however, is that at whatever times Thucydides may have written or revised its different parts, his *History* nevertheless possesses a fundamental unity. This unity is due to the omnipresence in the work of the singular intellectual temperament of the historian who created it. It is a unity that manifests itself in the *History*'s consistency of viewpoint, values, and interests; its passion for exactitude; its conception of human nature and concern with power; its dramatic qualities; and its depiction of the interplay of political judgment, unpredictable chance, and hard necessity in shaping human affairs and their outcome. These features help to make the *History*, despite its incompleteness and the length of time over which it was written, an integral achievement as an intellectual work of art and enduring contribution to western historiography.

Thucydides on the Causes of the War

> [T]he war . . . began when the Athenians and
> Peloponnesians violated the thirty years' truce
> concluded by them after the recapture of Euboea.
> Why they broke it and what were the grounds of
> the quarrel I will first set forth, that in time to
> come no man may be at loss to know what was
> the origin of this great war. The real though
> unavowed cause I believe to have been the
> growth of the Athenian power, which terrified the
> Lacedaemonians and forced them into war; but
> the reasons publicly alleged on either side were as
> follows. (1.23)

POLYBIUS, a Greek historian of the second century BCE and worthy successor to Thucydides, wrote a famous history of the rise of Rome to world power in which he included numerous observations on the requirements of a proper work of history. A point on which he laid great weight was the historian's obligation to tell not only what happened but why, that is, to explain the causes and reasons. "Nothing is so essential either for writers or for students of history," he said, "as to understand the causes underlying the genesis and development of any series of events." He stressed equally the need, when dealing with an event such as a war, to understand the difference between its occasion and beginning and its true cause.[1] Polybius's opinion is one that modern historians would commonly accept as axiomatic; for they agree that if a history is to provide an intelligible account of any part of the human past, whether of singular events like wars and revolutions, or of the evolution of nations and states, or of political, economic, institutional, cultural, social, intellectual, artistic, or other kinds of changes and developments, it must both establish and record the facts pertinent to its subject and explain the causes.

Unlike Polybius, Thucydides refrained from offering any general thoughts on the concept of causality, but dealt exclusively with the identification of the cause of the great war between the Spartans and Athenians that he had taken as his subject. As in the case of the two world wars of the twentieth century or of any other great war of the past, the Peloponnesian War was preceded by diplomatic tensions, localized conflicts, and international crises that foreshadowed its coming. In a part of the first book of his *History* Thucydides relates the quarrels and grievances that arose between Athens and Sparta and its allies in the years 435–431 as the immediate prelude to the war. They were largely due to the hostilities that broke out first between Corcyra and its mother city Corinth as a result of their conflict over Epidamnus, and the subsequent revolt of Potidaea, one of Athens's subject cities. The widening antagonisms, reactions, and interventions these events produced and the issues they posed led to the abrogation of the Thirty Year Peace concluded in 445 by Athens, Sparta, and their allies, and to the commencement of the war.

Although Thucydides did not theorize about the cause of the war, in addressing the subject he would have had to reflect on the sequence of developments and incidents that preceded the war in order to estimate their causal relevance in bringing it about. He gives no indication of his reasoning on the problem, but his terse and confident statement of the true cause of the war involves an implicit distinction between the cause as he saw it and other alternative causes, reasons, or explanations that contemporaries might have erroneously accepted. The meaning and implications of his remarks on the war's cause are among the important questions that arise when we read his *History* and to which Thucydidean scholars and historians of ancient Greece have devoted much attention.

If we return to Thucydides' words in the crucial passage in 1.23, we note that he says he will first give the reasons (*tas aitias*) why the parties broke the Thirty Year Peace and also describe the grounds (*tas diaphoras*) of their quarrel, that is, the disputes between them. He then points to the war's "real though unavowed cause" (*alethestaten prophasin, aphanestaten de logo*), namely, Athens's increasing power and the fear it inspired in Sparta. Other English versions translate this phrase as "the real but unavowed cause" (Crawley), "the truest explanation, although it has been least often advanced" (Smith), and "the true though

41

unavowed cause" (Hornblower, CT, vol. 1, p. 64). Finally, he contrasts this true cause or truest explanation which was not avowed or much spoken of, with the reasons publicly alleged for the quarrel, which he immediately proceeds to describe in 1.24 and thereafter in his account of the events such as the conflict between Corcyra and Corinth that culminated in the breaking of the Thirty Year Peace.

The Greek terms Thucydides used in speaking of the cause of the war had a wide range of meanings and were hardly precise. *Aitia*, for example, could mean a reason, a complaint, a cause of complaint, blame, or a cause, while *prophasis* might signify a plea, an alleged cause, a false excuse, and a true cause.[2] In present-day English, similarly, the word cause is often used synonymously with reason, in the sense of stating the reason why something happened, and also rather vaguely in such familiar expressions as the primary cause, major cause, minor cause, contributory cause, and so forth. In the century after Thucydides, Aristotle distinguished between four different kinds of causes—formal, material, efficient, and final—while modern discussions of causation by logicians, philosophers, and theorists of science have usually noted the distinction between a necessary and a sufficient cause.

To what extent did Thucydides' statement about the cause of the war depend on a prior analysis of the concept of causality on his part? In the early twentieth century F. M. Cornford maintained in a fascinating book that Thucydides was not a scientific historian, as commonly thought, and that he had no conception or understanding of causation.[3] In opposition to this extreme view, Simon Hornblower, one of the foremost contemporary students of Thucydides' work, declares that he explicitly formulated the distinction between "profound and superficial causes" and that this was arguably his "greatest single contribution to later history-writing," As he also puts it, Thucydides "developed, for the first time in European thought, a conscious, secular theory of causation in terms of deep and superficial political causes."[4] Other scholars have not gone quite so far as this, but have nevertheless tended to take the historian's statement of the war's cause in 1.23 to mean that he was consciously distinguishing between an immediate or superficial cause and a more remote and profound cause. Kagan, for example, calls Thucydides the inventor of the distinction between the underlying and remote causes and the immediate causes of war.[5] Werner Jaeger praises him as an innovator for recognizing the difference between the true cause of the war and "the disputed points which were its occasion."[6] J. H. Finley says he divided the war's causes into two classes: the inciting incidents and grievances that constituted the *aitiai* and *diaphorai* between Athens and Sparta, and the Spartan fear of Athens's growing power as the truest but least talked of explanation.[7] Jacqueline de Romilly thinks he subordinated the *aitiai* and *diaphorai*, the grievances and disputes which made up the immediate causes, to the *alethestate prophasis*, the true cause, which could be traced back fifty years before the actual outbreak of the war and lay in Athenian imperialism and the eventual fear it aroused in Sparta.[8] Albin Lesky explains that by *aitiai* Thucydides referred to particular motives, and by *alethestate prophasis* to the underlying cause deeply rooted in the nature of things, which compelled Sparta as if by a natural law to take up arms against the threat of Athens's increasing strength.[9] On the other hand, G.E.M. de Ste. Croix expresses a noteworthy dissent in his major work, *The Origins of the Peloponnesian War*, in which he denies that Thucydides made any distinction between an immediate or superficial and a more remote or profound cause. Noting that there is no inherent opposition between the terms *aitia* and *prophasis*, whose meanings often overlap, he believes that the point of Thucydides' statement was its contrast between the real or truest cause of the war, which was the least mentioned, and the publicly expressed grounds of complaint, which were a pretext.[10] This claim is part of Ste. Croix's larger argument that Sparta, not Athens, was the aggressor in the war and bore the main responsibility for breaking the Thirty Year Peace.

Thucydides' own loose and imprecise language makes it difficult to decide between these differing interpretations. He could have been intimating a distinction between the immediate or apparent cause of the war in the preceding incidents of 435–431 and its true underlying cause, but he could also have intended to contrast the true cause of the war, which was least spoken of, with the disputes and grievances that were publicly and commonly cited as its cause but which he considered specious or inadequate as an explanation. As his statement says nothing whatever about causality as a concept, perhaps the main significance of his opinion about the true cause of the war may lie in the fact that it represents his own independent and original historical judgment. Unwilling to be satisfied with an explanation of the war derived from the parties' own publicly alleged reasons, grievances, and justifications, he places in the foreground as the war's true but little mentioned or unavowed cause, operative over a lengthy period of time, Athenian imperialism and Spartan rivalry and fear of Athens's aggrandizement.

Modern scholars have been in disagreement as to whether Thucydides' statement of the true cause of the war was an early passage or a written at a late or a final stage in the composition of his *History* after the war ended. Whichever was the case, his view of the war's cause runs with complete consistency throughout the work. He reiterated it in two further passages in the first book. Reporting the vote of the Lacedaemonian assembly in 432 that the Thirty Year Peace had been broken, he makes the following observation:

> In arriving at this decision and resolving to go to war, the Lacedaemonians were influenced, not so much by the speeches of their allies, as by the fear of the Athenians and their increasing power. For they saw the greater part of Hellas already subject to them. (1.88)

In a subsequent passage forming the conclusion of the Fifty Years or Pentecontaeteia, his concise review in book 1 of the growth of Athenian power in the half-century preceding the Peloponnesian War, he makes a similar comment:

> Fifty years elapsed between the defeat of Xerxes and the beginning of the War; during these years took place all those operations of the Hellenes against one another and against the Barbarians which I have been describing. The Athenians acquired a firmer hold over their empire and the city itself became a great power. The Lacedaemonians saw what was going on, but during most the time they remained inactive and hardly attempted to interfere. They had never been of a temper prompt to make war unless they were compelled; and they were in some degree embarrassed by enemies near home. But the Athenians were growing too great to be ignored and were laying hands on their allies. They could now bear it no longer: they made up their minds that they must put out all their strength and overthrow the Athenian power by force of arms. And therefore they commenced the Peloponnesian War. (1.118)

His understanding of the cause of the war is confirmed in the first book by the words of the Corcyrans, whose conflict with Sparta's foremost ally Corinth, begun in 435, was one of the factors that led to the war. Having been attacked by Corinth, Corcyra, which was an independent city without any major allies, opened negotiations with Athens in 433 to obtain its aid against Corinth as well as an alliance. One of the principal inducements the Corcyrans offered Athens if it accepted them as allies was the strength of their navy. Their envoys told the Athenian assembly, "if any one thinks that the war [with Sparta] in which our services may be needed will never arrive, he is mistaken. He does not see that the Lacedaemonians, fearing the growth of your empire, are eager to take up arms, and that the Corinthians, who are your enemies, are all powerful with them. They begin with us, but they will go on to you" (1.33). The Athenians decided against a full alliance with Corcyra lest it involve them in the war with Corinth, which would have been a breach of the Thirty Year Peace. Instead, the two states concluded a defensive agreement to help each other should the territory or allies of either be attacked. The Athenians took this step, according to Thucydides, because they knew that war with the Peloponnesians was coming and "they had no mind to let Corcyra and her navy fall into the hands of the Corinthians" (1.44).

But what meaning should we read into Thucydides' insistence that the true cause of the war was Sparta's fear of Athens's growing power? Was he implying by this that the war was a clash between two opposing and irreconcilable political systems? The *History* contains no indication that this was what he thought. Although Athens was a democracy and Sparta a rigid oligarchy, he never suggests that the differences between their types of government and the distinctive values associated with each was the origin of the conflict between them. He records, moreover, that around 460 the Athenians sent troops to Sparta at its request to help it suppress a Messenian helot revolt (1.102). The two critical factors he highlights in explaining the war are fear and power. Fear is an emotion and a psychological response produced by the awareness of danger. Power is an attribute measured by the extent to which one actor in a situation can require the other actors to comply with his will or suffer penalties for refusal. The Spartans, famed above all other Greeks for their bravery, courage, and endurance, were not a fearful people, and as masters of a population of serfs who worked their land, they were also accustomed to living with the ever-present possibility of a slave insurrection against their rule. Perhaps Thucydides believed that only a great cause could explain a great war. His proffered explanation of the war is wholly political and follows alike from his conception of the relations between states as incessantly competitive in their quest for power and security, and from his conception of human behavior as strongly motivated by self-interest and the desire to dominate others. In his analysis of the situation, the Spartans went to war because they feared that Athens in its restless imperial ambition and growing strength was drawing ahead of them and presented a mortal threat to their hegemony over their allies and their status as a great power. It is quite obvious that in this explanation of why the war occurred, questions of justice and right or of who was responsible for breaking the Thirty Year Peace were of secondary importance and had little or no relevance to the determination of its cause.

In his statement of the true cause of the war between Athens and Sparta, Thucydides also held that the war was inevitable. He declares in 1.23 that the growth of Athenian power "forced" the Lacedaemonians into war, a passage Crawley translates as "made war inevitable." The Greek verb he used, *anankasai*, and its noun form, *ananke*, include the ideas of force, compulsion, and, more broadly, necessity. For Thucydides, necessity is one of the principles or powers that govern history and the affairs of men.[11] Its presence is seen in situations in which the human actors have few options and perhaps only one that they think viable. This need not imply in the case of the Peloponnesian War that the Spartans had literally no choice and were not free to opt for peace. Thucydides probably believed, however, that the expansion of Athens's empire and influence over the years confronted Sparta in 431 with a situation that drastically limited its alternatives. If it wished to avoid entering upon a decline, then necessity compelled it to choose war as the only means to arrest and reverse the growth of Athenian power. He could have been wrong, of course. Donald Kagan in his volume on the outbreak of the Peloponnesian War has reviewed and analyzed its antecedents and tried to prove that the war was not inevitable and need not have occurred.[12] Readers of Thucydides may scrutinize the facts he presents and come to their own conclusion as to whether he was right that the war was inevitable.

Thucydides inserted the Pentecontaetia or narrative of the Fifty Years into book 1 (1.89–118) chiefly to buttress and elaborate his judgment on the true cause of the war. Its stated purpose was to survey the growth of Athens's power during the period between the Persian and the Peloponnesian Wars, and it starts with a sentence that connects its subject with the earlier statement in 1.23 of the war's true cause: "How the Athenians rose to greatness I will now proceed to describe" (1.89). As a further reason for discussing this half-century, the historian also mentions its neglect by previous writers except for one, Hellanicus, who treated it very briefly and made chronological errors (1.97).

Beginning with the Greek victories against the Persians in 479, the survey tells how the Lacedaemonians desisted from participating in the war thereafter and thus left the leadership to Athens in continuing the resistance to Persia. Among the first things it records is Sparta's suspicion and opposition when Athens rebuilt its walls in the immediate aftermath of the Persian invasion and also completed the construction and fortification of its port, the Piraeus, with its three natural harbors. All of this work, Thucydides declares, was done at the advice of the Athenian leader Themistocles, who thought that a good harbor would greatly contribute to the extension of Athens's power and first dared to say that the Athenians must make the sea their domain, thereby laying the foundations of their empire (1.89–93).

The narrative goes on to relate the development of the Athenian empire. As the leader in the war against Persia, Athens decided which of its allied cities should contribute money and which of them ships. Although the allies were independent at first and met in a common assembly at Delos, in time Athens made such strides in power that it gradually brought them into subjection. In a reference to the revolt of Naxos that Athens crushed, Thucydides noted that this "was the first of the allied cities which was enslaved contrary to Hellenic law; the turn of the others came later" (1.98). As this comment shows, the historian neither moralizes about Athenian imperialism nor tries to conceal or justify its exploitative character. Treating it simply as a fact, he describes it bluntly as "exacting and oppressive," relying on "coercive measures" to compel the allies to pay tribute, furnish ships, and provide military service. Because the majority of them disliked military service, they contributed money instead of ships, as a result of which "the Athenian navy was proportionally increased, while they themselves were always untrained and unprepared for war when they revolted" (1.99).

On the occasion that Athens sent a force in 460 to assist Sparta in putting down a Messenian helot revolt, Thucydides records the "first open quarrel" between the two states. The Athenian troops were expected to help in siege operations; but knowing their "bold and original spirit" and fearing that they might be tempted to change sides if they remained, the Spartans took alarm and dismissed them. Much offended by this treatment, Athens then became Sparta's avowed enemy and allied itself with Argos, Sparta's great and traditional adversary (102–3).

The remainder of the Pentecontaetia covers the period of warfare starting in the 450s that went on sporadically on the Greek mainland and elsewhere between Athens, Sparta, and their allies for more than decade. It also provides some details on Athens's extended military and naval operations against the barbarians and others, including even expeditions to Egypt against the Persians, and to Cyprus. The narrative draws to a close with the adoption of the treaty of the Thirty Year Peace between Athens and Sparta followed a few years later in 440 by Athens's suppression of the revolt of Samos. Summing up the fifty years that elapsed between the Persian and Peloponnesian Wars, Thucydides declares that during this time "Athens acquired a firmer hold of its empire" and "became a great power," and the Lacedaemonians, no longer able to endure that their rival was growing so great, "made up their minds that they must overthrow the Athenian power by force of arms" (1.118).

As I have noted in a previous chapter, modern historians of classical Greece often use the title of the First Peloponnesian War to designate the earlier period of warfare between Athens and Sparta that Thucydides relates in the Pentecontaetia. They have also been critical of his account because of its numerous omissions of important facts known from other sources, its lack of a precise chronology, and its inadequacy in showing how Athens built up its empire. Gomme has discussed these defects and listed various omissions, among which he includes information about Athenian foreign policy, the organization of the Delian League as the foundation of the Athenian empire, the transfer of the League's treasury to Athens, and Athens's internal history and politics.[13] Many scholars have also criticized Thucydides' total silence about the cessation of hostilities between Athens and Persia, the so-called Peace of Callias, an important development which apparently occurred soon after 450 and removed a threat to the Athenian empire.[14] These faults may be at least partly explained by the fact that in the Pentecontaetia Thucydides did not intend to write a condensed history of the fifty years, but had the more restricted aim of describing the growth of Athenian power. In particular, he wanted to mention the events that alarmed the Spartans, and this might account for his omission of the peace with Persia.[15]

Within his understanding of the cause of the war, Athenian imperialism and Sparta's eventual determination to resist its expansion stand as the great central fact.[16] Several of the speeches in the earlier part of the *History* shed light on the empire as the Athenians and their adversaries saw it and likewise serve to reinforce the historian's explanation of the war.

At the congress in 432 at which the Spartans and their allies in the Peloponnesian League first debated the question of war or peace with Athens, Corinth was the most eager for war. Violently opposed to Athens and bent on revenge against it because of its alliance with Corcyra and other hostile actions, the Corinthians warned of its aggressive designs and called upon the Lacedaemonians to act promptly to prevent them. It happened at that time that some Athenian envoys were present in Sparta on other business and were allowed to address the meeting. They used the occasion chiefly to urge the Lacedaemonians to avoid war and settle their differences with Athens by arbitration, as provided for in the treaty of the Thirty Year Peace; but they also presented a surprisingly frank justification of Athens's imperial position. Recalling the great sacrifices and outstanding contribution Athens had made to the defeat of the Persian invasion, they asked whether "we deserve to be so bitterly hated by the other Hellenes merely because we have an empire." They did not acquire it by force, they argued, but because the allies voluntarily requested the Athenians to be their leaders against the Persians. Circumstances thereafter compelled them to develop their power, fear being their first motive, subsequently reinforced by ambition and self-interest. Once they had incurred the hatred of their allies, whom they had subjugated, and the Lacedaemonians, ceasing to be their friends, had become suspicious and hostile, they could not relax their hold without great risk, for if they were to do so, their subject cities would at once go over to Sparta. Having been offered an empire, they continued,

49

can you wonder that, acting as human nature always will, we accepted it and refused to give it up again, constrained by three all-powerful motives, ambition, fear, interest. We are not the first who have aspired to rule; the world has ever held that the weaker must be kept down by the stronger. And we think that we are worthy of power; and there was a time when you thought so too; but now, when you mean self-interest, you resort to talk about justice. Did justice ever deter any one from taking by force whatever he could? Men who indulge the natural ambition of empire deserve credit if they are in any degree more careful of justice than they need be under the circumstances. (1.75–76)

The Athenians therefore justified their possession of empire as due to necessity, because circumstances in the period following the defeat of the Persian invasion compelled them to acquire supremacy over their allies, and to the driving forces of human nature, fear, ambition, and self-interest, which are found in everyone. So far as they had any claim to empire, they based it on their superior power, in accord with the universal rule that the stronger must ever dominate the weaker. Not surprisingly, the Spartan ephor Sthenelaidas replied to the Athenians' speech by urging war to defend Sparta's allies and "withstand the advancing power of Athens" (1.86).

Amidst the final negotiations with the Lacedaemonians in 432, Pericles, the leader of the Athenian democracy, advised the people of Athens that necessity made war with Sparta inevitable and predicted that it would come (1.144).[17] Rather than yield to Sparta's demands, he was in favor of war. In the last of the speeches Thucydides attributes to him, delivered to the Athenian assembly in the second year of the war, after the city had suffered some reverses in addition to the terrible affliction of the plague, and had even made a vain overture of peace to Sparta, Pericles expressed his conception of the empire in an attempt to encourage the Athenians and raise their morale. Viewing the empire as both a symbol and proof of Athens's unequalled greatness, he reminded the Athenians that they held the unchallenged supremacy of the sea and exhorted them "to maintain the imperial dignity of your city in which you all take pride." Do not imagine, he told them, that "you are fighting about a simple issue, freedom or slavery", for at stake in the conflict was "an empire to lose," beside "the danger to which the hatred of your imperial rule has exposed you. Neither can you resign your power. . . . For by this time your empire has become a tyranny which in the opinion of mankind may have been unjustly gained, but which cannot be safely surrendered." Yet while admitting that it was a tyranny, Pericles nevertheless believed that the empire demonstrated Athens's preeminence as the possessor of "the greatest power of any state up to this day," which would assure the remembrance of its glory forever. Even if it were to decline, posterity would recall "that, of all Hellenes, we ruled over the greatest number of Hellenic subjects; that we withstood our enemies . . . in the most terrible wars, and that we were the inhabitants of a city endowed with every sort of wealth and greatness. . . . To be hateful and offensive has ever been . . . the fate of those who have aspired to empire. But he judges well who accepts unpopularity in a great cause" (2.62–63).

As the counter to this Periclean image of Athens's imperial rule as a great and glorious achievement, its enemies such as Corinth denounced Athens as "the tyrant city which has been set up in Hellas," a "menace to all alike" that had already enslaved many cities and whose victory would mean slavery for the rest (1.122, 124). Echoing this cry, the Lacedaemonians informed the Athenians on the eve of the war that peace could be preserved "if you will restore independence to the Hellenes" (1.139). As the war began, "the feeling of mankind," Thucydides records, "was strongly on the side of the Lacedaemonians; for they professed to be the liberators of Hellas. . . . [T]he general indignation against the Athenians was intense; some were longing to be delivered from them, others fearful of falling under their sway" (2.8). On preparing to attack Athens's ally Plataea, the Spartan King Archidamus told the Plataeans that "this great war had been undertaken" with a view "to the emancipation . . . of the . . . subject states" (2.72).

It is strange that despite the importance he assigned to the Athenian empire in his causal analysis of the war, Thucydides says hardly anything about the political groups or social classes in Athens who either promoted and benefited from the policy of empire or who opposed it. In Pericles' last speech, from which I have quoted above, the Athenian leader alludes in passing to certain "timid and inactive" citizens who it appears were not in favor of empire or the war, but does not identify them or whom they might represent (2.63–64). Thucydides' method is simply to personify the combatants in the war under the names of their city or territory, hence the Athenians, the Corinthians, the Spartans or Lacedaemonians, the Plataeans, and the like, without probing into their social composition, and to treat them all as single agents who are impelled by fear, ambition, interest, security, self-preservation, and the drive for power. As far as the Athenian empire is concerned, he seems to explain it as due primarily to Athens's desire for power in circumstances after 479 that favored its ambition. We should keep in mind, though, that the empire was the creation of the Athenian democracy which emerged and developed during the fifth century under a succession of outstanding leaders, one of whom was Pericles. For the large number of men, many of them poor, who constituted the democratic citizen body, the empire was a source of countless benefits because of the tribute, wealth, and prosperity it brought the state. As an imperial democracy, Athens was able to provide many of its people with employment in its navy and public works, on paid juries and in paid civic offices, and with allotments of land for settlement in the empire's subject cities. "No wonder," as Peter Brunt has commented, "that the poor were imperialists." And we may concur with his further observation that without the empire democracy would probably not have become a reality in Athens, since "popular rights would have meant little unless the principle of pay for public services, which was alien to oligarchy, had enabled the humblest citizens to take an active part in government and acquire some political and administrative experience."[18]

In the diplomatic negotiations between the Lacedaemonians and Athens immediately preceding the war, one of the matters in dispute stemmed from the grievance of Megara, which had previously become an ally of Athens but then revolted and joined the Spartan alliance (1.103, 114). The Megarians complained that Athens had excluded them from the Athenian market and all the harbors of its empire, contrary to the terms of the Thirty Year Peace. The Spartans insisted that if Athens wished to avert war, it must rescind its Megarian decree. This the Athenians were unwilling to do, alleging in justification that the Megarians were cultivating sacred land and receiving Athens's runaway slaves (1.67, 139).[19] The issue was debated by the Athenian assembly, where, according to Thucydides, many spoke, some favoring war and others affirming that the Megarian decree should be rescinded and not stand in the way of peace. Addressing the point in a speech that opposed any concessions, Pericles states,

> I would have none of you imagine that he will be fighting for a small matter if we refuse to annul the Megarian decree, of which they make so much, telling us that its revocation would prevent the war. . . . For in this seeming trifle is involved the trial and confirmation of your whole purpose. If you yield to them in a small matter they will think you are afraid, and will immediately dictate some more oppressive condition; but if you are firm, you will prove to them that they must treat you as their equals. (1.140)

He advises that Athens should answer that it would not exclude the Megarians from its markets and harbors if the Lacedaemonians agreed not to ban foreigners, whether Athenians or their allies, from Sparta (1.144). Endorsing his advice, the Athenians rejected all of the Spartan demands, saying they would do nothing under compulsion and offering arbitration to settle differences.

A widespread opinion in Thucydides' time and in some later ancient sources regarded the Megarian decree as the main cause of the war.[20] Thucydides, however, dealt with it quite cursorily, even though its repeal was one of the Spartans' principal demands. Modern historians have criticized the absence in his account of essential information about the decree, including its date, motives, and exact content, all of which remain in dispute. The issue is further complicated by the fact that there were two Megarian decrees, an earlier and a later, although Thucydides refers only to one. Some have also seen in the slight importance he gives the subject a proof that he failed to understand the significance of economic factors and commercial rivalry, particularly between Athens and Corinth, both of them maritime powers, as a cause of the war. Various explanations of the Megarian decree have been advanced: that it reflected the policy of Athens's mercantile class, which imposed it upon Pericles; that it was an embargo aimed at damaging Megara's trade; or that its objective was to put economic pressure on Megara to force it to leave the Peloponnesian League and become Athens's ally. Few if any historians today believe, however, that economic motives were a major determinant of Athenian policy or a cause of the war. Ste. Croix in particular, in a chapter on the relationship between Athens and Corinth, has devoted a detailed discussion to the refutation of the theory that the Peloponnesian

War was due to commercial rivalry. He has likewise exhaustively examined the evidence relating to the Megarian decree and concluded that it was a minor matter of which Sparta cleverly made use to accuse Athens of a breach of the Thirty Year Peace.[21] Pericles' refusal of any concession concerning it probably sprang from his belief that the Spartan demand was a test of Athenian resolve. We need not suppose that Thucydides was ignorant or unaware of economic matters because he said so little about the Megarian decree. Since he did not consider it a cause of the war, he had no reason to give it importance and therefore treated it simply among the grievances publicly alleged by one of the parties.[22]

The first book of Thucydides' *History* contains eight political speeches, a number exceeded only by the nine such speeches in book 6. As an essential and dramatic complement to the narrative, all eight are related to the same subject, the imminent coming of the war, which they help to explain. We have already quoted from several, but it is worth looking further at a few of them for the insights they offer into the attitudes and values of the parties.

The first speech Thucydides records is that of the Corcyrans, who were at war with Corinth because of the Corinthian intervention in Epidamnus, and had come to Athens in 433 to ask for an alliance. They call their request a "glorious opportunity" for the Athenians, to whom they offer two inducements: their lasting gratitude if they are accepted as allies when their vital interests are at stake, and their powerful navy, which would become available to Athens. They also assure the Athenians that war with the Lacedaemonians will come soon and that it would not be a breach of the Thirty Year Peace if they receive Corcyra as an ally, since it has been a neutral state. Stressing, finally, that it would be in Athens's "best interests" to ally itself with Corcyra "when war is . . . almost at the door," they also warn of the danger in the impending conflict should Corinth conquer and annex the Corcyran fleet (1.32–33, 35–36).

The Corcyran plea for an alliance focuses entirely on Athens's interests and omits any reference to justice. The Corinthians' speech follows immediately and was delivered at Athens on the same occasion to dissuade the Athenian assembly from making an alliance with Corcyra. Although it appears to take a higher ground, its strongest argument is also based on interest. After first castigating Corcyra for its criminal conduct against Corinth, the Corinthians then contend that Athens has no right to receive it as an ally, since the only purpose of its doing so would be to injure Corinth. "[I]f you become the allies of the Corcyrans," they warn, "you will be no longer be at peace with us, but will be converted into enemies." They also claim that the Athenians owed them a debt of gratitude for their past services in lending ships to Athens in the Persian War and opposing interference by the Peloponnesian League when Athens crushed the rebellion of Samos. Averring that the paths of expediency and of right coincided, the Corinthians urge Athens not to support Corcyra in injustice, and conclude that "in acting thus, you will act rightly, and will also consult your true interests" (1.37–43).

The Corinthian speech sought to persuade by appealing to reasons of both interest and of right, though the latter was pretty clearly self-serving. The Athenians obviously considered interest more compelling, and interpreting their own interest differently, they concluded a defensive alliance with Corcyra lest its navy be taken over by Corinth. This agreement provided that the two states should help each other if the territory or allies of either should be attacked (1.44).

The next four speeches were all spoken at Sparta in 432 in the debate over the question of war or peace with Athens. We shall examine only two of them, both of which were delivered at the meeting of the Peloponnesian League. The first of these, by the Corinthian envoys, strongly reproached the Spartans for their inertia and inaction in failing to move against Athens. Its most striking feature is the comparison it draws between the collective psychology of the Spartans and the Athenians. Whereas the former, according to the Corinthians, are conservative by nature, seeking to keep what they have, prone to procrastination, and dangerously slow to act, the Athenians "are revolutionary, equally quick in the conception and in the execution of every new plan . . . bold beyond their strength; they run risks which prudence would condemn; and in the midst of misfortune they are full of hope. . . . When conquerors, they pursue their victory to the utmost; when defeated they fall back the least" (1.70). This illuminating Corinthian analysis of the Athenian character also serves to alert us to Athens's resiliency and daring in waging the war that is to come. It regards Sparta as a status quo power, intent on preserving its position rather than augmenting it, and Athens as a dynamic, aggressive state, ever striving to make itself greater.

The second of these speeches, to which I have already referred, came from the Athenian envoys after the Corinthians had spoken, and cautioned the Lacedaemonians against war with Athens. While the envoys maintained that Athens was worthy of its imperial rule, they admitted that its empire was unjust and oppressive and acquired from motives of power, fear, and ambition. They contended, moreover, that if they seized every possible advantage, the same was equally true of the Lacedaemonians, who in the exercise of their supremacy managed the cities of the Peloponnesus entirely for their own advantage. "[I]f you, and not we," they argue, "had persevered in the command of the allies long enough to be hated, you would have been quite as intolerable to them as we are, and would have been compelled, for the sake of your own safety, to rule with a strong hand" (1.76).

Thucydides' view of the cause of the war quite evidently treats the conflict as a product of realpolitik between two states bound on a collision course.[23] His account of the disputes that formed the war's prelude certainly does not exonerate Athens from all responsibility. The Pentecontaetia highlights Athens's thrust for empire and domination, and the historian shows Pericles as desiring war and opposed to concessions on the Megarian decree or any other Spartan demand, though they might conceivably have averted the war. The Spartans too are seen to bear responsibility for the war by, among other things, their consistent disregard of Athens's offer of arbitration to settle differences. It was they, moreover, who, as Thucydides recorded, voted in their assembly by a large majority that Athens had broken the Thirty Year Peace (1.87). After taking this vote, they sent to the oracle of Apollo at Delphi to ask the god if it would be to their advantage to make war. His answer, according to Thucydides, was that if they did their best, they would be conquerors, and that he himself would help them (1.118). Sparta therefore had divine approval for its choice of war. It did not fight, of course, as it publicly claimed to do, for the independence and freedom of the Greek states. It had no general concern for freedom and took on the war in its own interest to prevent the growth of Athenian power and maintain its primacy over its allies and the Greek mainland.[24]

Thucydides and Pericles

> During the peace while he [Pericles] was at
> the head of affairs, he ruled with prudence;
> under his guidance Athens was safe and reached
> the height of her greatness in his time. When the
> war began he showed that here too he had
> formed a true estimate of the Athenian power.
> He survived the commencement of hostilities
> two years and six months; and, after his death,
> his foresight was even better appreciated than
> during his life. . . . Thus Athens, though still in
> name a democracy, was in fact ruled by her first
> citizen. But his successors were more on an
> equality with one another, and, each one
> struggling to be first himself, they were ready
> to sacrifice the whole conduct of affairs to the
> whims of the people. (2.65)

No READER of Thucydides' *History* will doubt that he took a keen interest in character and personality, though mainly from a political point of view. In the course of the work he presents a number of prominent men who held leadership positions in Athens, Sparta, and Syracuse before or during the Peloponnesian War. In book 1, for instance, in connection with an issue in dispute between the Spartans and Athenians, he looks back on the careers of two celebrated individuals whom he calls the "most famous Hellenes of their day" (1.138). One of them, the Spartan Pausanias, was the commander who led the Greeks in their victory over the Persians at the battle of Plataea. The other, the Athenian Themistocles, was an outstanding statesman, general, and the founder of Athens's naval power. A colorful figure notorious for his personal ambition and arrogant misuse of authority, Pausanias was put to death by the Spartans on suspicion of treasonable relations with Persia (1.128–34). Thucydides records the facts about him and his end without adding any evaluation. Themistocles, after having been banished by the Athenians, sought refuge with the king of Persia, who received him with honor and in whose service he died (1.135–38). In recounting these events of Themistocles' later life, the historian emphasizes the "natural force" that distinguished him above other men and the "native acuteness" that made him "the ablest judge" in a sudden emergency, so that even where he had no experience, he was more competent than anyone else to form a judgment and clearly foresee "the good or evil . . . hidden in the future" (1.138). This assessment of Themistocles is an obvious indication that judgment and foresight were among the qualities that Thucydides ranked highest and especially looked for in a political leader.

In some of the speeches he reports, Thucydides never names the speakers. When he does include the speaker's name, it was probably because he considered him to possess some importance. In the first book the speeches of the Spartan King Archidamus and the ephor Sthenelaidas convey, without any comment by the historian, a distinct idea of their characters from the advice they give. One defends a policy of putting off the war, the other demands prompt hostilities against Athens (1.80–86). Once the war begins, we hear no more about Sthenelaidas, but Archidamus appears as the commander of the Lacedaemonian troops in the first invasion of Attica in 431 and in other situations. In this position his dilatoriness and failure to wage war energetically brought severe blame upon him and seriously damaged his reputation (2.18).

Thucydides' *History* is concerned only with men, and women are scarcely mentioned in it. In a very few instances they are named in passing as some man's wife or daughter or as the priestess of a temple (e.g., 2.29; 4.107; 4.133; 6.55, 59), but otherwise they appear only as anonymous victims of the war and mourners of the dead. Pericles may have expressed a common Athenian attitude to women in a passage of his funeral oration directed to the wives of the men killed in the war: "[I]f I am to speak of womanly virtues to those of you who will henceforth be widows, let me sum them up in one short admonition: To a woman not to show more weakness than is natural to her sex is a great glory, and not to be talked about for good or evil among men" (2.45).[1]

Among the men beside Pausanias and Themistocles whom Thucydides singles out for particular notice are the Athenian politician and general Nicias and the demagogue Cleon, rivals for power after the death of Pericles; the Spartan general Brasidas, a very resource-ful, popular, and successful commander, killed at Amphipolis in 422, who in a speech before the battle exhorts his troops to show themselves true Spartans by their bravery and reminds them that "readiness, obedience, and a sense of honor are the virtues of a soldier" (5.9); the Athenian general Demosthenes, an inspiring leader eventually killed in Sicily, who initiated the occupation of Pylos in 425 and thus made possible the significant Spartan defeat and surrender that followed; the young Athenian aristocrat Alcibi-ades, who advocated and aspired to lead the invasion of Sicily; Hermocrates of Syracuse, an outstanding general and organizer of Sicilian resistance against the Athenian invader; and Gylippus, the Spartan commander in Sicily who played a vital part in the Athenians' defeat.[2]

In his treatment of character and personality, Thucydides does not touch upon personal matters. He offers no physical descrip-tion of individuals and no biographical details concerning their private lives. When he states that Alcibiades "was devoted to horse-racing and other pleasures that outran his means," he is reporting a fact that was politically relevant to Alcibiades' reputation and the "great position" which we are told he held among the citizens of Athens (6.15). For the most part, Thucydides refrains from com-menting on people directly, preferring instead to let their speeches and their actions in the movement of events reveal what they were like and indirectly intimate his judgment of them. The aspect that chiefly concerns him in dealing with individuals is the extent of their political intelligence and their ability and characteristics as leaders of a state or commanders in war. His approach to character was therefore somewhat limited, yet in depicting individuals by the methods he had chosen he was often able to endow them with a compelling reality.

Among the gallery of leading figures who appear in the *History*, Pericles occupies a unique and unequalled place. He receives more attention than any other man of the time and is given three sub-stantial speeches, the largest number by any individual who appears in the work. A celebrated personage in antiquity, Pericles rose to primacy in the greatest period of Athens's history. As one of his contemporaries, Thucydides undoubtedly knew a great deal about his life and career that he could have related but chose not to record. Plato, a critic of democracy, pictured him in his dialogue

Gorgias in an unfavorable light as a corrupting influence in Athens. The Greek author Plutarch, writing five hundred years later in the first century C.E., included Pericles in his collection of biographies, *Parallel Lives of Famous Greeks and Romans*, which contains a considerable amount of valuable information about the Athenian leader. Thucydides' image of Pericles is a purely political one. Partly through the latter's actions and especially through the presentation of his thoughts in his public orations on several different occasions, which were themselves also political actions, of course, the historian enables the reader to form a conception of Pericles' personality and caliber as a leader. He supplements this impression by his own explicit appraisal of Pericles, whom he portrays without a blemish as representing the highest type of statesmanship.

Born about 495, Pericles, the son of Xanthippus, a politician and general, was related through his mother to the ancient aristocratic and politically prominent Athenian family of the Alcmaeonidae, which in the seventh century had incurred a curse for the sacrilege of killing some suppliants who had taken refuge at the altar of the goddess Athena. A supporter of the democratic regime and active in its politics, Pericles became prominent in the 460s, and following the exile of his rival Cimon in 461, acquired a position of great influence. He was a constant promoter of the Athenian empire and took a leading part in the First Peloponnesian War against Sparta. During the 440s he emerged as Athens's dominant political figure by his hold on the democratic citizen body. The people repeatedly reelected him *strategos*, one of the ten generals whose office was the most important in the city politically as well as militarily, a place he occupied almost continuously from 443 to the time of his death in 429. He was one of the initiators of Athens's grandiose public building program, which included the construction of the Parthenon, the great temple of the city's divine patron Athena. Among the policies that brought him his popularity with the democracy was the payment of daily wages to citizens who served on the large Athenian juries. A highly cultured man, an intellectual as well as a politician, Pericles was the friend of some of the foremost artists, philosophers, and poets of the time. One of the teachers of whom he remained a disciple was the great fifth-century philosopher Anaxagoras, who taught that Mind was the animating principle of the universe and was prosecuted in

Athens for impiety. In his private life Pericles was well known for his relationship with his cultivated mistress and companion Aspasia, with whom he lived after divorcing his wife and by whom he had a son.[3]

Thucydides' earliest references to Pericles mention him merely as a successful military commander in several actions and do not trace his rise to power (1.111, 114, 116). In the negotiations of 432 prior to the war, the Spartans called upon the Athenians to drive away the curse associated with Pericles as a descendant of the Alcmaeonids. Thucydides recounts the origin of the curse and then explains that the aim of the Spartan demand, which Athens rejected, was not to honor the gods, but to cause Pericles' banishment if possible so that the Athenians would be more manageable, or else to discredit him with the citizens by making his curse appear partly responsible for the war. The historian then describes Pericles for the first time as "the leader of the state," "the most powerful man of his day," utterly opposed to the Lacedaemonians, against whom "he was always urging . . . the necessity of war" (1.126–27).

We may certainly credit to Pericles the Athenian foreign policy that provoked Sparta and its allies into war. His first speech, from which I have already quoted some passages in the previous chapter, is very important, since it is the first direct impression of him that Thucydides gives and serves to confirm the preceding characterization of him by the historian. It is clear from its tenor that he speaks as the city's leader and is proud of its greatness. Although his immediate purpose was to persuade the Athenian assembly to remain firm against the Lacedaemonians' demands, he supported his opinion by offering a broad strategic analysis of the coming war and the unequal capabilities of the opposing sides. At the outset he remarks on the unpredictability of events, often ruled by chance and capable of belying human calculation; but having said this, he proceeds nevertheless to appraise the situation of the parties in a thoroughly rational and objective manner. His first and main point is to oppose all concessions to the Spartans, arguing that they had tried to dictate terms while always refusing arbitration, and were forcing war upon Athens by their demands. Turning then to a review of the respective resources of the two sides, he emphasizes the great advantages Athens enjoyed by reason of its superior wealth and total control of the sea. The Spartans are poor in comparison, he states, lacking either private or public riches, and incapable of sustaining a long war that would take them away from their own homeland. While in a single pitched battle they and their allies were a match for all Hellas, they would be unable, he held to maintain a protracted war against a power like the Athenian one, which was different from their own and could sail into Spartan territory, raise fortifications there, and use its fleet to inflict reprisals on the enemy. He also notes some further weaknesses of Athens's adversaries, such as their inexperience in naval warfare and the defective organization of the Peloponnesian League, which, as a loose coalition, lacked the unity and political machinery to execute plans with speed and decision.

Pericles looked upon Athens's naval supremacy and empire as its greatest assets. Should the Peloponnesians "attack our country by land," he says, "we shall attack theirs by sea." He declares that the devastation of even a part of the Peloponnesus would do greater harm than would the ravaging of Athenian land in Attica, as the Spartans could only acquire new territory by force of arms, whereas the Athenians had ample land both in the Aegean islands and on the Greek mainland. For this reason, they could give up their lands and houses in the country outside Athens, as long as they kept a watch over their city and held the control of the sea. At this point, he unveils the strategy that he was confident would assure Athens of victory. The Athenians, he advises, "should not under any irritation at the loss of our property give battle to the Peloponnesians," who far outnumber them; for "if we conquer, we shall have to fight over again with as many more; and if we fail, besides the defeat, our confederacy, which is our strength, will be lost to us," because "our allies will rise in revolt when we are no longer capable of making war upon them." He therefore urges the Athenians to be willing if necessary to sacrifice their lands and houses in Attica rather than engage the enemy in a land battle. To this advice he adds the following prophetic warning: "I have many other reasons for believing that you will conquer, but you must not be extending your empire while you are at war, or run into unnecessary dangers. I am more afraid of our own mistakes than of our enemies' designs" (1.140–44).

Pericles' speech is manifestly that of a formidably intelligent strategic thinker. The Athenian assembly approved his policy, and while he may have touched his hearers' emotions when he appealed to them to be worthy of the ancestors, who had created their great empire, he mainly endeavored to convince them through reason and knowledge. The strategy he proposed was not a passive or purely defensive one. It counseled the Athenians to rely on their far greater financial resources and naval supremacy to defeat the Lacedaemonians while avoiding any major infantry engagements with them even if they invaded Attica. The hardest part of this advice was that the Athenians should abandon their houses and farms when they saw them being destroyed by the enemy. Athens was well fortified, however, and the long walls connecting it to its harbor at Piraeus secured its access to the sea. The city was therefore safe and provided a refuge for the population within its walls. Pericles also strongly cautioned against trying to expand the empire during the war. Pondering all these thoughts, however, the reader might wonder whether the Athenians, whom the Corinthians had previously described, in a comparison with the Spartans, as daring, enterprising, and quick to act, would have the patience and restraint to adhere to the sort of strategy Pericles laid out.

Thucydides presents the sequel to this speech early in the second book when the war had begun. As one of the ten Athenian generals, Pericles expected the invasion of Attica by Peloponnesian troops under King Archidamus. Anticipating that the king, who was a friend of his, might spare the lands he owned in the country either out of courtesy or to cast suspicion on him among his fellow citizens, he offered his property there to the public as a sign of his own integrity. With invasion imminent, he reiterated his previous advice, telling the people that they must prepare for war, bring their possessions into the city and defend the walls, but avoid battle. They did as he said, removing their families and goods into Athens, and sending their flocks and other animals to Euboea and adjacent islands (2.13–14).

When Archidamus entered Attica in the middle of the summer of 431, he hoped the Athenians would come out and fight rather than let their fields be ravaged, but they refrained. Advancing further, his army approached to within a few miles of Athens. As they witnessed the devastation of their country, the citizens, as Thucydides reports in a vivid picture of the excitement in the city, "felt the presence of the invader to be intolerable . . . and the whole people, the young men especially, were anxious to go forth and put a stop to it." Furious with Pericles and forgetting his previous warnings, "they abused him for not leading them to battle . . . and laid all their miseries to his charge." Despite their anger, however, he refused to change course. Certain that he was right, he avoided summoning a meeting of the Athenian assembly lest it make a bad decision in its hostile mood. He maintained a strong watch in the city, tried to calm the public irritation, and sent out units of horsemen from time to time to hinder the ravaging of the fields. Meanwhile, Athens dispatched a fleet of a hundred ships carrying a thousand hoplites and four hundred archers on an expedition around the Peloponnesus.[4] After the fleet's departure, the enemy troops in Attica, who were running short of food, withdrew to the Peloponnesus (2.19–23).

This episode, described with many details by Thucydides, conveys a distinct image of the temper and quality of Pericles' leadership. We next see him at the end of the summer commanding a very large Athenian army in an invasion of the territory of Megara (2.31), and soon afterward, in the winter of 431, delivering a second speech, a funeral oration for the Athenians who fell in the first year of the war. The Greeks attached great significance to the burial of the dead. In Athens, according to Thucydides, custom provided for a public funeral at the public cost for those who died in war. The ceremonies traditionally ended with an oration by a man whom the city chose for his ability and high reputation (2.34). Pericles' speech, the longest and most famous in the *History*, has been widely discussed and analyzed by scholars. It has come down from antiquity in Thucydides' version as one of the most eloquent of oratorical performances and a lasting expression of the Athenian civilization that it celebrates and memorializes. Its tone is lofty and solemn, its thoughts wide and commanding. The words Thucydides attributed to Pericles on this occasion constituted a unique tribute to Athens and its democratic polity.

It is worth pausing for a moment to compare his speech with another equally famous funeral oration, President Abraham Lincoln's Gettysburg Address in 1863. Lincoln's speech, which was much shorter, easily matched the solemnity of Pericles' but was also touched by religious feeling. Speaking during the American Civil War on the field of Gettysburg, where thousands of men had suffered death or injury in the battle to preserve the Union, he praised the sacrifice of the soldiers who lost their lives there and the cause for which they fought. His leading thought was that the war constituted a test of whether the new American nation, born in 1776 and dedicated to the principles of liberty and equality for all, would be able to survive. The climax of his address was a moving call for the renewal of American democracy—a resolve that the dead in the war shall not have died in vain and that the nation, "under God, shall have a new birth of freedom" so that government of, by, and for the people "shall not perish from the earth."

Unlike Lincoln, Pericles made no reference to the gods and, save for a mention of the sacrifices which the Athenians perform throughout the year (2.38), did not allude to religion. His vision of freedom was not universal, as Lincoln's might be said to be at least by implication, but was limited to those who enjoyed the rights of citizenship in Athens's democracy. In eulogizing the courage of the fallen, he tended to see their death on behalf of Athens as the highest moment of their existence. His speech was above all an encomium to the spirit of his city and its citizens.

After a few opening remarks, Pericles first voiced gratitude to the Athenians' ancestors and fathers, who had bequeathed to them a free state and brought Athens its great empire. Then, proposing to describe the principles of action by which Athens rose to power and the institutions and manner of life by which it became great, he spoke of the Athenian democracy as a form of government, in which "we live here as free men" (*eleutheros politeuomen*).[5] This part of his speech might almost be interpreted as a reply to the critics of democracy, while in much of what he says both here and afterwards we can also perceive a particular contrast with Sparta and its way of life. Athens is called a democracy, Pericles declares, because "the administration is in the hands of the many and not of the few." While its law "secures equal justice to all in their private disputes," the city also recognizes "the claim of excellence," since citizens distinguished by their ability are promoted in the public service as a reward of merit and none are prevented by poverty from benefiting their country. "[I]n our private intercourse," he continues, "we are not suspicious of one another," nor "angry with our neighbor if he does what he likes," while in public life "we are prevented from doing wrong" by respect for authority and the laws of the city written and unwritten (2.35–37). Moreover, he adds, we have provided for relaxation from toil by games and sacrifices throughout the year, and "at home our style of life is refined," things which all bring daily delight and banish melancholy (2.35–38).

Pericles further pictures Athens as a great center into which commodities flow from everywhere for the enjoyment of its people. "[O]pen to the world," it welcomes foreigners, who are free to see and to learn what they please. He boasts as well of its prowess and bravery in war compared to Sparta. While the Lacedaemonians from early youth onward are always practicing military exercises to make themselves brave, the Athenians "live at ease" and without laborious training are nevertheless "equally ready to face the perils" which their enemies face (2.38–39). Affirming that "our city is thus equally admirable in peace and war" (2.39), he rises to a still higher plane as he proceeds to praise the unique qualities of the Athenian character formed in an environment of democratic freedom:

> We are lovers of the beautiful, yet with economy, and we cultivate the mind without loss of manliness. Wealth we employ, not for talk and ostentation, but when there is a real use for it. To avow poverty with us is no disgrace; the true disgrace is doing nothing to avoid it. An Athenian citizen does not neglect the state because he takes care of his own household; and even those of us who are engaged in business have a very fair idea of politics. We alone regard a man who takes no interest in public affairs, not as a harmless, but as a useless character. The great impediment to action is, in our opinion, not discussion, but the want of that knowledge which is gained by discussion which is preparatory to action. For we have a peculiar power of thinking before we act and of acting too. . . . In doing good . . . we are unlike others; we make our friends by conferring, not by receiving favors. . . . We alone do good to our neighbors not upon a calculation of interest, but in the confidence of freedom and in a frank and fearless spirit. (2.40)

The speech's culminating moment is perhaps the passage that then follows:

> To sum up: I say that Athens is the school of Hellas [*Hellados paideusin*] and that the individual Athenian in his own person seems to have the power of adapting himself to the most varied forms of action with the utmost versatility and grace.

The proof of this truth, he says, is "the position to which these qualities have raised the state." Such is its superiority that no enemy is indignant when it suffers reverses at Athens's hands and "no subject complains that his masters are unworthy of him." It has left as witness of its power "mighty monuments . . . which will make us the wonder of this and succeeding ages. . . . For we have compelled every land and every sea to open a path for our valor and have everywhere planted memorials of our friendship and our enmity" (2.41).

With these words, Pericles returns to the praise of those whose death in the war proved that they were worthy of Athens. Mourning their loss, he links it once more with his exaltation of their city, telling his audience,

> I would have you day by day fix your eyes upon the greatness of Athens, until you become filled with love of her; and when you are impressed by the spectacle of her glory, reflect that this empire has been acquired by men who knew their duty and had the courage to do it, who in the hour of conflict had the fear of dishonor always present to them . . . and freely gave their lives to her as the fairest offering which they could present at her feast.

Speaking of the memory of the dead, he utters one of the most poetic passages of his address:

> For the whole earth is the sepulchre of famous men; not only are they commemorated by columns and inscriptions in their own country, but in foreign lands there dwells also an unwritten memorial of them, graven not on stone, but in the hearts of men. Make them your examples, and esteeming courage to be freedom and freedom to be happiness, do not weigh too nicely the perils of war. (2.42–43)

After offering his consolation to the family and survivors of the dead, Pericles concluded his oration, noting that the children of the fallen would be maintained at the state's expense until they were grown up (2.44–46).

To experience the full impact of this speech, a selection will not suffice; rather, it has to be read and pondered in its entirety as the astonishing praise of the Athenian civilization that Pericles holds in the highest regard. In the twenty-first century, most of us in the Western world may no longer be very partial to such fulsomely patriotic declarations. Having become thoroughly disenchanted with war and having ceased to glorify it, we may be repelled when we hear its waste of life extolled and justified in fine phrases about the young soldiers who did not die in vain. But Pericles was speaking to an Athenian audience for whom their city was their world and who were neither pacifists nor haters of war in which personal bravery was tested to the utmost. The question of how closely the Athenian leader's sentiments as transcribed by Thucydides resembled his actual thoughts is unanswerable, though most probably they did so to some degree.[6] Stylistically the speech abounds with antitheses, a device made popular by the sophist teachers of rhetoric. It contrasts words and deeds, the past and the present, the living and the dead, democracy and other types of government, private and public, political participation and non-involvement, work and recreation, versatility and specialization, wealth and poverty, ignorance and knowledge, speech and action, thinking and action, giving and receiving, and so on. It also synthesizes some apparent opposites: love of beauty with economy, intellectual cultivation with manliness, discussion with action. Its dominant theme is the individual freedom and political participation the Athenians enjoy as citizens of a democracy and how this shapes their lives. This was a thought that Pericles was not alone in expressing. Much later in the *History*, in his account of the Sicilian expedition, Thucydides reports the words of the Athenian commander Nicias to his troops at a desperate juncture when he reminds them that "they were the inhabitants of the freest country in the world," where "there was no interference with the life of any man" (7.69).

The human ideal depicted in the funeral oration is one of the free and many-sided development of personality, a life combining thought and action and consisting in the exercise of diverse faculties—intellectual, practical, and aesthetic—and last but not least, the supreme obligation of loyalty and service to the city. The opposition between this ideal and the narrow Spartan one based on discipline, military professionalism, and disparagement of learning, as we find it voiced earlier in the speech by King Archidamus in book 1 (1.80–85), is explicitly stated or implied in various parts of Pericles' speech.

A major aspect of the speech that should not be overlooked is its rationalization of Athenian imperialism. Pericles glorifies the creators of the Athenian empire and holds that Athens's superiority renders it worthy to rule others. Praising the dead, he is quite clear that in dying for Athens, they died for its empire. He boasts that the city has forced its way into every land and sea, leaving eternal memorials everywhere. When he proudly declares that "Athens is the school of Hellas," he is picturing his city as the educator of all Greece. After Greek civilization had passed away, later ages understood and concurred with this statement as a valid description of classical Athens's cultural primacy.[7] Possibly it means only that Athens stands as an example to the rest of Greece. But we may also want to read the statement as similar in spirit to the claim to be the carriers of a higher civilization that the Western imperialist powers in the nineteenth and twentieth centuries converted into an ideology to justify and rationalize their acquisition and rule over their colonial empires in Asia and Africa.

As soon as Thucydides has finished reporting Pericles' speech, he proceeds immediately to record the outbreak of the plague that struck Athens in 430. In its clinical detail and portrayal of human suffering, his account of the disease and its effects is one of the most powerful and brilliant parts of the *History*. His description of the social and moral breakdown the epidemic produced among the people of Athens—the universal violation of funeral customs in the disposal of corpses, the unrestrained indulgence in pleasure by many who felt themselves under sentence of death, the growth of lawlessness and criminality—seems to cast an ironic light on Pericles' ideal image of Athens in the funeral oration; "for the violence of the calamity was such," the historian relates, "that men, not knowing where to turn, grew reckless of all law, human and divine" (2.53).[8]

While the plague raged in Athens, a Peloponnesian invasion force was laying waste to Attica for the second time. Pericles, however, we are told, "continued to insist . . . that the Athenians should remain within their walls" (2.55). By now, though, weighed down by both the war and the plague, the mass of the people were no longer willing to heed Pericles, whom they accused of persuading them to go to war and of being the cause of their troubles. The city even sent envoys with an offer of peace to the Spartans, but without any success (2.59).

At this juncture we see Pericles again in his third and final speech, an address to the Athenian assembly intended to hearten the people, restore their confidence in him, and convince them to carry on with the war.[9] I have already quoted a bit from this speech in the preceding chapter. The thought of Athens's empire is much present in it, and it is also very remarkable for what it reveals about the character of Pericles as a democratic leader in his relationship to the citizen electorate to which he owed his power. Rather than try to appease popular feeling by mollifying words, he sticks to his convictions and endeavors to give the citizens some instruction. He first reproves them for their "inconsiderate anger against him, and want of fortitude in misfortune." Arguing that it was better that individual citizens should suffer and the state flourish rather than that citizens should flourish and the state suffer,[10] he exhorts them to stand by their country and not let their private calamities cause them to condemn not only him who advised the war but also themselves who had consented to it. Calling himself a lover of Athens and incorruptible, he protests that if they thought him a statesman when they decided to go to war, they were unfair now to accuse him of a crime. While he himself, he says, remained the same man, they had changed and decided that his advice was wrong because their characters were weak. Owing to the suffering their misfortunes caused, they lacked the strength of mind to persevere in their resolution and were not yet able to see the good that would come of it. He admits that a sudden and completely unexpected disaster like the plague could break the spirit, but reminds them that as "citizens of a great city and educated in a temper of greatness, you should not succumb to calamities however overwhelming, and darken the luster of your fame. . . . You should lose the sense of your private sorrows and lay fast hold of the common good" (2.60–61).

He then strives to raise their morale by telling them that their sufferings in the war would not be fruitless because they possessed an element of military superiority of which they were unaware. Their empire, he says, was not limited to their allies but also gave them absolute mastery over the sea. Wherever the Athenian navy chose to sail, neither the king of Persia nor any nation on earth could hinder it. In comparison to this great power, he maintains, the loss of their houses and lands meant nothing; for "if we cling to our freedom and preserve that, we shall soon enough recover all the rest. But, if we are the servants of others, we shall be sure to lose not only freedom, but all that freedom gives." Urging perseverance in the war, therefore, he assures the people that grounds of reason showed that they were stronger than the enemy. In a characteristic emphasis upon the importance of mind in war and politics, he points out that "courage . . . is fortified by the intelligence which looks down upon an enemy; an intelligence relying, not on hope, which is the strength of helplessness, but on that surer foresight which is given by reason and observation of facts" (2.62).

He thus called upon the citizens to maintain the imperial dignity of Athens in which they all took pride. Let them remember, he tells them, that they are fighting not only for their freedom but to keep an empire which has become a tyranny and which they dare not surrender because of the hatred it has brought upon them. They should not be led away by the bad advice of those who are angry with him, since the resolution in favor of war was theirs as well as his. Asking that they bear their sufferings with resignation and manliness, he appeals to their patriotism, a theme close to his heart, by recalling the fame and preeminence of Athens, "which has the greatest name in all the world because she has never yielded to misfortunes, but has sacrificed more lives and endured more hardships in war than any other; wherefore also she has the greatest power of any state up to this day; and the memory of her glory will always survive." Even if its greatness should somewhat decline, he forebodingly says, "for all things have their time of growth and decay," the recollection of its predominance would live (2.63–64).

The effect of his persuasion was that the Athenians "were again eager to prosecute the war." But Thucydides also reports that they felt their sufferings keenly, the poor having been deprived even of the little they possessed, while the more affluent had lost their estates in the country and their houses and rich furniture. Their anger was not pacified until they fined Pericles, but soon afterward, "with the usual fickleness of the multitude, they elected him general and committed all their affairs to his charge" (2.65).

After recording Pericles' final speech, Thucydides summed up his judgment of the Athenian leader in a significant passage of unusual length that is linked to the notice of his death in 429, two and a half years after the war began. He first points out how successfully Pericles guided Athens during the period of peace, in which the city reached its greatest height, while in war too he formed a true estimate of its power. After he died, "his foresight was even better appreciated than during his life," for the Athenians then proceeded to do everything he told them not to do, disregarding his advice that they would be victorious if they remained patient, looked to their navy, and avoided expanding their empire or endangering the existence of the city while the war continued. By the policies they adopted, which served only private ambition and interest, they did great damage to themselves and their allies and crippled the city in the conduct of the war. Thucydides placed the blame for this result on the difference between Pericles as a leader and the inferior men who followed him. The reason for this difference, he explains, is that Pericles,

> deriving authority from his capacity and acknowledged worth, being a man also of transparent integrity, was able to control the multitude in a free spirit; he led them rather than was led by them; for, not seeking power by dishonest arts, he had no need to say pleasant things, but on the strength of his own high character, could venture to oppose and even to anger them; his words humbled and awed them; and when they were depressed by groundless fears, he sought to reanimate their confidence. Thus Athens, though still in name a democracy, was in fact ruled by her first citizen. (2.65)

His successors, however, who were more or less equal to each other and competed to be first, sacrificed the conduct of affairs to the people's whims and were guilty of many errors. Among these, Thucydides mentions particularly the failure of the Sicilian expedition, launched fourteen years after Pericles' death, which cost Athens the greater part of its army and its fleet. He attributes the Athenian defeat in Sicily not to a miscalculation of the enemy's power, but to the faults of the democracy. Yet even after this and other reverses, he points out that Athens was still able to carry on the war and was finally overthrown not by its enemies but by internal dissensions. Hence he drew the conclusion that Pericles was fully justified in his foresight that Athens "would win an easy victory over the unaided forces of the Peloponnesians" (2.65).

Thucydides' prescience, when writing of events in 429, concerning Athens's fall twenty-five years later, shows, as I have noted in an earlier chapter, that he must have written his evaluation of Pericles in hindsight after the war ended. Contemplating Athens's defeat and the loss of its empire, which occurred after Pericles was no longer present to guide its destiny, the historian admires his leadership without any qualification. The three speeches by Pericles that he presents in books 1 and 2 make up a united whole. They express both an image of the speaker and an exposition of his policy which remain consistent throughout.[11] The Athenian statesman lives for Athens and to enhance its greatness. He is devoid of selfish interests and thinks only of the good of the state with which the well-being of its citizens is bound up. He has an ideal conception of the uniqueness and superiority of Athens because of the free individuality and versatile intelligence of its citizens, which set it off from all the other cities of Greece. He prizes mind, forethought, and discussion as the begetter of successful action. He believes in the necessity of power and is an imperialist for whom Athens's independence and freedom and its imperial dominion are intertwined and inseparable. It is striking that he did not shrink from calling the empire a tyranny. Yet he looks upon it as a magnificent achievement that not only serves Athens's material interests but stands as a measure of the city's glory and power that will cause it to be eternally remembered. His policy is especially directed to the maintenance of Athens's naval supremacy, which he sees as the guarantee of victory over Sparta and its allies. As long as Athens controls the sea and avoids pitched battles with the Lacedaemonians, the city can afford losses on land, carry the war wherever it wishes, and by reason of its wealth outlast its enemies. Finally, his policy is also moderate and prudent, intent on keeping the city safe and insisting that it should not try to expand its empire while fighting the war.

Modern historians have differed over whether Pericles' mainly defensive war strategy was the best for Athens.[12] Thucydides expresses no doubt that it was and fully approves of it. He did not think much of democracy unless it was fortunate enough to have at its head someone as able and incorruptible as Pericles.[13] We should not take too literally, though, his statement that Athens during Pericles' sway was a democracy in name only and was really ruled by its great leader, since the latter could not have governed as a general and politician unless he retained the confidence and support of the citizenry. In the view of Thucydides, Pericles' dedication to Athens, aristocratic integrity, and embodiment of the union of thought and action exemplified the highest virtues of a statesman. That the historian, with all his effort at impartiality, regretted and mourned Pericles' loss is evident. His passing from the scene early in the war and replacement by lesser men who abandoned his policy was a landmark event for Thucydides. It is commemorated by his very exceptional comments in 2.65 on the departed statesman, which were written in the sad light of his later knowledge of Athens's ultimate defeat.

Scenes from the Archidamian War

MYTILENE, PLATAEA, CORCYRA, PYLOS

> This day will be the beginning of great evils for
> the Hellenes. (2.12)

THE GLOOMY prophesy above, which was fully confirmed by events, was uttered by the Spartan envoy Melesippus after the Athenians refused to receive him on a last mission to persuade them to yield, and while King Archidamus and his Peloponnesian army were already marching to invade Attica. Thucydides began his narrative of the Ten Year or Archidamian War with the opening of the second book and continued it through book 5.25. In the latter passage, while mentioning the accord of 421 that terminated this first period of the war, he also anticipates the short life of the peace treaty and the war's renewal. Book 2 relates the commencement of the war in the spring and summer of 431 in two separate episodes: the surprise attack by Sparta's ally Thebes upon its neighbor city Plataea, the ally of Athens, followed eighty days later by the Peloponnesian invasion of Attica (2.2–6, 10, 18–19).[1] Thucydides briefly describes some of the immediate preparations that each side made for the war and also gives a complete list of both the allies of Sparta and of Athens (2.7, 9). In the case of Athens, his summary in indirect discourse of a speech by Pericles presents a number of important facts about the city's large reserves of treasure and its military manpower at the outset of the war. The latter included 29,000 hoplites, 16,000 of whom occupied the fortresses and manned the walls of the city to defend against an enemy invasion. Besides these soldiers, Athens had 1,200 cavalry including archers, plus 1,800 foot archers. As for its fleet, the city had three hundred triremes fit for service (2.13). Each of these ships was a long vessel with a heavy battering ram sheathed in bronze attached to its prow at the water line. It was propelled by three banks of rowers numbering as many as 170 men and also manned by marines and sailors. Although the historian states that the Peloponnesians intended to increase their navy to five hundred ships (2.7), he supplies no information on their financial resources or the size of their military forces at the beginning of the war, for the reason, probably, that he was unable to obtain it.

At the outbreak of the First World War in August 1914, the nations on both sides hailed the event with wild enthusiasm, never imagining the length of the coming conflict or the unparalleled carnage and destruction it would cause. The start of the Franco-Prussian War of 1870, too, was greeted with acclaim by the French and German people. Thucydides throws some light on the prevailing mood in 431 when the great war began between Athens, Sparta, and their allies. Both sides, he said,

> were full of enthusiasm: and no wonder, for all men are energetic when they are making a beginning. At that time the youth of Peloponnesus and the youth of Athens were numerous; they had never seen war, and were therefore very willing to take up arms. All Hellas was excited by the coming conflict between her two chief cities. (2.8)

Thucydides presents many graphic scenes of combat on sea and land, but does not give an account of the nature of warfare at this period, which he could assume that his readers understood well enough. The fighting forces of both the Athenians and Peloponnesians were comprised very largely of male citizens, one of whose duties was to serve their city in war. In sea battles the triremes fought by trying to ram the side of the enemy's ships with their beaked prows to damage or disable them so that they could be captured and towed away or possibly sunk. The other tactic was to close with and board an enemy ship in order to take it in hand-to-hand combat. In battles on land, although cavalry, archers, and lightly armed troops equipped with javelins might play a part in flanking attacks, the decisive offensive element was the heavily armed hoplite infantry massed in phalanx formation. The hoplites of the period had to supply their armor and weapons at their own expense and hence were usually recruited in Athens and other cities from the somewhat better-off male members of the population. They were equipped with a crested bronze helmet, breastplate, and greaves, a tall shield borne on the left arm, a sword, and a long spear held in the other hand. Positioned in a horizontal line and in columns of about eight men deep, each man shoulder to shoulder with his neighbor and all carrying their shields before them like a wall, the phalanxes of the hoplite army marched forward across the field at an increasing pace to the sound of shouts and war cries, striving to hold their close order as they neared the enemy advancing toward them in similar formation. Thucydides noted that "all armies, when engaging, are apt to move outwards towards their right wing . . . because every soldier individually fears for his exposed side, which he tries to cover with the shield of his comrade on the right, conceiving that the closer he draws in the better he will be protected" (5.71). The charge of a hoplite army could be such a terrifying sight that sometimes the soldiers of the other side would simply turn and run. Thucydides described the Spartans' advance in the great battle of Mantinea in 418 against Argos and its allies, where they were victorious. Their custom was to move forward slowly "to the music of many flute players, who were stationed in their ranks, and played, not as an act of religion, but in order that the army might march evenly and in true measure, and that the line might not break, as often happens in great armies when they go into battle" (5.70). When the two opposing bodies of men crashed against each other with an awful shock, the hoplites behind the front rows of warriors pushed forward hard against the backs of the men ahead of them in order by their weight and momentum to force a breach in the enemy line. As soon as the ranks of either side gave way or broke, the fighting became a melee of individual combat and killing in which the army that retreated and ran was defeated. Thucydides pictures a scene of this kind at the battle of Delium in 424 involving thousands of infantry on both sides, at which Sparta's allies the Boeotians defeated the Athenians. "The two armies met at a run," he reports, and although the right and left wings of both never engaged "the rest closed, and there was a fierce struggle and pushing of shield against shield" (4.96). Hoplite battle, though a fearsome and ferocious ordeal, did not last long, usually no more than a few hours of a single day, and pursuit of a defeated enemy was limited. After the battle the victorious side erected a trophy and at the enemy's request returned its dead. In these combats, it was quite common for the battlefield commanders, who took part in the front rank with their men, to be killed in the fighting.[2]

In the conduct of war, the Greeks had tended to recognize certain rules or conventions. Among them were that sacred places should not be violated nor should persons under the protection of the gods, like suppliants and heralds, be harmed. Prisoners, too, and enemies who surrendered were not to be killed. All of these prohibitions often gave way during the Peloponnesian War, which witnessed many atrocities, including the killing of ambassadors and suppliants, the execution of prisoners and enemies taken after surrender, and wholesale massacres.[3]

Athens's strategy in the war was at first the one laid out by Pericles, who, as Thucydides reported, assured the Athenians that they would win if they avoided land engagements with Sparta, maintained their fleet and the defense of the city, and refrained from trying to expand their empire during the war. After his death in 429, the Athenians resorted to a more offensive policy by damaging assaults directly on Spartan territory, which they were able to launch by means of their naval superiority. Thucydides does not explicitly discuss the Spartan strategy when the war began, but we can infer that it was based on the plan of invading and ravaging Attica to such an extent that Athens would soon be forced to make peace on Sparta's terms. During the decade of the Archidamian War, the Peloponnesians invaded Attica five times and certainly hoped and expected at first that the Athenians would come out to meet them in battle. The longest invasion was the second in 430, which lasted forty-five days, while the shortest in 425 lasted fifteen. Thucydides noted that the second invasion and a third in 427 caused the greatest distress to the Athenians (3.26). It was cruel for them, of course, to see their lands and houses outside the city ravaged and burned, and the recurrence and effects of the plague intensified their suffering. Nevertheless, the Spartan strategy did not sap the Athenians' will and had no success in compelling Athens to end the war.[4]

In his third book Thucydides recorded three incidents of the war in close succession which occurred in the same year, 427. The first was Athens's punishment of its ally Mytilene for rebelling against it. The second was Sparta's punishment of Athens's ally Plataea after its capture. The third was the revolution in Corcyra and its consequences. The narrative of the first two events includes reports of speeches, and in the case of the third, the longest personal statement by Thucydides in the entire history. The fact that he chose to devote so much attention to these three incidents suggests that he considered them exceptionally noteworthy in their representative significance. His treatment of the issues they presented is profoundly revealing for what it tells about the play of power and the passions of the war, the Greek moral horizon, Athenian politics after Pericles, and his own attitudes and values.

ATHENS AND MYTILENE (3.3–18, 25–50)

Mytilene, the largest city of the island of Lesbos off the coast of Asia Minor, was an ally of Athens that revolted against Athenian domination in 428 and compelled most of the other towns of Lesbos to join with it. Thucydides describes the development of the revolt, a movement long planned, and Athens's actions to suppress it. Hoping to obtain aid and an alliance from the Lacedaemonians, Mytilene, whose polity was oligarchic, sent ambassadors to plead its case at a meeting of the Peloponnesian allies in Olympia during the Olympic Games. In their speech they acknowledged that Mytilene's position in the Athenian empire was an exceptional one, because unlike nearly every other ally of Athens it still remained autonomous and not enslaved; but they also contended that its fear that it would soon be subjugated justified its rebellion. The Peloponnesians heard them favorably and, accepting Mytilene as an ally, promised to assist it against Athens. Not long afterward, a large Athenian fleet reinforced by a thousand hoplites blockaded and cut off Mytilene by land and sea. Salaethus, a Spartan envoy who managed to get through the blockade and take command in the city, assured the Mytileneans that forty Peloponnesian ships would soon arrive to help them. By the time this fleet drew near, however, Mytilene had already fallen to the Athenians, and so it sailed home. What had happened meanwhile was that as the besieged city ran short of provisions, an insurrection of the lower classes who demanded their share of food forced the ruling oligarchy to negotiate a surrender with the Athenian general Paches. Its terms provided that Mytilene's fate in the wake of its rebellion should be decided in Athens and allowed the civic magistrates to send a delegation to Athens on their own behalf. After occupying Mytilene with his troops, Paches dispatched Salaethus and about a thousand men implicated in the revolt as prisoners to Athens.

When these captives reached Athens, the Spartan Salaethus was immediately executed. In the alarm and anger provoked by the

Mytilenean revolt, the Athenian assembly voted to kill not only the prisoners held in Athens but all the adult males of the rebel city and to enslave the women and children. A ship was promptly sent to Mytilene with an order to Paches to carry out this sentence immediately. No sooner had the Athenians made this decision, however, when they were overcome by qualms as they began to reflect, according to Thucydides, "that a decree which doomed to destruction not only the guilty, but a whole city, was cruel and monstrous" (3.36). This feeling was so widespread that on the following day the assembly held another meeting to reconsider the matter.

Thucydides' narrative up to this point sets the stage for what must have seemed to him the most important and illuminating part of the whole affair: the dramatic debate concerning the treatment of Mytilene and the first appearance in the *History* of the popular figure Cleon, the man who proposed the decree of the previous day condemning the Mytileneans to death and slavery. His was one of the two speeches on the renewal of the issue of Mytilene that Thucydides reports. Cleon was one of the new politicians who had succeeded Pericles in the leadership of the Athenian democracy. The son of a wealthy tanner and thus of inferior social origin, audacious, coarse, and self-confident, he had risen to a dominant position in Athenian politics by his talent in appealing to the populace. He was in favor of the ruthless prosecution of the war and while serving as a general was later killed at Amphipolis in 422 toward the end of the Archidamian War. Upon introducing him, the historian comments that "he was the most violent of the citizens and at that time exercised by far the greatest influence over the people" (3.36). From this and several later references, it is clear that the patrician Thucydides felt a strong antipathy to Cleon, whom he considered a cheap, dishonest demagogue and unfit leader of the foremost city of Hellas. Of all the persons who appear in his *History*, Cleon is treated with the least impartiality.[5] Although Thucydides never says so, we might guess that he did not approve of Cleon's draconian policy toward Mytilene after the suppression of its revolt.

Cleon's speech on the subject is an able performance that mixes an aggressive attempt to discredit his opponents with crude populist flattery and an appeal to justice (*to dikaion*) understood as deserved retribution for wrongs done to Athens. Paradoxically, its readiness to criticize the Athenians and its allusions to the Athenian empire contain echoes of Pericles' speeches. It is altogether contrary to Pericles' spirit, however, in its contemptuous attitude towards political discussion and its discouragement of further deliberation on the question of Mytilene. Determined to prevent a reversal of the assembly's previous decision, Cleon starts by blaming the Athenians for their weakness in regretting their condemnation of the Mytileneans, a fault he denounces as dangerous and showing that a democracy is incompetent to govern others. He admonishes them to remember that their empire is "a despotism exercised over unwilling subjects" who neither love them nor obey in return for any kindness on Athens's part but are "held down by force." It is detestable, moreover, "to be perpetually changing our minds." A state with imperfect but unalterable laws is superior to one with good laws that are not observed. He goes on to praise the simple sort of people as better citizens than the more astute, who, wishing to be thought wiser than the laws, take the lead in debates in the assembly where they speak their minds to display their cleverness and whose folly generally brings ruin to their country. Questioning the good faith of speakers who oppose his view, he reproves the listeners beguiled by their rhetoric, whom he describes as more like spectators at a performance of sophists than counselors for the state's welfare.

Coming to the heart of his speech, he asks his hearers to understand that Mytilene had done greater injury to Athens than had any other single city; for while it was possible to make allowances for a state that found Athenian rule too heavy to bear or was compelled by the enemy to revolt, Mytilene had no such excuse. Athens had allowed it its independence and treated it with the highest consideration, yet it joined with Athens's greatest enemies to destroy it. "We should from the first," he says, "have made no difference between the Mytileneans and the rest of our allies, and then their insolence would not have risen to such a height; for men naturally despise those who court them, but respect those who do not give way to them" (3.39). Since Mytilene had preferred "might to right," it should be deservedly punished for its crime. This punishment, he insists, must include not only the upper classes, but also the common people, who had likewise taken part in the revolt. Urging that the Athenians must not let pity, the charm of words, or a too forgiving temper—three weaknesses fatal to empire—induce them to reverse their decision, he emphasizes both the expediency (*ta xumphora*) and the justice of treating the rebels with the utmost severity in order to deter other allies who might want to revolt. If they take the opposite course, he tells them, "you will be self-condemned," because if the rebels "were right in revolting, you must be wrong in maintaining your empire. But if, right or wrong, you are resolved to rule, then rightly or wrongly they must be punished for your own good" (3.40). In his conclusion, pleading with his hearers not to be soft-hearted but to remember the danger that had hung over their heads, Cleon repeats his call to chastise the wrongdoers as they deserve and "prove by an example to your allies that rebellion will be punished with death" (3.40).

The second speaker was Diodotus, of whom virtually nothing is known and who is not mentioned again by Thucydides. At the previous meeting of the assembly, he had been the main opponent of the decree condemning the Mytileneans. Reiterating his opinion in a speech no less able than Cleon's, he ignores justice altogether and bases his case wholly on expediency and Athenian self-interest.

Diodotus begins with an affirmation of the value of debate and deliberation in order to assure that the Athenians are given wise advice. Observing that "haste and passion were the two things most adverse to good counsel," he praises the reconsideration of Mytilene's sentence and "the practice of deliberating more than once about matters so critical." He censures speakers who use slander to terrify their opponents and the audience, thereby depriving the city of its counselors by fear. "The good citizen," he maintains, "should prove his superiority as a speaker, not by trying to intimidate those who will follow him in debate, but by fair argument" (3.42). All these statements, of course, were aimed at Cleon. Diodotus goes on to criticize the Athenians for being a difficult people to advise, because their excessive cleverness, he says, causes them to suspect any speaker who delivers his advice in plain terms of having corrupt motives or trying to deceive them.[6]

Coming to the case of the Mytileneans, he argues that the right question to consider is not the magnitude of their crimes, "but what is for our interest" (3.44). However great their guilt, he avers, he would not advise their death unless it was advantageous, and similarly, even if there was some excuse for them, he would not want them spared unless it benefited the state. From this perspective he rules out justice as an issue and proceeds to contradict

Cleon's claim that inflicting death on the Mytileneans would deter future revolts. States over time, he points out, had continually increased their punishments by prescribing death for many offenses, yet without preventing future transgressions. "[D]eath deters nobody," he contends, and it is absurd to suppose that human nature, when hope and desire leads it to embark upon some enterprise, can be restrained by the law or any other terror (3.45).

Having thus impugned the deterrent effect of the death penalty, Diodotus warns that Athens should avoid driving rebellious subjects to despair. For if they once rebelled, they would resist to the last, knowing that it would make no difference to their fate whether they surrendered or not. After being finally conquered, their cities would be left in ruins and yield no benefit to Athens. Since the Athenians would only injure themselves by treating offenses with the severity of a judge, they should look to the future and impose only moderate penalties on rebellious subjects in order to profit from their wealth and service. He couples this opinion with the insistence that the true safeguard against revolt is not the severity of the penalties but extreme vigilance beforehand to prevent subjects from even thinking of rebellion. Finally, he attacks Cleon's error in proposing to kill not only those responsible for Mytilene's revolt but the entire male population. Here he makes the point that the common people are invariably supporters of Athens.[7] To execute them would not only be a crime but play into the hands of ruling oligarchies, who if they induced a city to revolt would have the people on their side because the latter knew that Athens's policy was to punish everyone whether guilty or innocent. Denying Cleon's view that justice and expediency could be combined, he concludes that it is "far more conducive to the maintenance of the Athenian empire, to suffer wrong willingly, than for the sake of justice to put to death those whom we had better spare" (3.47).

These speeches present another of those dramatic confrontations of opposing policies and values that are one of the hallmarks of Thucydides' work. Both the speakers stood forth as champions of Athenian imperialism. But while Cleon appeared as a vengeful orator demanding the extreme penalty in the name of justice, Diodotus presented himself as a wise and reasonable adviser counseling moderation in the name of expediency.[8] When it came to a vote, Diodotus's motion prevailed by a small margin. A ship departed immediately for Mytilene to overtake the first vessel bearing the order of execution, which had started on its voyage twenty-four hours earlier. Fortunately, the latter had not hurried on its mission, and the second ship, whose oarsmen ate while they rowed and rowed and slept in turns, arrived shortly after the first one just in time to stop Paches from carrying out the sentence. "So near," Thucydides says, "was Mytilene to destruction" (3.49).

In recounting this episode in his *History of Greece*, the great Victorian scholar George Grote commented that "the Athenians, on the whole, [were] the most humane people in Greece (though humanity, according to our ideas, cannot be predicated of any Greeks)."[9] If we consider Thucydides' description of the actual punishment that Athens finally meted out to Mytilene for its revolt, it was certainly far from moderate. All the thousand or more Mytilenean prisoners in Athens were put to death; the city's walls were demolished and its fleet confiscated; the territory of Mytilene and the other rebel towns was divided into three thousand allotments, most of which were leased to Athenian colonists and cultivated by the natives who paid the colonists an annual rent; and Athens took possession of the towns Mytilene held on the Asia Minor mainland. "Thus," writes Thucydides in conclusion, "ended the revolt of Lesbos" (3.50).

The Plataean Debate (3.52–68)

Situated in Boeotia near the border with Attica, Plataea, long allied with Athens, was renowned as the site of the great battle that defeated the Persian invaders in 479. Six hundred of its men fought alongside the other Greeks against King Xerxes' host, and every five years the city held the *eleutheria* or Freedom Festival to commemorate the battle and Greek victory. The surprise attack on Plataea by Sparta's ally Thebes in the spring of 431 was one of the two events Thucydides marked as the beginning of the Peloponnesian War. The Plataeans succeeded in expelling the Theban troops, killing some and taking almost two hundred others as prisoners whom they put to death despite promising to spare them. After this event, Athens sent a force to help hold Plataea while many of the citizens removed their wives and children to Athens for safety. Two years later King Archidamus, instead of invading Attica, led a Peloponnesian army against Plataea, intending to devastate its territory. The Plataeans sent him a protest, reminding him that after the battle of Plataea the Spartans had sworn an oath promising to preserve and defend the city's independence. Archidamus answered that he would respect its autonomy if it was willing to help Sparta to liberate the Greeks from Athenian subjection, or at least to remain neutral. When the Plataeans declined this offer, Archidamus asked them to allow the Lacedaemonians to take over their city and property, promising that everything would be returned to them at the end of the war. After hearing this proposition and fearing for their existence, they consulted the Athenians, who replied that they would protect Plataea to their utmost power and that it should not forsake the Athenian alliance. The Plataeans accordingly resolved to stick with Athens. Thereupon Archidamus, after first appealing to the gods and heroes of Plataea to recognize the righteousness of his cause, began a long siege and blockade of the city, which his troops surrounded with a wall.[10]

All these developments Thucydides relates at intervals in his second book. Resuming the story in book 3, he describes the hopeless situation of the besieged city as it was deprived of food, and the successful attempt of about two hundred of the men inside to break out and escape (3.20–24). Athens, of course, did not bring it help, because that would have required engaging the Lacedaemonians in battle; Plataea, moreover, did not have much military importance. Finally, in the summer of 427, the starving city surrendered on the Lacedaemonians' terms that no one would be punished without a just cause. Within a few days, five judges arrived from Sparta, who, rather than bringing any specific charges against the Plataeans, simply asked each of the remaining defenders of the city whether they had done any service to the Lacedaemonians or their allies during the war. Hoping to avoid answering this cynical question, the Plataeans obtained permission to speak at greater length and chose two of their number to make their case (3.52).

This was the prelude to the two speeches, the first by the Plataean spokesmen, the second by their bitter enemies the Thebans, that Thucydides reports verbatim. Here again antitheses encounter each other and policies and values clash. Possibly it was the deliberate plan of the historian that the Plataean speech should appear somewhat disorganized. With their lives at stake, the speakers give the impression of being so terrified that they have difficulty putting their thoughts in order. What stands out most of all is the pathos and hopelessness of their situation, forced to plead before judges who were really their prosecutors and in the presence of Sparta's Theban allies, who wanted their blood.

The main argument the Plataeans advanced in their defense was based on the claims of gratitude and justice. They recalled Plataea's part in repelling the Persian invasion, when it fought at the Spartans' side, and how it afterward aided Sparta to put down a helot rebellion. If it then became Sparta's enemy, this was because prior to the war, when the Plataeans asked Sparta for help against the violence of the Thebans, it refused their request, and so they turned to Athens. The Athenians having been their benefactors, they could not betray them. The Thebans had done them many injuries and tried to seize their city, and they should not have to suffer for defending themselves and punishing the aggressor, as a universal law allowed. They expressed fear, however, that their Spartan judges would not be impartial, but take expediency and hatred as the measure of justice. Unable to leave the subject alone, they reverted once more to Plataea's contribution to the defense of Greek freedom against the Persians. At that time, they said, the Spartans held them in high honor for their principles of loyalty, yet now the same principles, which had led them to an alliance with Athens, would prove to be their destruction.

They went on to plead with their judges not to blemish the Spartan reputation for nobility by passing an unjust sentence which would arouse the indignation of mankind. Again they spoke of the Persian War and of the Plataeans as "benefactors of Hellas." Would it not be monstrous, they asked, if the Lacedaemonians destroyed their city and for the sake of the Thebans blotted out an entire people? The Plataeans, they lamented, "who were zealous in the cause of Hellas even beyond their strength, are now friendless, spurned and rejected by all. None of our old allies will help us, and we fear that you, O Lacedaemonians, our only hope, are not to be depended upon" (3.37).

From this point on, their speech becomes mostly an appeal to pity. They had surrendered and stretched out their hands as suppliants, they told their judges, and "the custom of Hellas does not allow suppliants to be put to death." They begged that the Spartans remember their ancestors killed by the Persians on Plataean soil, whose tombs the citizens of Plataea honored annually with public offerings. If the Spartans put the Plataeans to death and allowed Thebes to annex Plataea, they would "enslave the land in which the Hellenes won their liberty" and "bring desolation upon the temples in which they prayed when they conquered the Persians" (3.58). They ended with a call for mercy, in which they asked the Spartans to think also "of the uncertainty of fortune, which may strike anyone however innocent." They beseeched them not to deliver the Plataeans, "who were so loyal to the cause of Hellas," into the hands of Thebes, their worst enemy. "Be our saviors," they prayed. "You are liberating the other Hellenes; do not destroy us" (3.59).

The Thebans' answer to this affecting statement was a brutal indictment of Plataean wrongdoing and an insistence that justice was on their side. An embarrassing point they had to deal with first was the historical fact that Plataea was the sole Boeotian city that had joined the Greek resistance to the Persian invasion, while Thebes itself chose to help the Persians. "[T]his is [the Plataeans'] great glory," the Thebans said, "and our great reproach." They charged, however, that the only reason the Plataeans did not side with the Persians was because "the Athenians did not," and that afterward Plataea was alone of all the cities of Boeotia in standing with Athens in its attack upon the liberties of Hellas (3.62). They thus sought to equate Thebes's previous support of Persia with Plataea's support of Athens. They also extenuated Thebes's conduct at the time of the Persian invasion by the argument that the city was then ruled by a small despotic group which compelled it to support the Persians; but that after Thebes had freed itself and obtained a constitution, it had fought consistently against Athenian aggression.

The Thebans then proceeded to denounce Plataea's record. Disallowing its claim of obligation to Athens, they accused it of betraying all the Greeks by following the Athenians in "the path of injustice" and helping them to enslave all their allies (3.64). They refused to accept any blame for their attack on Plataea, contending that they were invited by some of the latter's richest and noblest citizens "who wished to withdraw [it] from a foreign alliance [meaning of course the alliance with Athens] and to bring [it] back to the national institutions of Boeotia" (3.65). And they particularly condemned the Plataeans for the crime of slaughtering the

Theban prisoners whom they had captured and first promised to spare as suppliants.

The Thebans closed their address with an exhortation to the Spartans not to let their hearts be softened by the Plataeans' tales of their ancient virtues or their pitiful lamentations and appeals to the Spartan fathers' tombs. "Men," they said, "who suffer an unworthy fate are indeed to be pitied, but there should be joy over those who suffer justly" (3.67). The Plataeans had only themselves to thank for their plight. They could have chosen the worthier alliance, but preferred Athens instead. Possessed by the spirit of hatred, they did injury to Thebes. before Thebes ever injured them. "Maintain then, Lacedaemonians," the Theban speakers urged, "the common Hellenic law which [the Plataeans] have outraged, and give to us, who have suffered contrary to law, the just recompense of our zeal in your cause. Do not be moved by their words to spurn and reject us, but show Hellas by example that, when a cause is tried at your tribunal, deeds and not words will prevail" (3.67).

In the debate over Mytilene, the Athenians proved to be more merciful than were the Spartans at Plataea, although both of them acted in accord with expediency and the dictates of power rather than justice. Thucydides' narrative diminishes the credit of the Spartan judges by stating that they pretended to have believed that the Plataeans would remain neutral because of a treaty they had made with Sparta after the Persian War (3.68). As Plataea had not been neutral, the judges could conclude that the Spartans were released from any obligation to them. The hearing they gave the Plataeans was in any case a mere formality with a predetermined outcome. Taking no notice of the latters' plea, the judges resumed the procedure of asking all the prisoners separately whether they had done any service to the Lacedaemonians and their allies in the war. As each gave his negative answer, he was led away and killed. Two hundred of them were put to death that day, along with twenty-five Athenians. All the women taken in the siege were enslaved. About a year later the Thebans razed Plataea to its foundations, erecting on the site a temple to the goddess Hera and a large inn close by. They made the city's territory into public land that they divided up and leased to individuals. Thucydides declared that the Lacedaemonians' severity to the Plataeans sprang from "a desire to gratify the Thebans, who seemed likely to be useful allies to them in the war just then beginning. "Such was the fate of Plataea," he concludes his account of the city's tragic end, "which was overthrown ninety-three years after the Plataeans entered into alliance with Athens" (3.68).[11]

The Revolution in Corcyra (3.70–83)

The Greek word *stasis* means civil strife, sedition, or internal war and can also be translated as revolution. In the fifth century, the *staseis* or revolutions that occurred in the Greek city-states were usually struggles by partisans of oligarchy to overthrow democracies or by partisans of democracy. to overthrow oligarchies. Oligarchies signified the rule of the state by the *oligoi* or few, a minority consisting of propertied citizens, sometimes a very small minority, who alone possessed political rights. Democracy signified the rule of the state by the *demos* or people, the entire body of (male) citizens, who all possessed political rights. Because oligarchy was based exclusively on the wealthy and well-born, and democracy to a considerable extent on common men of little or no property, *stasis* was frequently a conflict between the city's rich and poor.[12] In the early part of his work Thucydides takes passing notice of revolutions in several Greek cities, such as the one against the oligarchy that occurred in Epidamnus in 435, which he reports in the first book (1.24), because by causing the rival intervention of both Corinth and Corcyra, it was one of the developments that led to the war. It is only when he comes to the revolution in Corcyra in 427, however, that he pictures its events in some detail followed by a number of remarkable reflections on the phenomenon of revolution itself.

At the beginning of the war, Corcyra (modern Corfu), an island located in the Ionian Sea on the northwest coast of Greece, was a democracy allied with Athens. An oligarchic party backed by Corinth, the ally of Sparta, attempted to detach the city from the Athenian alliance. Disturbances ensued in which the supporters of oligarchy, charging that Corcyra was in danger of enslavement by Athens, murdered the leader of the pro-Athenian democrats and about sixty of his followers. Encouraged by the Corinthians and the Spartans, they forced the Corcyraean assembly to declare its neutrality in the war. The people then resisted and violence broke out. A Peloponnesian fleet arrived, ravaged some of Corcyra's land,

and threatened to attack the city, but sailed away when a larger Athenian fleet of sixty ships appeared. Within the city the adherents of the democratic popular party began killing their political adversaries. Some fifty of the latter who had taken refuge as suppliants in the temple of Hera were persuaded to come out and condemned to death. A much larger number of others, refusing to leave the temple enclosure when they saw what had happened, either killed each other or committed suicide by hanging themselves on trees or in some other manner. During the seven days that the Athenian general Eurymedon and his fleet remained at Corcyra, Thucydides reports that

> the Corcyraeans continued slaughtering those of their fellow citizens whom they deemed their enemies; they professed to punish them for their designs against the democracy, but in fact some were killed from motives of personal enmity, and some by the hands of their debtors because of the money they owed them. Every form of death was to be seen and everything, and more than everything that commonly happens in revolutions, happened then. The father slew the son, and the suppliants were torn from the temples and slain near them; some were even walled up in the temple of Dionysus, and there perished. And this seemed to be the worst of revolutions, because it was the first. (3.81)

Of course, this was not actually the first *stasis* which Thucydides had mentioned, but perhaps he calls it the first because it exceeded all the previous ones in the scale of its violence and slaughter and must have seemed to him to present a paradigm of the nature of revolution.

The following two chapters, 3.82–83, convey the heart of Thucydides' thought on revolution.[13] In them he first records the spread of civil convulsions throughout the Hellenic world, as the oligarchic and democratic parties in every city struggled to bring in either the Athenians or the Lacedaemonians. This could not have happened in time of peace, he explains, when there would have been no excuse or desire to introduce outsiders; but in the midst of war, both sides could easily obtain allies to give them help and injure their enemies, and the dissatisfied party was accordingly only too ready to call in foreign aid:

> Revolution thus brought many calamities upon the Greek cities such as have been and always will be while the nature of mankind remains

the same, but which are more or less aggravated and differ in character with every new combination of circumstances. In peace and prosperity, both states and individuals are actuated by higher motives, because they do not fall under the dominion of imperious necessities; but war which takes away the comfortable provision of daily life is a violent teacher, and tends to assimilate men's characters to their conditions. (3.82)

In these comments upon revolution, Thucydides attributes its basic cause to human nature as acted upon by the harsh conditions of war. He shouldn't be taken to imply, though, that future revolutions will necessarily be a repetition of the past, for while they may have their motives in a common human nature and hence must recur, he expects that they will differ from one another in degree and character according to circumstances.

Up to this point the historian has remained rather objective in relating the events at Corcyra, although we may certainly perceive a moral revulsion at the slaughter he recounts. As he pursues his analysis, however, and notes that the revolutions that successively struck the cities of Greece strove to outdo each other in the extremity of their methods and revenges, his deepest feelings seem to be engaged. Speaking in his own person with a passion both moral and intellectual, he proceeds to offer a series of remarkable observations—what Hornblower well terms "a display of generalizing fireworks"[14]—that expose the pathology of the revolutionary spirit and its effects. That spirit as he sees it is composed of a factionalism and fanaticism totally indifferent to any considerations of humanity or law. It characteristically expresses itself in a perversion of moral and political language and valuation. Hence "words," he says, "changed their meaning in relation to things," being twisted as men saw fit. "Reckless daring" was called "loyal courage," "prudent delay" became "the excuse of a coward," and "moderation" was regarded as "the disguise of unmanly weakness." The lover of violence was trusted, and his opponent held in suspicion. A plotter was admired, but the cleverness of someone who detected a plot was admired still more, and one who kept clear of plots was thought a coward and disrupter of party. He who outstripped others in evildoing was applauded and so likewise was the man who incited another man to evil which he had never thought of. Ties of party were stronger than those of blood, because a partisan was more ready to dare without asking a reason. Party associations themselves were not based on law or the public good, but on self-interest in defiance of the law. The bond of good faith was no longer divine law but partnership in crime. Revenge was preferable to self-preservation. Agreements to which parties swore when they could do nothing else only lasted until one or the other had the power to break them. Partisans took more pleasure in a treacherous act against an enemy than in an open act of revenge (3.82).

"The cause of all these evils," he explains, was "the love of power" originating in "greed and ambition," and the party spirit the latter created. Here Thucydides has identified those drives or passions in human nature that, conquering reason and humanity, were the begetters of revolution. The party leaders of both sides used specious names,

> the one party professing to uphold the political equality of the many under law, the other the wisdom of an aristocracy, while in reality they made the public interest, to which in name they were devoted, their prize. Striving by every means to overcome each other, they committed the most monstrous crimes; yet even these were surpassed by the magnitude of their revenges . . . neither party observing any definite limits either of justice or public expediency, but both alike making the caprice of the moment their law. . . . Neither faction cared for religion, but praised any fair pretence which succeeded in effecting some odious purpose. (3.82)

Thucydides concludes these observations on the horrors that *stasis* brought upon the Greek city-states with a final comment:

> Thus revolution gave birth to every form of wickedness in Hellas. The simplicity which is so large an element in a noble nature was laughed to scorn and disappeared. An attitude of perfidious antagonism everywhere prevailed; for there was no word binding enough, nor oath terrible enough to reconcile enemies. Each man was strong only in the conviction that nothing was secure; he must look to his own safety, and could not afford to trust others. Inferior intellects generally succeeded best. For aware of their own deficiencies, and fearing the capacity of their opponents . . . they struck boldly and at once. But the cleverest sort, presuming in their arrogance that they would be aware in time . . . were taken off their guard and easily destroyed. (3.83)[15]

It would be difficult to overstate the intellectual power of this entire analysis, which is one of the landmarks of Greek historical thought. Modern partisans of revolution may condemn Thucydides' treatment as prejudiced and one-sided, but it is hard to deny its truth. There have been many notable theoretical discussions of the nature of revolution by philosophers, historians, and revolutionaries themselves, including Aristotle, Edmund Burke, Tocqueville, Marx, Lenin, Mao Tse Tung, and others.[16] Thucydides was the first historian to attempt this task, and he produced a wealth of insights on the subject. His reflections, as Gomme has observed, move from *stasis* in Corcyra to *stasis* in the Greek world and the war between democratic Athens and oligarchic Sparta as one of its causes, to the universal conditions of *stasis*, and then back to Greece.[17] He says little about the goals and sociopolitical causes of revolution in the Greek city-states, but beside stressing the importance of great-power intervention in these conflicts, he concentrates on their psychology as a basic manifestation of human nature, the murderous party and individual hatreds they released, and the distortions they wrought in linguistic meaning and moral description. It has been argued that his condemnation of the evils revolution inflicted on Hellas shows that he made no distinction between the moral judgments applicable to the conduct of states and those applicable to the conduct of individuals within states, subjecting both of them to the same standards.[18] This conclusion seems to me to be doubtful when we recall how often he depicts, without any moral comment, the self-interest, desire for aggrandizement, and determination to maintain empire and great-power status that dominated Athens and Sparta in their relations with their allies and with one another. Thucydides seems to treat the situation of the city-state during revolution as a special case in which the political community, having disintegrated into civil and party violence, has ceased to exist. When this has happened, it is no longer the city that acts, but the factions that control it, and it is to this condition that his moral strictures apply.

The most striking and original part of his discussion of revolution is his account of its effect on language and moral valuation under the influence of party interests and passions. His pointed observations on this subject may remind the present-day reader of the totalitarian society modeled mainly on Soviet communism that the British writer George Orwell pictured in his famous dystopian novel *Nineteen Eighty-Four*. In this society too words have changed their meaning, as is exemplified in the three slogans of the ruling party: "War Is Peace," "Freedom Is Slavery," and "Ignorance Is Strength." Modern readers may also call to mind the comparable shifts in linguistic meaning in the history of the twentieth century, when the one-party states of the communist world used to entitle themselves "people's democracies" and describe their system of voting with only a single candidate on the ballot as "freedom of election." They may likewise remember the moral principles taught in the Soviet Union, the People's Republic of China, and other communist states, which included the approval of spies and informers, secret police, and the killing of political enemies, as well as the moral principles propagated in Nazi Germany, which included approval of race hatred, aggressive nationalism, and genocide against the Jewish people.

Thucydides may have revealed his innermost personal feelings about the evils of revolution in his statement that "the simplicity [*to euethes*] which is so large an element in a noble nature [*to gennaion*] was laughed to scorn and disappeared" (3.83).[19] What did he mean by "simplicity" in this context? I believe that he probably had in mind candor, straightforwardness, absence of deviousness and cunning. These were a great part of a noble nature, and their extinction, which Thucydides perceived in the revolutionary party struggles that tore cities apart, was one of the things he most lamented.[20]

Following his account of "the passions which the citizens of Corcyra first of all the Hellenes displayed toward one another" (3.85), Thucydides brings the story of the Corcyraean revolution to a quick completion in several more chapters. He leaves the revolutionary scene in Corcyra with the democrats in control, while about six hundred survivors of the oligarchic party, who had fortified themselves in a mountain on the island, launch damaging attacks on the city's inhabitants (3.85). He returns to it two years later, in 425, when the Corcyraean democrats, assisted by Athenian troops, assaulted and captured the mountain fortress and its occupants. In a harrowing final episode, he relates how they forced their prisoners in groups of twenty to pass between two files of armed men who struck and pierced them before they were led away with whips and killed. Other prisoners, refusing to come out of the building in which they were being held, were slain by attackers who made an opening in the roof through which they shot arrows and hurled missiles. Many of the prisoners took their own lives. The slaughter continued for a day and a night, and at dawn the Corcyraeans flung the bodies of the dead on wagons and removed them from the city. All the prisoners perished while the women taken with them were reduced to slavery. Thus the people destroyed their opponents in Corcyra, and at least during the rest of the Peloponnesian War, Thucydides writes, "there was nothing left of the [oligarchic] party worth mentioning" (4.46–48).

PYLOS (4.3–23, 26–40)

The Archidamian War, which continued in a number of theaters, concluded four years later. During this period, Thucydides, while serving as one of the Athenian generals, was banished in 424 for failing to prevent Amphipolis, a colony and ally of Athens in northeast Greece, from being captured by the Spartan general Brasidas. He spent the next twenty years as an exile in Thrace and other places, working on his *History*.

The most important military success of this period of the war was the Athenians' occupation in 425 of Pylos on the west coast of the Peloponnesus less than fifty miles from Sparta, followed by their blockade and conquest of a Lacedaemonian force on the island of Sphacteria adjoining Pylos. In his fourth book Thucydides presents an enthralling account of the two-and-a-half-month sea and land operation comprising these events.

It was only by chance that the Athenians under the command of Demosthenes occupied and built a fort at Pylos after a storm drove their ships there. The Spartans, confident of capturing the fort, prepared to assault Pylos both from land and with ships, and also sent a body of 420 hoplites to hold Sphacteria lest the Athenians seize it. They were defeated in several days of fighting in which they failed to regain Pylos, while their soldiers on Sphacteria were blockaded and cut off from the mainland by Athenian ships. In fear that these men on the island would be starved out and lost, the Spartans suspended hostilities, made a truce with the Athenian commanders at Pylos that allowed food to be brought over to Sphacteria, and sent envoys to Athens with a proposal of peace. Their concern for the fate of their blockaded warriors, so great that they were willing to make peace to free them, is very understandable. Sparta's population and military manpower were declining in the fifth century, and the 420 hoplites trapped on Sphacteria amounted to fully one-tenth of the Spartan army.[21]

The speech the Spartan envoys delivered at Athens, of which Thucydides gives a verbatim version, struck a conciliatory tone. Although admitting that Sparta had suffered a calamity at Pylos, they attributed it to error, not to any decline in Spartan power. They reminded the Athenians that fortune would not always favor them and that reverses and disasters were bound to occur, Hence they urged the wisdom of making peace to avoid further risks and while Athens remained powerful. In exchange for the return of their fighting men on Sphacteria, they offered Sparta's lasting friendship and an alliance. "Now, if ever," they said, "is the time of reconciliation for us both, before either has suffered any irremediable calamity" that would cause "an inveterate hatred" between the two states. Peace would bring relief to all the Greeks, they stated, and if Sparta and Athens were at one, then "the rest of Hellas, which is less powerful than we, will pay to both of us the greatest deference" (4.18–20).

The Athenians rejected this offer under Cleon's influence, just as five years previously the Spartans had dismissed an offer of peace from Athens. Thucydides explains that the reason was greed. Thinking they could make peace at any time because they had the Spartan troops on Sphacteria in their power, the Athenians "wanted more" from Sparta (4.21). Encouraged by Cleon, they made a number of territorial and other demands that led to the failure of the negotiations. The Spartan envoys went home persuaded, Thucydides says, that Athens would not make peace "on any tolerable conditions" (4.23). His account seems to imply that the Athenians should have seized the opportunity for peace.[22]

With the truce ended, the Athenian forces at Pylos found themselves getting short of food and water. Nearby them on the mainland lay a Spartan army. The Spartans paid rewards to anyone who would carry supplies through the Athenian blockade to the men on Sphacteria, and by this means the latter were able to endure and maintain their resistance. The blockade accordingly dragged on instead of coming to a quick end. In Athens the people now began to regret their refusal of the Spartan peace offer and to blame Cleon. He in turn attacked the generals, particularly his political rival Nicias, for their failure to take the island. Despite a total lack of military experience, he boasted that he could do it himself if he were general. Nicias promptly offered, with the approval of the Athenian assembly, to hand over to Cleon the command of an expedition to conquer Sphacteria. Although he tried to back out, popular pressure compelled him to accept the assignment, and he pledged that within twenty days he would either bring back the Spartans from Sphacteria alive or kill them all. "His vain words," Thucydides records, "moved the Athenians to laughter" (4.28). Choosing as his colleague Demosthenes, the commander who was already at the scene, and taking with him some additional troops, he arrived shortly in Pylos. Demosthenes wanted to attack Sphacteria and was encouraged by a fire that destroyed most of the wooded cover on the island and thus made movement much easier. The two generals first called upon the Spartan troops to surrender, promising them good treatment if they did so. When they refused this demand, the Athenians assaulted Sphacteria and succeeded after hard fighting in surrounding their enemy, whom they greatly outnumbered. Stopping their attack, the generals gave the surviving Spartans, who now faced destruction, the chance to surrender. A truce was then made, during which the Spartans communicated with their army on the mainland to ask what they should do. In answer, they were told to "act as you think best, but you are not to dishonor yourselves" (4.38). Thereupon, after consulting together, they all surrendered and were obliged to hand over their arms. The Athenians captured 292 Lacedaemonian fighting men on Sphacteria, 120 of whom were Spartiate warriors. All of them were brought back to Athens as prisoners to be held there until the end of the Archidamian War. Although Thucydides' bias against Cleon is visible in his account, he acknowledges that the latter's "mad promise . . . was fulfilled; for he did bring back the prisoners within twenty days, as he had said" (4.39).

After this victory, the Athenians decided that if the Spartans should again invade Attica, they would kill the Spartan prisoners. They garrisoned Pylos, and allowed Messenians to occupy it and ravage Spartan territory in Laconia. Sparta had never before experienced irregular warfare of this kind and was also forced to

contend with the desertion of helots to its enemy. It tried to negotiate with Athens in the hope of recovering Pylos and its prisoners,
but without result.

Athens's victory at Pylos was its biggest success of the war and
did considerable damage to Sparta's morale and military reputation. "Nothing which happened during the war," Thucydides says,

> caused greater amazement in Hellas; for it was universally imagined
> that the Lacaedemonians would never give up their arms, either under
> the pressure of famine or in any other extremity, but would fight to the
> last and die sword in hand. No one believed that those who surren-
> dered were men of the same quality with those who perished. (4.40)

From 424 on, however, the Athenians suffered a number of reverses at the hands of the brilliant and popular Spartan general
Brasidas and became more receptive to the idea of peace. War
weariness also affected the two sides. The death at Amphipolis in
422 of both Cleon and Brasidas, whom Thucydides calls "the two
greatest enemies of peace" (5.14), removed a major obstacle to
the termination of the war. Finally, in the spring of 421, following
lengthy negotiations, Sparta and Athens concluded a fifty-year
treaty—the peace of Nicias, named after the leading Athenian
politician and general who was eager to put an end to the war. Its
terms, which Thucydides transcribes (5.18), provided that, with a
few exceptions, both parties should give back what they had
gained in the war. While most of the Peloponnesian allies voted for
the peace, several of them, including Corinth, were opposed and
refused to accept it. Sparta and Athens also agreed to a defensive
alliance promising to help one another if their territory were invaded by another power. Although Thucydides doesn't make any
such claim himself, most historians maintain that Athens won the
Archidamian War, because the Spartans abandoned their attempt
to destroy the Athenian empire and also ignored the interests of
some of their own allies in order to make peace. On the other
hand, the war cost Athens a high price in lives and wealth; it also
failed to force the Spartans to accept the legitimacy of the Athenian empire or to consider the latter henceforth as invulnerable. If
Athens, therefore, emerged from the war with a balance of advantage, it was not very great.[23]

Writing from hindsight, Thucydides depicts the peace of Nicias
as no more than an interval of truce in a single, very long war. He

points out the great mistrust that prevailed between the parties after they made the peace and the violations of the treaty which both sides committed. Sparta failed, for instance, to restore Amphipolis to Athens and Athens refused to hand back Pylos to Sparta (5.26, 36). In keeping with his explanation of the true cause of the war, he must have continued to believe that the great-power interests and ambitions of Sparta and Athenian imperialism were too opposed to be reconciled for long. Discussing the fragility of the peace of Nicias, Russell Meiggs, the historian of the Athenian empire, says that "fundamentally, Periclean imperialism had generated too much energy and appetite to allow the Athenian demos to settle down to a stable peace. Had there been the will the way could have been found, but underlying suspicions were too deep-rooted."[24] Looking forward from the conclusion of the peace in 421, Thucydides declares:

> For six years and three months the two powers abstained from invading each other's territories, but abroad the cessation of arms was intermittent, and they did each other all the harm they could. At last they were absolutely compelled to break the treaty made at the end of the first ten years, and to declare open war. (5.25)

Dialogue at Melos, the Sicilian Expedition

> Of the gods we believe, and of men we know,
> that by a necessary law of their nature wherever
> they can rule they will. This law was not made
> by us, and we are not the first who have acted
> upon it; we did but inherit it, and shall bequeath
> it to all time, and we know that you and all
> mankind, if you were as strong as we are, would
> do as we do. (5.105, the Athenians to the the
> Melians)

THE GREATER PART of Thucydides' fifth book—the shortest in the *History* save for book 8, which was never finished—describes the fragility of the peace of Nicias, the fighting that occurred between various states in the aftermath of the treaty, and the de facto resumption of the war between Athens and Sparta even before the treaty was publicly declared broken. Some of Sparta's most important allies, such as Corinth, Megara, and Thebes, who had refused to join in the peace, became disaffected, and its military reputation lay under a cloud because of its loss of Pylos and surrender at Sphacteria. Argos, a democracy in the Peloponnese and a longtime rival of Sparta that had remained neutral in the Archidamian War, aspired to displace the Lacedaemonians from their supremacy. During the next three years, however, Sparta overcame these challenges, repairing its earlier alliances and consolidating its hegemony over the Peloponnesian League while its relations with Athens worsened. In recounting these developments, Thucydides directs attention for the first time to one of the most conspicuous figures of the age, the brilliant, youthful Athenian politician Alcibiades, who thereafter occupies a prominent role in the *History*. Thucydides introduces him as a member of the war party in Athens and "a man who would have been thought young in any other city, but was influential by reason of his high descent." The one quality of Alcibiades that he mentions is his pride (5.43).

The decisive event in the reestablishment of Sparta's ascendancy was its victory, with the help of some of its allies, over Argos and its allies at Mantinea in the summer of 418. Athens, which had made an alliance with Argos at Alcibiades' urging, came to its support. A very large number of troops were engaged in this battle, which Thucydides calls "by far the greatest of Hellenic battles that had taken place for a long time, and fought by the most famous cities" (5.74). The united forces under the command of the Spartan King Agis at Mantinea numbered about twenty thousand hoplites plus some cavalry and light-armed infantry, while the coalition led by Argos consisted of about sixteen thousand hoplites as well as lightly armed troops but no cavalry.[1] Among the Spartan troops were several hundred helots who had been freed because of their service in the Spartan army (4.34; 5.67). Thucydides, who was keenly interested in military organization and tactics, describes the Spartan chain of command and battle formation. "Almost the whole Lacedemonian army are officers," he observes, "who have officers under them, and the responsibility of executing an order devolves upon many" (5.66). Orders passed from King Agis personally to the polemarchs (generals), to the commanders of divisions, and thence to the commanders of fifties, commanders of platoons, and the platoons themselves. Agis's army consisted of seven divisions in the field plus a body of six hundred Sciritae, Arcadian troops especially trained to fight on the left wing. Each division contained four companies of fifty men divided into four platoons for each company. Four men fought in the front rank of each platoon. The depth of the line was not uniform but left to the discretion of the commanders of divisions, though on average it was eight men deep. Beside the Sciritae, the front line consisted of 448 men (5.66–68). In his detailed account of the actions of the two armies, Thucydides highlights the Spartans' outstanding discipline and courage, concluding that by this single victory "they wiped out the charge of cowardice, which was due to their misfortune at Sphacteria, and of general stupidity and sluggishness then current against them in Hellas. They were now thought to have been hardly used by fortune, but in character to be the same as ever" (5.75). Following its defeat in the battle of Mantinea, Argos was compelled to renounce its alliance with Athens and made a treaty of peace and alliance with Sparta for fifty years.[2]

The Melian Dialogue (5.84–113)

Thucydides' narrative contains frequent references to the massacre and enslavement of entire populations of cities. In 423, for example, Scione in northern Greece, a city subject to Athens, revolted and joined the Spartans under King Brasidas. The Athenians were so enraged by its defection that they passed a decree ordering its destruction and the death of all its people. When they captured Scione two years later, they executed the adult men, enslaved the women and children, and gave the city's land to the Plataeans for settlement (4.122; 5.32). Thucydides reports this atrocity flatly without the slightest comment. In a similar manner, he mentions briefly how the Lacedemonians, during an invasion of Argos's territory in the winter of 417, seized a place called Hysiae and slew all the free men whom they caught there (5.83).

The Athenian destruction of Melos in 416, recorded at the end of the fifth book, was another such atrocity, though on a much larger scale and far more notorious. In this case, Thucydides chose to depict the situation at considerable length by first reporting the discussion that took place between the Athenians and the Melians prior to the fall of Melos. The Melian dialogue is deservedly famous as a dramatic presentation of conflicting principles and ideas. Dealing with issues that were central to Thucydides' thinking, it gave him, as Jacqueline de Romilly has said, "an opportunity . . . to analyze in the widest possible fashion a general policy that could be attributed to Athens as a whole."[3] Its form as a direct exchange of views by the unnamed spokesmen of the two sides is unique in the *History*. A possible literary influence upon its rapid crossfire dialogue was the device used in the Greek tragic drama of the fifth century of alternating single lines of speech by the characters.[4] Although doubts have often been expressed about the Melian dialogue's authenticity, the fact noted by Thucydides, that the Athenians addressed only the magistrates and chief men of Melos, which had an oligarchic government, not the whole people (5.83), seems to indicate that he possessed a report of the proceedings and may even have had some Melian sources.[5]

An Aegean island colonized by settlers from Sparta centuries earlier, Melos was neutral in the Archidamian War. Because it refused to join the Athenian alliance, Athens attacked it in 426, but failed to subdue it. Determined to conquer the defiant islanders, in the summer of 416 Athens sent an expedition of thirty-eight ships and about twenty-seven hundred hoplites plus other troops against Melos. Once they landed on the island, the Athenians offered to negotiate, hoping that Melos would surrender to superior force without a fight. Although the Melians were willing to talk, they would only permit the Athenian envoys to address a select number of the city's elite rather than the entire citizen body. Accepting this arrangement, the Athenians began the dialogue with the proposal that instead of each of the parties delivering set speeches, the Melians should reply to the Athenian statements whenever they disapproved them. The latter agreed that such a proceeding was reasonable, but contended that the Athenians' warlike movements belied their words; for "we see," they say, "that, although you may reason with us, you mean to be our judges; and that at the end of the discussion, if the justice of our cause prevail and we therefore refuse to yield, we may expect war; if we are convinced by you, slavery" (5.86). To the Athenians, this objection was pointless, and they declined to continue the discussion unless the Melians' purpose was to face reality and save their city. The latter had no alternative but to acquiesce and agree that "this conference has met to consider our preservation" and that the argument should go forward on that basis (5.88).

With these preliminaries out of the way, the verbal duel could proceed. It is apparent from the start that its terms were unfair because they were dictated by the Athenians. The fundamental issue in the ensuing debate, that of justice versus power, had already been intimated. The Athenians, however, did not wish to consider justice. They state bluntly that the two sides should aim "only at what is possible," since both know that "the question of justice" enters into the discussion of human affairs "only when the pressure of necessity is equal"; otherwise, "the powerful exact what they can, and the weak grant what they must" (5.89). This brutally frank dictum that justice applies only between equals subject to the same necessities, not between the stronger and weaker, focuses the discussion on the question of interest or expediency and represents the Athenian attitude throughout. Although the Melians may strain to introduce moral arguments, the Athenians see them as irrelevant. Disdaining the use of "fine words" (5. 89), they make no effort to prove that right is on their side, and are concerned exclusively with the pragmatism of power.

103

The Melians attempt to circumvent the Athenian position in different ways. They first point out that even if justice is set aside, it is still very much in the Athenians' interest to respect a principle that serves the common good by allowing someone in peril to use any plea of right to help his cause, for if Athens ever falls, it will incur the heaviest vengeance and stand greatly in need of such a principle. The Athenians answer that they are not worried that their empire may fall; they even assert that the Spartans "are not cruel to their vanquished enemies" (5.91). What they want, they insist, is to take Melos with the least possible trouble and that "it is for the interests of us both that you should not be destroyed" (5.91). To the Melians' reply that it cannot be in their interest to become Athens's slaves, the Athenians respond that this is the only way they can preserve themselves. When the Melians wonder why they cannot be Athens's friends while still remaining neutral, the Athenians state that they consider Melos's friendship more harmful to them than its enmity, because the subjects of their empire would regard it as a sign of weakness if Athens should fail to compel the Melians, who are "insignificant islanders," to submit to its power (5.97).

The Melians, however, cannot refrain from voicing the conviction that they would be base and cowardly not to defend their freedom against Athenian enslavement. The Athenians, who consider this opinion absurd in light of their superior power, rejoin that it is no disgrace to yield to overwhelming force and that the question for the Melians is not honor but prudence. They urge the latter to think of their weakness and avoid deluding themselves by relying on luck or hope if they decide to resist. But the Melians are unconvinced that their confidence in the possibility of resistance is blind or stupid. Since they are righteous and the Athenians unrighteous, they reply, they may justifiably hope for the favor of the gods or for aid from their kinsmen the Lacedemonians. The Athenians counter, however, that they too expect the favor of the gods and that their conduct is in no way contrary to the common opinion about either the gods or human affairs. It is at this juncture that they advance the crushing claim quoted at the head of this chapter: "Of the gods we believe, and of men we know, that by a necessary law of their nature wherever they can rule they will. This law was not made by us, and we are not the first who have acted upon it . . . we know that you and all mankind, if you were as strong as we are, would do as we do" (5.105). They add that the Melians are foolish to expect help from the Lacedemonians, who, while very virtuous among themselves, in their dealings with others always equate honor with what is agreeable and expediency with justice; moreover, even if they should send help, Athens has never once retired from a siege for fear of attack by another enemy (5.105, 111).

The dialogue winds down with the Athenians' final admonition to the Melians that they had failed during the entire discussion to say anything "which would give a reasonable man expectation of deliverance." Accusing them of lacking sense, they beg them to discard their false belief in honor, a mere name that was luring them to irretrievable disaster. If they were wise, they would see that it was no disgrace to yield "to a great city which invites you to become her ally on reasonable terms, keeping your own land, and merely paying tribute." They should therefore reflect again after the Athenians withdraw, understanding that they are deliberating about "their one and only country, which may be saved or . . . destroyed by a single decision" (5.111).

After consulting together, the Melians resolve to defend their freedom, trusting, they say, to "good fortune . . . by the favor of the gods," and to "human help from the Lacedaemonians." On hearing this answer, the Athenians tell them, "you are the only men who deem the future . . . more certain than the present," and that "the more you cast yourselves upon the Lacedaemonians, and fortune, and hope, and trust them, the more complete will be your ruin" (5.112–13).

With this dire prediction the dialogue concludes. The Athenians promptly began hostilities, initiating a siege extending into the winter. No help came from the Spartans, and the Melians were forced to surrender. What followed next was inevitable. The Athenians, Thucydides writes, "put to death all who were of military age, and made slaves of the women and children. They then colonized the island, sending thither five-hundred settlers of their own" (5.16). The historian's narrative is quite detached. If he feels any horror at Athens's action, he does not express it. Possibly the sympathy he had for the Melians was qualified by the fact that they had brought their fate upon themselves by their unwillingness to grasp the reality of their situation. Many if not most readers are likely to agree that they were irrational to choose resistance against such overwhelming odds. Although the terms the Athenians offered would have cost Melos its independence, they were not so onerous. They were surely preferable to the alternative of the death and destruction of the people and city.

The moral focus of the dialogue, nevertheless, is not upon the Melians, whatever their imprudence or foolishness, but on the Athenians. It is important to avoid the mistake of thinking that they identified might with right and held that justice is merely a convention and does not really exist. We find this opinion propounded by the sophists Callicles and Thrasymachus in Plato's dialogues *Gorgias* and *Republic*, but it was not the view Thucydides attributes to the Athenians. Rather, they maintain that an appeal to justice is beside the point in this particular case because justice applies only between equals. Accepting it as obvious that the weak must submit to the strong, they claim that this principle accords with human nature and experience and with the practice of the gods. In desiring to subjugate Melos, they are moved partly by their ambition for conquest but also by fear for their empire. Always in their mind is the danger that their allies might revolt if they show weakness, and so they are determined to demonstrate that the Melians must pay highly for their defiance.

In the Melian dialogue Thucydides proffers a masterly portrait of the rationale and methods of Athenian imperialism. Grote called the Melian tragedy "one of the grossest and most inexcusable pieces of cruelty combined with injustice which Grecian history presents to us."[6] He is not the only scholar who has found it significant that Thucydides placed this episode at the end of his fifth book, immediately before beginning his narrative of the Sicilian expedition in book 6. In the juxtaposition of the two events Grote perceived a dramatic unity, since Athens's decision to conquer Sicily, which followed its destruction of Melos by only a few months, brought upon it "the most ruinous catastrophe known to ancient history."[7] But by relating them in sequence, did Thucydides mean to imply that the slaughter Athens committed at Melos and its calamitous defeat in Sicily were morally linked and that the latter should be seen as a retribution for the former? This seems most unlikely. His account of the Sicilian expedition does not suggest at any point that its failure was a punishment designed to right the moral balance, but he treats it rather as due entirely to human factors that might conceivably have been different.

Most modern readers would probably like to believe that the Melian dialogue was intended as a moral condemnation of Athens. Such was reportedly the opinion of Thucydides' modern editor, Gomme, who said that it was meant to show Athens's moral decline. Unhappily, though, Gomme did not live long enough to deal with the Melian dialogue in his Thucydides commentary. Andrewes, his successor as editor, disagreed with him on this subject and observes that "the view of the Dialogue as an indictment of Athens is mistaken."[8] There seems to be no way to resolve this difference, since nothing in the dialogue betrays Thucydides' own moral position.

Irrespective of his personal attitude, however, the Melian dialogue does show clearly and in no uncertain terms that great powers are guided by their own interests, unaffected by considerations of justice. Thucydides regards this truth as a universal law founded in human nature. Although he has made the same observation about the actions of states in previous parts of his *History*, he reiterates it here in a particularly dramatic way. This may well be the essential point of the dialogue from the author's perspective, rather than any moral judgment we may be tempted to read into it.[9]

THE SICILIAN EXPEDITION (6–7)

Athens first intervened in Sicily at an earlier point in the war when it sent a small fleet of twenty ships in 426 to help its ally Leontini against Syracuse, the greatest, most powerful of Sicilian cities. At that time, according to Thucydides, the Athenians were already considering the possibility of "getting the affairs of Sicily into their hands" (3.86). Ten years later they resolved to send out a much larger expedition in the hope of conquering the island. "Of [Sicily's] great size and numerous population," the historian says, "most of them knew nothing, and they never reflected that they were entering upon a struggle almost as arduous as the Peloponnesian War" (6.1). He explains that while the Athenians "virtuously professed" that they were going to Sicily to support their recently acquired Sicilian allies against Syracuse, their true motive was to acquire "the empire of Sicily" (6.6). It is striking that in this statement he uses the identical phrase, *alethestate prophasis* (truest cause or reason), which he had previously used in 1.23 to explain the true cause of the war as a whole. Athens's decision to invade Sicily may be considered comparable in its consequences to Nazi Germany's decision in the Second World War to invade the Soviet Union. Assuming that they would gain a rapid victory, both powers made an enormously costly strategic mistake, in the German case because it involved Germany in a prolonged, ultimately fatal two-front war in both the east and the west, and in the Athenian case because Athens took on the burden of conquering the western island of Sicily while also being engaged in a taxing war in Greece to maintain its empire. The Athenian effort in 415 to besiege and capture Syracuse may be likened to the German siege and effort to capture the Soviet city of Stalingrad in the winter of 1942. Not only did both fail, but in each instance the defenders in these campaigns withstood the aggressors, counterattacked and forced their surrender, and destroyed the invading army.

Thucydides' narrative of the Sicilian expedition occupies the sixth and seventh books of his *History*.[10] It is one of the most vivid and gripping representations of war in western historiography. The graphic power of its depiction of the military and naval actions in Sicily and their sequel has never been surpassed. The eminent English historian Lord Macaulay called Thucydides' seventh book, which includes the description of the Athenians' withdrawal after their defeat in the harbor of Syracuse, "the *ne plus ultra* of human art."[11] In its chronicle of the expedition, the *History* knits together a brief background survey of Sicily's original inhabitants and the peoples it contained; the political and diplomatic aspects of the Athenian invasion and the response it aroused in Sicily; speeches by politicians and generals that illuminate their policies, acts, and personalities; concurrent developments of the war in Greece; interesting technical details of the fighting; a list of the allies who fought on both sides; and the actions of the Spartan general Gylippus and his Peloponnesian forces, who were sent to help the Syracusan resistance to the Athenians. Well before Thucydides begins this account, he has already given the reader a foreknowledge of the fate of the Sicilian expedition. He conveys this information in his proleptic comments in the second book on the death of Pericles and its aftermath. There he speaks of the inferior caliber of Pericles' successors in the leadership of imperial Athens, who catered to the people's whims and were guilty of many errors, the worst being the Sicilian expedition in which the Athenians lost "the greater part of their fleet and army" (2.65). In Thucydides' eyes intervention in Sicily represented a complete abandonment of Pericles' policy. But even though the reader knows that it will have a bad end, he does not know the events that were part of the Sicilian expedition, and the telling of these is full of dramatic incident, suspense, and human interest. And while one may regard the humbling of an aggressive, overreaching Athenian imperialism as highly deserved, it is impossible not to sympathize with the defeated Athenians in their terrible fate in Sicily. Thucydides spares us none of its horrors, and we cannot but feel pity at the suffering of the Athenian army in its final retreat and annihilation.

When the Athenians voted in 415 to send a fleet to Sicily to assist the city of Segesta against Selinus, which was allied with Syracuse, they appointed Nicias and Alcibiades as two of the three commanders.[12] Nicias, a very rich man and an experienced, successful general, was then about sixty years of age. Not only had he played a crucial part in achieving the peace of 421 with Sparta, but he opposed the renewal or expansion of the war and therefore tried to rescind the decision authorizing the Sicilian expedition. Alcibiades, on the other hand, was strongly in favor of the expedition. Thucydides records the speeches of both men in a debate on the issue in the Athenian assembly. Nicias's objections to invading Sicily were those that any prudent statesman might put forward: its many uncertainties and perils, its untimeliness in light of Athens's numerous current problems and the enmity of the Lacedaemonians, and the difficulties of achieving its aims. Contending that Sicily posed no threat to Athens, he warned that it "is a populous and distant country, over which, even if we are victorious, we shall hardly be able to maintain our dominion. And how foolish it is to select for attack a land which no conquest can secure, while he who fails to conquer will not be where he was before" (6.11). These last were prophetic words. But Nicias also went on to launch a personal attack against Alcibiades without naming him. He alluded to the latter, who was then about thirty-five years old, as someone eager to hold a command but far too young for the responsibility it entailed and heedful only of his own interests. In an appeal to the older citizens against this brilliant figure and his youthful supporters, he urged them "on behalf of our country, now on the brink of the greatest danger . . . she has ever known," not to vote for a war in Sicily (6.13).

Alcibiades, an aristocrat born with all the blessings of fortune, was handsome, rich, charming, and talented. He grew up with Pericles as his guardian and was notorious for his profligate habits and the excesses of his private life. A close friend of Socrates, he appears as one of the major characters in Plato's beautiful dialogue *The Symposium*. His ambition seems to have been limitless, and he wanted to lead the democracy although he was not a democrat himself. In fact, as events were to show, he had no real political commitments and was intent only upon his own aggrandizement.

As a prelude to Alcibades' speech, Thucydides, who perhaps knew and gathered some information from him directly,[13] sheds light on his situation and motives. He was the most enthusiastic advocate of the Sicilian expedition, not only opposed to Nicias as a political enemy, but intensely eager to command so that he might become the conqueror of Sicily and then even of Carthage as well. His costly devotion to horse racing and other pleasures led him to seek to repair his private fortune and gain money as well as glory by serving as general. Although he held a great position among the citizens, they feared "his lawless self-indulgence" and the "far-reaching purposes" behind his actions. Suspecting that he aimed to establish a tyranny, the people distrusted and set themselves against him, even though "his talents as a military commander were unrivalled." His wild courses, according to the historian, "went far to ruin the Athenian state;" yet he also says that by their unwillingness to entrust Alcibades with the administration of the war and giving it to others, the Athenians soon shipwrecked the state (6.15). These judgments were based on future knowledge, of course, as prior to the Sicilian expedition Alcibiades had not shown any proof of outstanding ability as a military leader nor had he yet been guilty of conduct that could contribute to the state's ruin.

Alcibiades' speech first asserted his right to command by reason of his personal superiority and previous achievements on Athens's behalf. He asked the Athenians not to fear his young years but make use of his services while he was in the flower of his days. To convince them not to reverse their decision on the Sicilian expedition, he offered several arguments to prove that Sicily would be an easy conquest. Athens must conquer Sicily, he maintained, in the interests of its empire; if it remained inactive it ran the risk of losing its power, for "if we are not rulers, we shall be subjects."

Sicily's acquisition, moreover, would lead to the mastery of all of Hellas. And whether the Athenians succeeded in their enterprise and remained or had to depart, "in either case our navy will ensure our safety, for at sea we shall be a match for all Sicily" (6.18). The prediction in this last statement turned out, of course, to be completely wrong. Criticizing Nicias for trying to set the old against the young, he called for unity between the two and for the Athenians to strive together to increase their city's greatness.

If Nicias had enjoyed the political authority of a Pericles, he might have succeeded in changing the popular mind. But after listening to Alcibiades and a plea for assistance from the Sicilian cities of Segesta and Leontini, the Athenians were even keener to extend the war to Sicily. Nicias then spoke for a second time, now professing to accept their decision but still hoping to dissuade them from it by emphasizing the magnitude of the force that would be needed for such a vast undertaking. So overwhelming was their support for the expedition, however, that his speech had the opposite effect. Instead of discouraging them, as well it might have, it made them more resolute to provide whatever resources in men and equipment might be required to insure the expedition's safety and success Thucydides notes that "the city had recovered from the plague and . . . constant pressure of war; a new population had grown up; there had been time for the accumulation of money during the peace." Hence, "there was abundance of everything at command" (6.26). He also indicates that among the reasons for the expedition's popular support was that those who would fight "expected to receive present pay, and to conquer a country which would be an inexhaustible mine of pay for the future" (6.24).

As the preparations for the Sicilian invasion moved toward completion, a sensational scandal of religious profanation occurred in Athens. In a single night, unknown malefactors mutilated nearly all the Hermae, the statues depicting a phallus and image of the god Hermes that stood everywhere at the doorways of Athenian temples and private houses as a protection against evil influences. With religion as closely intertwined with family and public life as it was in Athens and throughout Greece, the vandalizing of these effigies caused an uproar in the city. The people, angry at this act of sacrilege, feared that it might be an ill omen of the fate of the expedition and attributed it to a conspiracy to overthrow their democracy. Suspicion fell upon some riotous young men and principally on Alcibiades, who was accused of instigating the defacement of the Hermae and also of certain earlier violations, including the profaning of the Mysteries, religious cults with secret rites in which membership required initiation. The impieties alleged against him were seen as evidence of a plot against the state. He denied the charges and asked to be tried before the Sicilian expedition left. His political enemies succeeded in delaying his trial, however, in order to gain more time to incite popular feeling against him. He was therefore permitted to go as a commander so as not to delay the expedition, but on condition that he return when recalled to stand trial.[14]

The Sicilian expedition set sail in midsummer of 415. The entire population of Athens went down to the port of Piraeus in high spirits to cheer its departure. "No armament so magnificent." Thucydides states, "had ever been sent out by any single Hellenic power." After describing the lavishness with which the fleet had been equipped, he adds, possibly with a touch of irony in view of what happened later, "never had a greater expedition been sent to a foreign land; never was there an enterprise in which the hope of future success seemed to be better justified by actual power" (6.31). When Athens's ships and warriors gathered with those of its allies at Corcyra on the way to Sicily, the entire invasion force consisted of 134 triremes plus a large number of supply and other vessels, 5,100 hoplites, and nearly 500 archers and additional lightly armed troops (6.43).

Thucydides fills out the picture with several speeches that describe the reaction in Syracuse, a democratic polity, to the reports of the Athenian invasion which began to reach the city. At first the people refused to believe them. Then at a meeting of the popular assembly, Hermocrates, a prominent political figure, stated that he had reliable information that the Athenians were coming with a great fleet and army because they coveted Sicily and especially Syracuse. Confident that they could be defeated, he called upon the city to take immediate measures to defend itself and also to send out envoys to unite all of Sicily in the face of the common danger (6.33–35). Athenagoras, a popular leader of the democracy, disagreed with Hermocrates. Insisting that the Athenians were not mad enough to try to conquer Sicily, he attributed the reports of the invasion to a plot by the oligarchic party to seize power in the city and destroy its liberty (6.36–40). A Syracusan general ended the debate by declaring that he and his colleagues would investigate the situation and collect information which they would communicate to the people (6.41). Soon afterwards the Syracusans learned that the Athenian fleet was already at Rhegium on the Italian side of the straits of Messina. Now their doubts were at an end and they fell to work at once to prepare themselves for the rapidly approaching war that was almost at their gates.

When the Athenians reached Sicily, the three generals—Nicias, Alcibiades, and Lamachus—held a council of war. Instead of immediately assaulting Syracuse while it was still unprepared, as Lamachus first proposed, they followed Alcibiades' advice to try by diplomacy to gain some allies in Sicily. After failing to achieve an alliance with the city of Messina, they seized Catana to the north of Syracuse on the east coast of Sicily, which they made their main base. There a ship arrived with an order from Athens to Alcibiades and some others to return to the city to stand trial. On their homeward voyage, the accused men escaped and the Athenians subsequently sentenced them to death for their nonappearance. Alcibiades now made his way to Sparta, determined to help the Spartans against Athens. Despite their mistrust, they were willing to receive him because he knew so much about the Athenians' plans and resources. In a shrewd, very effective speech, he persuaded them to heed Syracuse's call for assistance by sending a fighting force to Sicily, and also to resume direct war with Athens by the occupation and fortification of Decelea in Attica. This advice was to prove very damaging to Athens. His oration, which showed how best to fight the Athenians and explained and justified his own conduct, was notable for its effrontery and sophistry. Alcibiades called himself a lover and true patriot of Athens who was only seeking to regain his lost country. He urged the Spartans to use him to the full in accord with the saying, "the more harm I did you as an enemy, the more good I can do you as friend." By intervening in Sicily, he told them, "[Y]ou . . . may overthrow the Athenian power once and for ever . . . and be leaders of all Hellas, which will follow you, not upon compulsion, but from affection" (6.92).

In Sicily, meanwhile, the Athenians sailed to Syracuse, where they landed and defeated the Syracusans in an indecisive battle. They then returned to Catana and nearby Naxos for the winter

113

season. Even though most of the Sicilian cities feared the domination of Syracuse, they refrained from joining Athens in the war. Seeking to enlist Camarina as an ally, the Athenians sent a representative to address its citizens, who first heard a speech by Hermocrates as the representative of Syracuse. The latter appealed for Sicilian unity against Athens as the enslaver of Hellas and promised help from the Peloponnesians who, he said "are far better soldiers than the Athenians" (6.80). The Athenian spokesman Euphemus responded with a justification of Athens's imperial position, rather tactlessly arguing that "we rule . . . in the first place because we deserve to rule," and that fear for their security compelled the Athenians to maintain their empire. Nevertheless, he assured the Camarinaeans that "we have not come to enslave you but to save you." Athens's policy, he stated, was determined by its interests, which in Sicily "require, not that we should weaken our friends, but that our friends should be too strong for our enemies." It was thus in the Athenian interest to preserve the independence of the Sicilian cities against the threat of falling under the yoke of Syracuse, which would use its enhanced power to aid the Peloponnesians. "We rule over the cities of Hellas," Euphemus declared, "in order to maintain our independence, and we emancipate the cities of Sicily that they may not be used against us. And we are compelled to adopt a policy of interference because we have many interests to guard." He urged Camarina to insure its own security against Syracuse by joining Athens as an ally (6.83–87).

The Athenian speech at Camarina reflected the same hard realism on the subject of empire that had been consistently expressed in earlier statements by Athenian spokesmen which Thucydides quotes. It made perfectly clear that Athens as an imperial power based its policy in Sicily as elsewhere solely on self-interest and expediency. Camarina's response was of course equally dictated by these same factors. Since it feared both Athens and Syracuse, it decided not to assist either one of them for the time being. Somewhat later, though, perceiving that Syracuse might win without its help, Camarina gave the Syracusans a moderate amount of aid.

The Athenians finally began their campaign to conquer Syracuse in the following spring of 414. Thucydides gives an enthralling account of the changing fortunes of the subsequent military operations, in which, despite some successes, the Athenians suffered two great reverses that determined the outcome of the Sicilian campaign. The first was the failure of the siege of Syracuse. After landing their forces north of the city, the Athenians captured the heights of Epipolae, the plateau on Syracuse's northern outskirts. From there they set out to build a wall that would extend south and north down to the sea at either end and thus encircle and cut off the city by land. The first Syracusan efforts to halt the wall's progress were unavailing, although the Athenian general Lamachus was killed in one of the engagements. The Athenian fleet also moved meanwhile into Syracuse's Great Harbor. As the wall speedily lengthened, the desperate defenders were on the verge of defeat and ready to capitulate when the arrival of the Spartan general Gylippus at the head of a mixed army of three thousand Sicilians and Peloponnesians inspired them to fresh resistance. At that moment, Thucydides records, the Athenian wall had advanced so far that Syracuse was "near . . . to destruction" (7.2). In the next days the Syracusans succeeded in building and protecting against attacks a counterwall on Epipolae that traversed the end of the unfinished Athenian wall and prevented it from going further. Once this occurred, the Athenians no longer had any hope of investing the city.

The Syracusans were now also preparing to fight at sea and expected further reinforcements from within Sicily and from Greece. The Athenian troops had seized and occupied Plemmyrium, which lay at the mouth of Syracuse's Great Harbor. Encamping there, they built three forts, but were continually harassed by enemy cavalry when they went out to fetch water and forage. They themselves were hampered throughout their Sicilian campaign by a lack of cavalry. Now very much concerned about the danger of defeat, Nicias, who was in sole command since the death of his co-commander Lamachus, sent an urgent letter to Athens, which Thucydides quotes, describing the deteriorating situation of both his soldiers and naval crews. "We who are supposed to be the besiegers," he reported, "are really the besieged, at least by land; and the more so because we cannot go far even into the country, for we are prevented by their horsemen" (7.11). Mentioning this and the other difficulties his forces faced, he insisted nonetheless that the generals and soldiers had done their duty. But with all Sicily united against them and another Peloponnesian army on the way to help Syracuse, he asked Athens either to recall the expedition lest it be lost, or to reinforce it with another large fleet and army bringing plenty of money. He also made the personal request to be relieved of his command because he was suffering from kidney disease (7.11–15).

This communication reached Athens in the winter of 413. Its dark, hopeless tone contrasted sadly with the bright, confident spirit in which the Sicilian expedition had set out in the summer of 415. The Athenians decided, in answer, not to replace Nicias, but to send two more generals, Demosthenes and Eurymedon, to join him. They also resolved to send out a second fleet and army to Sicily. Meanwhile, although the Athenians won a sea fight against the Syracusans, Gylippus led an attack that captured Plemmyrium and its forts, where large quantities of Athenian supplies were stored. Its loss was a serious blow to the Athenians, making it far harder for them to obtain provisions, and creating general gloom throughout the army. In Greece King Agis of Sparta invaded Attica with a Lacedemonian army which took and fortified Decelea, where it remained permanently and despoiled the surrounding country. The Athenians suffered great losses, their sheep and cattle were killed, thousands of their slaves deserted, and their cavalry had to ride out daily to keep guard over the country or make raids against Decelea. The city was also forced go to much more trouble and expense to import food for the population. Grain and other provisions could no longer come overland through Decelea, but had to be carried by sea on a much longer route. In their financial straits, the Athenians imposed a new 5 percent tax on their allies on all seaborne imports and exports.

These developments introduce the sequence of events leading to the second crucial Athenian reverse in Sicily, the prevention of the expedition's withdrawal. By now the war had entered a new stage in which the increasingly self-confident Syracusans were manifesting the same exceptional qualities of initiative and daring that had hitherto distinguished the Athenians in all their enterprises. "The same reckless courage," Thucydides pointed out, "which had often enabled the Athenians, although inferior in power, to strike terror into their adversaries, might now be turned against them by the Syracusans" (7.21). Yet he emphasized that notwithstanding "the cruel necessity of maintaining two wars at once," the people of Athens "carried on both with a determination which no one would have believed unless he had actually seen it" (7.28).

Marveling at their resilience, he described their situation at the time as follows:

> That, blockaded as they were by the Peloponnesians, who had raised a fort in their own country, they should refuse to let go Sicily, and themselves besieged, persevere in the siege of Syracuse, which as a mere city might rank with Athens, and—whereas the Hellenes generally were expecting at the beginning of the war . . . that they would survive a year [or] two or perhaps three years, certainly not more, if the Peloponnesians invaded Attica—that in the seventeenth year from the first invasion, after so exhausting a struggle, the Athenians should have been strong enough and bold enough to go to Sicily at all, and to plunge into a fresh war as great as that in which they were already engaged—how contrary was all this to the expectation of mankind! (7.28)

At this point in the saga he was relating, he interspersed a brief notice of another atrocity of the war, perhaps the worst of all, which occurred in mainland Greece. A body of Thracian warriors whom the Athenians had first hired as mercenaries and then discharged to save money assaulted and captured the town of Mycalessus in Boeotia. They sacked its houses and temples and killed all the inhabitants, sparing "neither old nor young, but cut down, one after another, all whom they met, the women and children, the very beasts of burden, and every living thing." The Thracians, he notes, "could be as bloody as the worst barbarians" when they dared. Amidst the wild panic in the town, every kind of destruction occurred. When the killers came upon a boys' school, they massacred every child. "No greater calamity than this," according to the historian, "ever affected a whole city;" and considering its size, "no calamity more deplorable occurred during the war" (7.29–30). Mycalessus, a small and insignificant place, was of no military consequence. In choosing to tell its tragic story, Thucydides laid aside his usual impersonality in order to express his sorrow and pity for the hapless victims as well as his moral reprobation of the barbarism of those who slew them.

In the summer of 413, Demosthenes and Eurymedon arrived in Syracuse with a fleet of some seventy-three ships carrying another five thousand Athenian and allied hoplites, many lightly armed troops, and abundant supplies. The Syracusans were amazed and dismayed that their enemy was still capable of raising such a large

117

force nearly equal in size to the first expedition. Demosthenes, an efficient leader who had been mainly responsible for the earlier Athenian victory against the Spartans at Pylos, wanted to strike at once by attempting to seize the counter-wall with which the Syracusans had stopped the Athenian wall on Epipolae. Convinced that Nicias had made a great mistake on coming to Sicily in failing to take advantage of surprise by an immediate attack on Syracuse, he had no wish to repeat this error. He held that if the Athenians could capture the enemy counter-wall, the city would fall, and that if they failed, then the expedition should abandon Sicily and go home. The other two generals having agreed, the Athenians launched a daring night assault on Epipolae in which they were driven back after hard fighting with many casualties.

Demosthenes and Eurymedon now demanded that with the army so discouraged and its situation hopeless, the expedition should immediately leave Sicily. Nicias, though, was unwilling to do so. He hesitated to make such a confession of weakness and insisted that the Athenian people "would not forgive their departure if they left without an order from home" (7.48). He also argued that a party in Syracuse wanted to surrender the city and that the Syracusans were in an even worse condition than the Athenians. He therefore urged persisting in the effort to take Syracuse and wear out its defenders. Amid these divided counsels, the army remained where it was. In the meantime the Spartan Gylippus brought to Syracuse a new army made up of fresh forces collected in Sicily and newly arrived Peloponnesian troops. Facing a strengthened enemy who was preparing to attack on land and sea, the three Athenian generals now finally agreed that they must withdraw from Sicily at once. Just as their fleet was preparing to sail, an eclipse of the moon occurred; the date has been ascertained as 27 August 413. Thucydides described the Athenians' terrified reaction to this portentous event: "[T]he mass of the army was greatly moved and called upon the generals to remain. Nicias himself, who was too much under the influence of divination and omens, refused even to discuss the question of their removal until they had remained thrice nine days" (7.50). Religious fears and scruples consequently delayed the expedition's departure at a time when immediate action was imperative. The historian's disapproval of the reason for this decision and Nicias's superstitious attitude is evident.

Some days later the Syracusans were victorious in a sea battle in the Great Harbor in which the Athenians lost a number of ships and Eurymedon was killed. Thucydides paints the effect of this defeat on the Athenians in the darkest colors, a prelude to the final disaster. They were in "utter despair," regretting "that they had ever come. . . . They had failed at almost every point, and were already in great straits, when the defeat at sea, which they could not have thought possible, reduced their fortunes to a still lower ebb" (7.55). Following this action, the Syracusans closed the mouth of the harbor, which was about a mile wide, with a line of vessels to prevent the rest of the Athenian fleet from sailing out. Their aim was to trap and capture the entire expedition.

At a council of war, the Athenian generals and officers decided to throw all their forces into an attempt to break the blockade of the harbor. They agreed that if they conquered, they would go to Catana; if they failed, they would burn their ships and retreat overland to some friendly territory. Before the battle, Nicias made a stirring speech telling his men of the army's readiness to fight, warning of the consequences of defeat, and calling on their patriotism to remember that "you are both the fleet and army of your country, and . . . on you hangs the whole state and the great name of Athens" (7.61–64). Gylippus and the Syracusan generals likewise exhorted their men, holding out the prospect of the glory they would win by their conquest of the Athenians, their worst enemies, who had come to their land to enslave them (7.66–68).

Leaving a body of infantry ashore to guard their baggage and the sick against the Syracusan army, the Athenians boarded their ships with as many fighting men as possible. At this critical point, Thucydides chose artfully to concentrate again on Nicias, whose state of mind he reveals for a pathetic moment. Overwhelmed by the gravity of the situation and feeling that he had not yet done or said enough, Nicias speaks to the captains, calling each man by his name, his father's name, and his tribe. He entreats them to think of their ancestors, of Athens's hereditary fame, of the freedom it gives to every man, exceeding that of any other country, and of their wives, children, and their fathers' gods (7.69). "As men will at such a time," Thucydides strikingly comments, "they do not care whether their commonplace phrases may seem to be out of date, but loudly reiterate the old appeals believing that they may be of some service at that awful moment" (7.69).

A fierce, confused battle followed within the enclosed space of the harbor in which almost two hundred ships were engaged, over one hundred of them Athenian. Thucydides includes numerous particulars. "The crash," he says, "of so many ships dashing against one another took away the wits of the sailors, and made it impossible to hear the boatswains, whose voices in both fleets rose high, as they gave directions to the rowers or cheered them on in the excitement of the struggle" (7.70). From shore the Athenian and Syracusan troops who were stationed there watched the shifting fortunes of the naval battle in an agony of suspense. In the end, the Athenians failed to break out of the blockaded harbor. The Syracusans destroyed some of their ships and drove the others back to land. Panic struck the Athenians, whose plight the historian compares to that of the Spartans at Pylos some years before: "[F]or at Pylos the Lacedemonians, when they saw their ships destroyed, knew that their friends who had crossed over to the island of Sphacteria were lost. . . . And so now the Athenians, after the rout of their fleet, knew that they had no hope of saving themselves by land unless events took some extraordinary turn" (7.70).

The generals, who still had sixty ships, wanted to try once more to break through on the following morning, but the demoralized crews refused to go. So "overwhelmed by their misery" were the Athenians that "they never so much as thought of recovering their wrecks or of asking leave to collect their dead" (7.72). The only alternative left them for survival was a retreat by land to a safe place in Sicily. Three days after the naval battle they started to move. The narrative rises to its climax as it pictures the final phase of the expedition in its dreadful march. There were at least forty thousand men, filled with fear and despair and shedding tears at having to abandon their sick and wounded comrades despite the latters' pleas and lamentations. Nicias and Demosthenes went among the troops to try to hearten them by appealing to their patriotism and bravery. In what the reader cannot but see as a great irony, Nicias spoke to them of hope, invoking that same delusive hope which the Athenians had dismissed three years earlier when they bade the unfortunate Melians not to rely on hope as they faced slavery and death. Since he had passed his days, he said, in the performance of religious duties and many just and blameless actions, he still had hope in the future. He exhorted the soldiers to hope that if their expedition had provoked the jealousy of any god, "by this time we have been punished enough," and that the gods "will be more merciful to us, for we now invite their pity rather than their jealousy" (7.77).

Marching inland westward for three days with the plan of eventually getting to Catana, the Athenians found themselves blocked by the enemy's troops and turned south to reach the sea the next day at dawn. Harassed by Syracusan cavalry and light infantry, they moved parallel with the shore, intending to turn inland again along one of the rivers that ran to the coast. The rear division of the army, which Demosthenes led, was attacked by Syracusan forces, surrounded, and surrendered after a daylong resistance on the condition that the soldiers' lives would be spared. Six thousand men gave themselves up and were taken to Syracuse as captives. Many others had been killed in the previous fighting. Over the next two days Gylippus and the Syracusans caught up with and continually attacked Nicias and his men, who were lacking in food and very tired. On learning that Demosthenes had surrendered, Nicias offered on behalf of Athens to pay the Syracusans for their expenses in the war if they let his army go, but they rejected his proposal. Pursued on every side by enemy cavalry and missiles, the remaining Athenian force reached the river Assinarus, where all discipline vanished as crowds of soldiers rushed down to the water to cross or drink. Many were trampled and drowned, many others died in the terrible carnage that the Syracusans standing on the steep riverbank inflicted on the men below in the stream. At last Nicias surrendered to Gylippus, who commanded his troops to stop the killing and take prisoners.

The Athenian expedition existed no more. As he draws the story of its destruction to a close, Thucydides describes the subsequent fate of those who remained alive. Both Nicias and Demosthenes were executed. Of the former, he comments, "No one of the Hellenes in my time was less deserving of so miserable an end; for he lived in the practice of every customary virtue" (7.86). Although this statement surely expresses a human compassion, it appears to be no more than a praise of Nicias's conventional piety and private character, and certainly not of his military leadership. At least seven thousand of the prisoners became captives of the state, more became the property of Syracusan soldiers, and others escaped after an interval of slavery, so that survivors of the Athenian army were scattered throughout Sicily. A considerable number were imprisoned without shelter in the stone quarries of Syracuse, where they died of hunger, thirst, and exposure to the scorching sun and the cold autumn nights. The Athenian expedition, as the historian pronounces its epitaph, was the greatest of all recorded Hellenic actions, "most glorious to the victors, most ruinous to the vanquished." The Athenians and their allies "were utterly and at all points defeated, and their sufferings were prodigious. Fleet and army perished from the face of the earth; nothing was saved, and of the many who went forth few returned home" (7.87).

What were the reasons for the expedition's defeat? Thucydides includes no discussion of this question, but it is possible to deduce some of his thoughts on the subject. In the first place, he considered the expedition a great mistake, one due to the deviation from Pericles' policy on account of the decline in the quality of political leadership in Athens after the former's death in 429. This is probably his main explanation. Yet he also comments that the Athenians had not "miscalculated their enemies' power" (2.65); and at one place he appears to suggest that the recall of Alcibiades, whose "talents as a . . . commander were unrivalled," was the cause of the expedition's defeat (6.16). In the war itself, he devotes the most attention among the Athenian generals to the role of Nicias, quoting three of his speeches to his troops, as well as his letter to the Athenian assembly asking that the expedition be recalled or reinforced. Although many historians have placed the chief responsibility for the expedition's failure on Nicias's incompetent generalship,[15] Thucydides never blames or criticizes him directly. Nonetheless, he seems to share the view of the Athenian co-general Demosthenes that Nicias should have begun his attack on Syracuse as soon as the Athenian army arrived in Sicily instead of going into winter quarters at Catana (7.42). Although Nicias was personally brave and even heroic as the expedition neared its end, his heart was never in the attempt to conquer Sicily, and he showed his reservations by his inaction at the beginning of the Sicilian campaign. Later, at a critical moment, he foolishly rejected the advice of the other two generals to leave Sicily after the Athenians' defeat in their attempt to take the Syracusan counter-wall on Epipolae. He maintained this position largely because of his fear of the discredit and condemnation he might incur with the people of Athens, for which personal reason he was willing to risk the existence of his army. An even more egregious error, as Thucydides obviously regards it, was Nicias's superstitious terror at an eclipse of the moon, which led him to delay the Athenian removal from Sicily with fatal consequences. Despite his tribute to Nicias's virtue, Thucydides' previous characterization of him in the *History* helps to explain his defects as a commander of the Sicilian expedition. Speaking of his eagerness for peace with Sparta, Thucydides states that as "the most fortunate general of his day," Nicias desired,

> whilst he was still successful and held in repute, to preserve his good fortune; he would have liked to rest from toil, and to give the people rest; and he hoped to leave behind him to other ages the name of a man who in all his life had never brought disaster on the city. He thought that the way to gain his wish was to trust as little as possible to fortune, and to keep out of danger, and that danger would best be avoided by peace. (5.16)

A man who thought in this way was not well fitted to lead the Athenians to victory in Sicily.

But Thucydides also brings out the ability and fighting qualities of the Syracusans as the Athenians' adversaries. He notes that the Sicilian cities were the only ones the Athenians had ever encountered which were

> similar in character to their own, enjoying the same democratic institutions and strong in ships, cavalry, and population. They [the Athenians] were not able by holding out the prospect of a change of government to introduce an element of discord amongst them which might have gained them over, nor could they master them by a decided superiority of force. (7.55)

He likewise observes how the Syracusans improved their skill in naval warfare in successive engagements and increasingly manifested the boldness and initiative that had previously distinguished the Athenians. "To daring men like the Athenians," he comments, "those who emulated their daring were the most formidable foes" (7.21). In the last book of his *History*, he states in passing that "the Syracusans, who were most like [the Athenians], fought best against them" (8.96).

The defeat and loss of the Sicilian expedition was a tremendous material and political blow to Athen's imperial position. Nevertheless, the city went on fighting and was able to carry on the war for nine more years before it succumbed.

Endings

> The news was brought to Athens, but the
> Athenians could not believe that the armament
> had been so completely annihilated, although
> they had the positive assurances of the very
> soldiers who had escaped from the scene of
> action. At last they knew the truth; and then they
> were furious with the orators who had joined in
> promoting the expedition—as if they had not
> voted it themselves—and with the soothsayers,
> and prophets, and all who by the influence of
> religion had at the time inspired them with the
> belief that they would conquer Sicily. Whichever
> way they looked there was trouble; they were
> overwhelmed by their calamity, and were in fear
> and consternation unutterable. The city mourned
> and the citizens mourned. (8.1)

The End of the *History*

With this graphic description of the reaction in Athens to the fate
of the Sicilian expedition Thucydides begins the eighth book of
his *History*. The same book also rings down the curtain on the entire work, whose narrative stops suddenly in the summer of the
year 411.[1] Although the Peloponnesian War continued for another
seven years, the great guide who has led us through its preceding
events is no longer available to us. It is not known why he left the
work unfinished, but this last book contains a number of indications that parts of it were a draft consisting of separate reports
that he would have probably revised.[2] Since his account is the
main source not only for the war but for the entire period of
Athenian and Greek history that it covers, its failure to describe
the remainder of the war down to its conclusion is a grievous loss
to historical knowledge of the Greek world at the end of the fifth
century.

The passage from the *History* quoted above contains an implicit criticism of Athenian democracy in its pointed comment that the people, though enraged against those who promoted the Sicilian expedition, were nevertheless responsible for approving it. But Thucydides goes on to record that the shock of their calamitous loss in Sicily did not shatter the Athenians' will or undermine their commitment to the war. "[T]hey determined," he says, "under any circumstances not to give way," and resolved to rebuild their navy, to make sure of their allies, to raise money, and to cut the city's expenses. They likewise decided to elect an emergency council of elders that would advise the people on necessary measures in this time of crisis (8.1). "After the manner of a democracy," the historian adds, "they were very amenable to discipline while their fright lasted" (8.1). Beside the Athenians' determination to prosecute the war, the beginning of the eighth book reports the excited response in Greece to Athens's overthrow in Sicily. States that had previously been neutral were now willing to join in attacking the imperial city, while Sparta's allies were more eager than ever to carry the war to victory. Athens's subject cities, convinced that it could not survive for another summer, "were everywhere willing even beyond their power to revolt." The Lacedaemonians themselves, greatly encouraged, looked forward to the successful termination of the war which would assure them "of the undisputed leadership of Hellas" (8.2).

This is the scene as Thucydides depicts it in the late summer of 413 in the nineteenth year of the war. After the enthralling experience of books 6 and 7, readers are apt to find the eighth book of the *History* something of an anticlimax. The two former books have a powerful dramatic unity and coherence built around the story of the Sicilian expedition, while the latter, by comparison, lacks a unifying theme and seems somewhat fragmented. It is the only book that contains no direct reproduction of speeches, and its narrative is sometimes confusing and difficult to follow because the events it describes are so dispersed and intricate. In place of one predominant military enterprise, it reports many scattered actions, battles, and events in Greece itself, in the coastal and island cities of western Asia Minor, and in the region of the Hellespont. The previous two books focused on a few outstanding individuals, principally Nicias and Alcibiades, but also the Athenian commander Demosthenes, the Sicilian leader Hermocrates, and the Spartan general Gylippus. The eighth book presents a much larger cast of characters, of whom Alcibiades is the most prominent. He played a larger role in this period of the war than did any other person, but Thucydides also directs attention to numerous other men—Athenians, Spartans, and Persians—who emerge into temporary prominence. There are also obscurities and gaps in the sequence of events in this book that modern scholars have tried to remedy with the help of other sources.

If Thucydides hadn't indicated earlier in the *History* how the war would end, we wouldn't discover from the incomplete book 8 that Athens was destined to final defeat and the loss of its empire. In fact, his narrative as far as he takes it shows Athens holding its own, sending out fleets, striving to repress rebellious allies, and winning a great sea battle in 411 against the Spartans and their allies at Cynossema in the Hellespont. The Athenians' ability to endure against a host of enemies ought not to surprise us if we keep in mind Thucydides' earlier statement in book 2, one of the most important in the *History*, in which he spoke of the future after memorializing the death of Pericles. There he emphasized Athens's ability to sustain the conflict for a number of years in spite of the destruction of its navy and army in Sicily, revolts by its allies, and civil strife at home. Even after the Persians joined the war on the side of the Peloponnesians, he said, the Athenians "continued to resist, and were at last overthrown, not by their enemies but by themselves and their own internal dissensions" (2.65).

Amid the welter of developments related in book 8, it is not difficult to pick out the major strands or factors whose interplay shaped this final stage of the Peloponnesian War. One of the most important was the entry of Persia into the war as Sparta's ally. Throughout most of the *History*, Thucydides has said very little about Persia, although he has mentioned that at the outset of the war both the Spartans and Athenians hoped to enlist Persian assistance (2.7). From other sources it is also known that around 424 Athens and Persia probably renewed the previous peace agreement between them.[3] Nevertheless, in 413 the Persian satrap Tissaphernes, governor of the province of Sardis in Asia Minor, offered support to the Spartans on behalf of his master, King Darius.[4] The probable reason for this action was that the Athenians were assisting Amorges, a rebel against Darius, whom the king had ordered Tissaphernes to bring in dead or alive; the king, moreover, held Tissaphernes responsible for collecting the arrears of tribute due from the Greek cities in his province, which the Athenians apparently prevented from being paid (8.5).[5] Soon the Persian monarch made an alliance with Sparta and its allies to carry on the war in common against Athens. Their treaty was twice revised in 412, all three texts being recorded by Thucydides. In its last, definitive version, the Spartans and their allies agreed, in exchange for the promise of Persian money, supplies, and ships, of which they were badly in need, to recognize the king of Persia's rule and freedom to act as he pleased in all his Asian possessions. Both parties also pledged to make peace with Athens on the same terms (8.58). The scope of the clause concerning the Persian king's possessions in Asia is not clear. As these possessions, however, included some of the Ionian Greek cities of Asia Minor to which the Persian monarchy laid claim and from whom it demanded tribute, Sparta's alliance with Persia showed how little it really cared for the independence and freedom of Greece for which it professed to be fighting the war against Athens.[6]

A second major factor that marked this period of the war was the widespread rebellions that broke out among Athens's subject allies. One of the largest was the revolt of the wealthy commercial city of Chios, which joined with Sparta and encouraged Lesbos, Miletus, and other smaller cities of the Athenian empire to do the same. The Athenians fought hard to put down these revolts. In the case of Chios, they attacked its ships and landed upon the island troops who defeated the Chian forces and devastated their territory, but failed to take the city. Thucydides noted the prudence and moderation of Chios, which did not venture to revolt until other cities were ready to follow and Athens was in an obvious state of weakness. If the Chians, he added, "were deceived through the uncertainty of human things, this error of judgment was common to many who, like them, believed that the Athenian power would speedily be overthrown" (8.24). Although the Athenians crushed the revolt of Lesbos, their efforts to reconquer Miletus were frustrated by Spartan assistance to the Milesians, and Rhodes also rebelled and joined the Peloponnesian alliance.

A third significant factor in this period of the war was the change of sides of Alcibiades, whose intrigues and maneuvers Thucydides follows. After leaving Sicily in 415, he had rendered very useful service to the Spartans in their war against Athens. Later he was highly instrumental in instigating and bringing Spartan aid to the revolts of Chios and other subject cities of the Athenian empire. But Sparta's King Agis hated him as a rival and personal enemy, while the Spartans generally distrusted him (8.12, 45). It is likely that the cause of Agis's enmity, unmentioned by Thucydides, was that Alcibiades had been the lover of Agis's wife and had fathered one of her children.[7] Although the historian refrains from probing Alcibiades' psychology or driving passions, it seems pretty clear that he was an adventurer governed by a thirst for power and glory and above all by a concern for his own survival in a political situation that was highly precarious and fraught with dangers. In an unusual flashback in time, Thucydides relates that prior to the revolt of Rhodes, Alcibiades had learned while he was at Miletus that a message was on its way from Sparta ordering his execution. He therefore left the Spartans and fled to the Persian satrap Tissaphernes, whose close adviser he now became. In that capacity he "did all he could to injure the Peloponnesian cause" (8.45). So he was twice a renegade, first from Athens, then from Sparta. The information the *History* conveys about his policy at this juncture must very likely have been obtained either from Alcibiades himself or from someone in his confidence. He advised Tissaphernes to withhold financial assistance from the Peloponnesians and not to be in a hurry to end the war, but rather to play each side of the Greeks against the other so that both would be exhausted. He also proposed that the Athenians would be better partners for the Persians than would the Lacedaemonians because they had no ambition to increase their possessions on land. If the Persians were to help Athens maintain its mastery of the sea, he suggested, then the Athenians would in turn help the Persian king to subjugate the Greeks who lived in his territory. Thucydides judged that Tissaphernes heeded Alcibiades' advice to prolong the war and therefore did nothing to aid Persia's Peloponnesian allies. He explains that while Alcibiades truly believed that his counsel was in Persia's interests, he also had an additional motive. This was to prepare the way "for his own return" to Athens, because "he knew that, if he did not destroy his country altogether, the time would come when he would persuade his countrymen to recall him; and he thought that his arguments would be most effectual if he were seen to be on intimate terms with Tissaphernes" (8.46–47).

The last of the major factors of this period of the war was the outbreak of *stasis* or internal conflict among the Athenians, which resulted in a revolutionary coup against Athens's democracy in 411. Thucydides describes the development of the antidemocratic conspiracy. It was first hatched among a number of Athenian officers at Samos, which Athens had made the base for its operations against its rebel allies and the Peloponnesian forces in the eastern Aegean. They were in communication with Alcibiades, who they believed would bring the Persians over to Athens's side in the war. Eager to return to Athens, Alcibiades played on these officers' hopes that he would use his influence upon Tissaphernes to make the Persians their friend if they agreed to abolish the villainous democratic regime which had driven him out and establish an oligarchy in its place. Partly because of these messages, Thucydides says, "but still more of their own inclination, the captains and leading Athenians at Samos were now eager to overthrow the democracy" (8.47). They told their soldiers that the King of Persia would help and supply them with money "if Alcibiades was restored and democracy given up." The Athenian general Phrynicus, "a man of great sagacity" (8.27) and enemy of Alcibiades, opposed their scheme. He told the authors of the conspiracy that the Persian king had no reason to join the Athenians, whom he distrusted, and would remain allied with the Peloponnesians, who had never done him any harm. He also argued, and rightly, according to Thucydides, that Alcibiades "cared no more for oligarchy than he did for democracy, and in seeking to change the existing form of government was only considering how he might be recalled and restored to his country at the invitation of the clubs" (8.48). The clubs in question were the *hetairiai* or *xunomosiai*, political associations in Athens that existed to promote the mutual benefit of their members in lawsuits and elections, and some of which consisted of aristocrats who were in favor of oligarchy.[8]

The leaders of the conspiracy nevertheless proceeded with their plans. At the end of 412 they sent envoys to Athens, with Peisander as their spokesman, to persuade the people that if they restored Alcibiades and changed their government, they might obtain Persian help and defeat the Peloponnesians. Meeting with strong opposition, Peisander told them that there was no hope of saving Athens without the support of the king of Persia and that a Persian alliance was impossible unless they removed the democracy. "Do not let us be dwelling on the form of constitution," he said, "which we may hereafter change as we please, when the very existence of Athens is at stake. And we must restore Alcibiades, who is the only man living capable of saving us" (8.53). Because they saw no alternative to this plan, and even though they still retained the hope of reverting to democracy, the citizens finally agreed to authorize negotiations with Tissaphernes and Alcibiades. Before leaving Athens, Peisander went around to all the political clubs, urging that they unite to put down the democratic regime (8.54).

The negotiations that followed between the Athenians and Tissaphernes failed because the Persian satrap demanded too much. In Athens, however, the subversion of the democratic order was already well under way with the help of the oligarchic political clubs. Androcles, a popular demagogue who had been the chief mover in the earlier exile of Alcibiades, was assassinated, together with a number of other partisans of democracy. No search was made for the assassins, who were never brought to trial. The champions of oligarchy announced that no more than five thousand people consisting of those most able to serve the state in person and with their money should have a share in the government. Thucydides declares that this proposal was merely a pretense "to look well in the eyes of the people, for the authors of the revolution fully meant to retain the government in their own hands" (8. 66). Amidst a climate of fear and suspicion, the Athenian assembly continued to meet; but the organizers of the oligarchic coup controlled its agenda and proceedings, so that nothing was said or done but what they approved. The historian comments that when they saw the strength of the conspiracy,

> the citizens were afraid . . . and if anyone did utter a word, he was put out of the way. . . . [T]he people were so depressed and afraid to move that anyone who escaped violence thought himself fortunate, even though he had never said a word. Their minds were cowed by the supposed number of the conspirators, which they greatly exaggerated, having no means of discovering the truth, since the size of the city prevented them from knowing one another. (8.66)

Such was the situation in Athens when Peisander and the other envoys from Samos returned to the city in the spring of 411, bringing with them some heavily armed troops to complete the overthrow of the democratic polity. On their voyage to Athens, they acted to install oligarchies in a number of its subject cities.

After their arrival they convened the Athenian assembly, which elected a committee to frame a new constitution that was shortly presented to the people. It provided for a council of Four Hundred, which was to have absolute authority and could summon at its discretion the Five Thousand, a body that as yet had no institutional existence (8.67).

Beside Peisander, Thucydides names several other ringleaders of the oligarchic revolution in Athens whom he praises for their ability. Those he mentions were the general Phrynicus, the politician Theramenes, and most notably Antiphon, "the real author . . . of the whole scheme . . . inferior in excellence [*arete*] to none of his contemporaries, and possessed of remarkable powers of thought and gifts of speech." Of Antiphon in particular he says that "when the government of the Four Hundred was overthrown and became exposed to the vengeance of the people, and he being accused of taking part in the plot had to speak in his own case, his defense was undoubtedly the best ever made by any man tried on a capital charge down to my time." From Thucydides this was high praise.[9] He goes on to observe that with such capable men guiding the movement, it was no wonder it succeeded; "for an easy thing it certainly was not, one hundred years after the fall of the tyrants, to destroy the liberties of the Athenians, who were not only a free, but during more than half of this time had been an imperial people" (8.68).

The Four Hundred took power without any opposition, as the people were too terrified to resist. They changed the democratic system completely, according to Thucydides, and "governed the city with a high hand," killing, imprisoning, and exiling their political enemies (8.69–70). They also made a futile peace offer to the Spartans.

But on the island of Samos, meanwhile, where there were many Athenian troops, ships, and sailors, a democratic counterrevolution broke out against the oligarchic government of the Four Hundred in Athens. Led by two officers, Thrasybulus and Thrasyllus, the soldiers bound themselves by solemn oaths to maintain a democracy, remain united, prosecute the war vigorously, and treat the Four Hundred as an enemy. They deposed their generals and elected new ones, including Thrasybulus and Thrasyllus. Backed by the Athenian forces there, the leaders of this democratic movement recalled Alcibiades, who came to Samos and delivered a speech that promised Persian help and inspired his listeners with hopes of victory. The Athenian soldiers not only immediately appointed him as one of the generals, but "placed everything in his hands" (8.82). Now the dominant figure, he continued to hold out the deceptive prospect that his favor with Tissaphernes and the Persians would bring them around to support the Athenians in the war.

The Four Hundred dispatched envoys to try to achieve an accommodation with the hostile Athenian forces in Samos who supported the democratic polity. Refusing to listen, the soldiers cried out, "Death to the subverters of the democracy" (8.86). The envoys defended the Four Hundred, denying that they intended to betray Athens to its enemies, and promised that every Athenian citizen would in turn become a member of the Five Thousand. They failed to pacify the troops, who proposed sailing to Athens at once to remove the oligarchy. Had they done this, they would have abandoned Ionia and the Hellespont to immediate conquest by the Peloponnesians, whose own ships and forces lay nearby at Miletus. The intervention of Alcibiades saved the day. He restrained the angry soldiers, protected the envoys from the menaces of the crowd, and sent them back to Athens after telling them that he was not against the Five Thousand but that the Four Hundred had to go. He urged them to remain firm against the enemy and that if Athens were preserved, the parties might be reconciled. Although Thucydides merely summarizes Alcibiades' speech at Samos in this tense situation, it is not hard to imagine the audacity, oratorical skill, and personal charisma with which Alcibiades succeeded in persuading his auditors. No one else, Thucydides believed, "could have restrained the multitude," and he pays him the high tribute at this point of having done "as eminent a service to the state as any man ever did" (8.86).

When the representatives of the Four Hundred reported Alcibiades' views in Athens, some of the leaders of the oligarchic revolution, foreseeing the likelihood of a change of government, lost their nerve. They therefore proposed that the Five Thousand should actually be established and the polity made more equal. Analyzing their motives, Thucydides says that they were dominated by personal rivalries and ambition of the kind "more fatal than anything to an oligarchy succeeding a democracy. For the instant an oligarchy is established the promoters of it disdain mere equality and everybody thinks he ought to be far above everybody else." What most affected them was their fear of "the great power of Alcibiades at Samos, and an impression that oligarchy was not likely to be permanent," hence "every one was struggling hard to be the first champion of the people" (8.89). The most extreme oligarchic leaders, however, were determined to preserve the regime of the Four Hundred, even if that required making peace with the Spartans on the best terms they could get. So they initiated another attempt at negotiations, hastily sending an embassy to Sparta, which again met with no success. On its return, Phrynicus, one of its members, was murdered, and the Four Hundred were suspected of preparing to bring in the Spartan enemy. Thucydides devotes some detail to a description of the dissensions between the extreme partisans of oligarchy and the supporters of popular rule, which broke out in the city and port of Piraeus and threatened to lead to civil war.

Just at this time a Peloponnesian fleet defeated and captured a number of Athenian ships near Euboea, the long island adjacent to the east coast of Attica, whose cities then revolted and joined the Peloponnesians. These reverses dealt Athens a severe blow. The panic-stricken people, Thucydides reports, were even more terrified than after the ruin of the Sicilian expedition. Their army in Samos was in revolt, they had no ships in reserve or crews to man them, there was revolution in their own city, and the defection of Euboea meant the strategic loss of an essential supply route. Worst of all, they feared the Peloponnesians would immediately attack Piraeus, where there were no ships left to fight. The historian thought the Peloponnesians might have won the war at that moment if they had invaded or blockaded Piraeus. They did not venture to do so, however, a failure he attributed to the Spartans' habitual cautiousness, which made them, he said, "the most convenient enemies the Athenians could have had" (8.96).

At this critical juncture, the Athenians met in an assembly, deposed the Four Hundred, and established the Five Thousand as the government. This institution was to include everyone who could provide himself with the heavy armor required by hoplites (which meant all the citizens who possessed the financial means to do so). No one was to be paid for holding office, as had been the case under the democracy. The people also voted to recall Alcibiades and others from exile, and exhorted him and the forces in Samos to act vigorously. Most of the leading supporters of the Four Hundred fled for refuge to King Agis at Decelea. Some were exiled or executed, Antiphon being among the latter. Thus ended the oligarchical revolution, which, according to Thucydides' account, was carried out by means of terror, force, and deceit. In a rare personal comment, he says that the new government of the Five Thousand, a tempered combination of oligarchy and democracy or "moderate mixture [*metría xunkrasis*] . . . of the few and the many," was "during its early days . . . the best which the Athenians ever enjoyed within my memory." After the miserable state into which Athens had fallen, "the city was again able to raise its head" (8.97–98).[10]

With the recounting of internal developments in Athens down into the late summer of 411, Thucydides' narrative almost reached the point where it breaks off. What mainly remains of book 8 is his brief account of naval operations in the Hellespont and the Athenian victory over the Peloponnesians at Cynossema. When news of this success arrived in Athens, he reports, "the Athenians could hardly believe their good fortune, and after the calamities which had befallen them in Euboea and during the revolution, they were greatly encouraged. They thought that their affairs were no longer hopeless, and that if they were energetic they might still win" (8.106). The eighth book ceases with a mention of the activities of Alcibiades at Samos and of the movements and intentions of the Persian Tissaphernes in his relationship with the Peloponnesians. These events occurred near the conclusion of the twenty-first year of the Peloponnesian War.

AFTER THUCYDIDES: THE END OF THE WAR

Every survey of Greek and Athenian history in the fifth century relates the developments of the final years of the Peloponnesian War following the end of Thucydides' narrative.[11] Forced to do without the latter, historians have been able to reconstruct this final period from several other ancient authors and sources. The most important of these and nearest in time to their subject are the *Hellenica* or Greek history by the versatile Athenian Xenophon (c. 428–354), a disciple of Socrates, and the work by the anonymous so-called Oxyrhynchus historian, which has survived in fragments

135

among a collection of papyrus documents first discovered at Oxyrhynchus in Egypt in 1906. Both of these writers were younger contemporaries of Thucydides who undertook continuations of his *History* some years after his death.[12]

For a few years after 411 Athens's fortunes continued to improve. Its forces were successful in the Hellespont in some small engagements with the Peloponnesians and in the spring of 410 they defeated the latter and the Persians in a great naval battle at Cyzicus in which Alcibiades was the top commander. Prior to the battle he had ceased to be on good terms with Tissaphernes, who, ordered by the Persian monarch Darius to prosecute the war against the Athenians, imprisoned him. He managed to escape after a month, then sailed to Lesbos, and from there brought some ships to join with the Athenian fleet in the Hellespont, which was victorious at Cyzicus. In the aftermath of the latter, the Spartans made a peace offer to Athens based on the status quo that would have permitted each side to keep the cities then under its control. Due to popular pressure and renewed self-confidence, the Athenians unwisely refused this proposal, which despite their losses would still have enabled them to retain a considerable part of their empire.

In the summer of 410, following the victory of Cyzicus, democracy was peacefully reestablished in Athens and the government of the Five Thousand, which had lasted for only nine months, ended its rule. The restored democratic regime reinstated payment for holding office and introduced the *diobelia*, a two-obol daily dole to poorer citizens. Alcibiades, who had not yet returned to Athens and could no longer claim to be an intermediary with Persia, was nevertheless elected annually to the office of general because of his great reputation as a military and political leader.

Although the Athenians and Peloponnesians were both very hard pressed for resources and money to carry on the war, the latter received the support of Persia, which assisted them with financial subsidies. For a few years the two sides maintained an indecisive war of attrition, conducting scattered operations against one another's possessions. Alcibiades scored some notable successes in his attacks on Persian territory in Asia Minor, from which he extracted money and booty, and he also recaptured the city of Byzantium from the Spartans. In 407 the Persian monarch sent his son Cyrus to govern the coastal provinces of Asia Minor and help the Spartans. Alcibiades, now at the height of his reputation, finally returned to Athens in June 407. He was welcomed and acclaimed by cheering crowds, who showered him with honors, including the supreme command of the Athenian forces. While there were those in Athens who hated and opposed him, a great many of the citizens placed high hopes of victory and the preservation of their empire in his leadership.

In the period thereafter, however, the course of the war turned against Athens and sealed its fate. The Spartans appointed a new commander, Lysander, a capable, energetic general and strategist whose efforts were aided by a supply of Persian money from Cyrus to pay his crews. In August 407 Alcibiades left Athens with a large military force and one hundred ships. His first actions were unsuccessful, and in 406 a large portion of his fleet led by his deputy Antiochus was defeated by Lysander in an engagement at Notium in which twenty-two Athenian vessels were lost. Some of his own soldiers submitted complaints against Alcibiades in Athens and public opinion shifted against him, so in 406 he was not re-elected as one of the city's generals and was replaced by Conon. Fearing that he might be put on trial (for the Athenian democracy frequently punished its generals for their failures), he retreated to a fortress in Thrace.

In 406 the Athenians triumphed in a big naval battle at the Arginusae Islands lying off the coast of Asia Minor near Lesbos. The Spartans, who were commanded by Lysander's successor, lost over seventy ships to the Athenians' twenty-five. Unfortunately, a large number of Athenian survivors who were left clinging in the rough sea to disabled vessels were not rescued by their compatriots. The joyful news of the victory was clouded over in Athens by the people's grief and anger at the loss of these men, and the generals in command were held responsible for failing to save them and for not recovering the bodies of the dead. Six of the generals were tried and executed for their fault; only Conon was spared, while two others saved themselves by refusing to return to Athens to undergo examination for their actions.

After Arginusae the Spartans made a further offer of peace, which the Athenians rejected. The allies of Sparta called for the reappointment of Lysander, who returned to action nominally as deputy commander, since Spartan law prohibited a second term as commander. In the late summer of 405 he inflicted a decisive defeat on the Athenians at Aegospotami in the Hellespont by means of a surprise attack. One hundred and seventy-one ships, almost the entire Athenian fleet, were captured, as well as the Athenian encampment on the shore and several thousand prisoners. He executed many of the prisoners and sent the rest back to Athens, where they added to the numbers of people whom the state had to provide with food. In the autumn, Lysander's ships arrived before Athens's harbor at Piraeus, while the army of the Peloponnesian League and the troops of King Agis at Decelea advanced up to the city's walls to lay it siege.

Although the Athenians tried briefly to resist, they no longer possessed the strength or resources. Forced to surrender, they asked for peace and sent an embassy to Sparta. Many of Sparta's allies, notably Corinth and Thebes, demanded that Athens be destroyed, its men slaughtered, and its women and children enslaved. But the Spartans refused to impose this dreadful punishment on the city that had rendered unforgettable service to Greece in the Persian War. Perhaps they also deemed it most imprudent to leave such a vacuum of power in Attica. The terms of peace to which Athens agreed required the destruction of its fortifications and the Long Walls connecting the city to Piraeus; the surrender of all its ships except for only twelve vessels; the abandonment of its empire; the return of exiles; and a commitment to follow Sparta's leadership and have the same friends and enemies. With the peace concluded, Lysander's ships moved into the Piraeus in the spring of 404 and the Peloponnesians began the demolition of the Athenian Long Walls to the music of flutes. Xenophon wrote that the day was thought to mark "the beginning of freedom for the Greeks."[13] In reality, it was nothing of the sort. Rather than bringing freedom, what it signified was the commencement of Sparta's domination in Greece for the next three decades.

Thucydides as a Philosophic Historian

> If he who desires to have before his eyes a true
> picture of the events which have happened, and
> of the like events which may be expected to
> happen hereafter, given the human condition,
> shall pronounce what I have written to be useful,
> I shall be satisfied. My history is an everlasting
> possession, not a prize composition which is
> heard and forgotten. (1.22)

IN THIS concluding chapter, we must return to the famous words about his work that Thucydides placed at the beginning of his *History*. Far from being a vain boast, they proved to be a plain statement of fact. How shall we explain the enduring greatness of his account of the Peloponnesian War? What are the qualities of mind he put into it that give it its distinction as a classic history of the highest rank and one of the preeminent cultural monuments of the fifth-century Greek and Athenian civilization from which it sprang? The answer to these questions, I believe, lies principally in the explanatory power founded on the large world of ideas it reveals to the reader, and in Thucydides' belief that events similar to those he related "may be expected to happen hereafter" in accord with what he called *"to anthropinon,"* the human condition (1.22).

Aristotle's *Poetics*, a treatise on literary and aesthetic theory written in the century after Thucydides, declared that poetry is more philosophical than history because its statements are concerned with universals and what might be, whereas the statements of history deal with singulars and what has actually happened.[1] Whatever we may think of this distinction, it would need to be qualified in the case of Thucydides, whose intellectual temper was quite obviously philosophical. He was to an exceptional degree a generalizing historian. While he set himself a high standard of accuracy, impartiality, and truthfulness in matters of fact, he was not content to write a chronological year-by-year narrative detailing

139

the particular events, incidents, and interrelations of the war as they unfolded. He was equally concerned to explain them, to penetrate their reasons and causes, and to comprehend the war's background and its importance in the history of Hellas. Throughout his work, along with the scenes of war he evoked so vividly that they often appear before our eyes, we encounter general reflections that shed light on the actions he relates and contribute to a fuller understanding of their nature and significance. He continually sought to see the facts in relation to a wider whole or general truth.[2] This was an intrinsic part of his historical method, which involved a deep preoccupation with ideas touching on such matters as the nature of man, reason and passion, justice and power, chance and necessity in the shaping of events, and the relation between thought and action. These characteristics justify our view of him as a great philosophic historian.[3]

The high intellectualism and philosophic perspective that Thucydides brought to the writing of history cannot be understood outside the context of his involvement in the Greek Enlightenment, centered in Athens, which coincided with his own lifetime and extended down into the fourth century.[4] The astonishing efflorescence of literature, art, philosophy, and philosophic argument that occurred in Athens during the fifth century accompanied the growth of Athenian democracy and the emergence of the city after the Persian War as a powerful imperial state. The unprecedented ferment of ideas that marked this period, the progress of rationalism, and the radical questioning of religion and traditional beliefs and values that were a part of the intellectual scene must have affected Thucydides' mind in many ways. Reason, as one scholar has written, exulting in a new freedom and confidence, also turned its searchlight upon itself not only to discover its potential but to understand the irrational aspects of human nature.[5]

The generalizing and philosophic reflections contained in Thucydides' *History* are to be found in its narrative of events, in the speeches of the historical actors, and in the author's own infrequent direct comments. They are not detached abstractions imposed upon the story, but integrated observations that grow out of and form an organic part of the work as it proceeds, thereby adding immeasurably to its scope and depth. Among other things, they also provide us with an insight into Thucydides' worldview and personal vision. In the case of the speeches, although he was their author, we should take care to avoid simply identifying his own opinions and judgments with the ones he attributes to the speakers, as has often been done. We can infer his attitude and convictions only from the statements he makes *in propria persona*, from clues in the narrative, and sometimes also from his silences. But while he was not necessarily in agreement with the thoughts expressed in many of the speeches that he invented, he strove, as he explains in 1.22, to report faithfully the substance or point of what the speakers had actually said and to assign them opinions that in each instance would be appropriate to their situation. The speeches therefore expose a wide range of opposing arguments, assumptions, motives, values, rationalizations, and policy options that quite commonly have a general and abstract philosophical character.

We have noted a number of Thucydides' generalizations in preceding chapters, but two further examples can serve at this point to highlight the vital explanatory function they perform in his work. The first is the elaborate comparison he drew between the Athenian and Spartan national characters, which makes its first appearance in book 1. At the conference of the Peloponnesian allies in 432 to discuss the question of war with Athens, the Corinthians, who were most eager for war, reproached the Spartans for their failure to respond to Athenian aggressions and injuries. "[Y]ou have never considered," they said on that occasion,

> what manner of men are these Athenians with whom you will have to fight, and how utterly unlike yourselves. They are revolutionary, equally quick in the conception and execution of every new plan; while you are conservative, careful only to keep what you have, originating nothing, and not acting even when action is most necessary. They are bold beyond their strength; they run risks which prudence would condemn, and in the midst of misfortune they are full of hope. Whereas it is your nature, though strong, to act feebly; when your plans are most prudent, to distrust them; and when calamities come upon you, to think you will never be delivered from them. They are impetuous, and you are dilatory; they are always abroad, and you are always at home. For they hope to gain something by leaving their homes; but you are afraid that any new enterprise may imperil what you have already. When conquerors, they pursue their victory to the utmost; when defeated, they fall back the least. Their bodies they

devote to their country as though they belonged to other men; their true self is their mind, which is most truly their own when employed in her service. When they do not carry out an intention which they have formed, they seem to have sustained a personal bereavement; when an enterprise succeeds, they have gained a mere installment of what is to come; but if they fail, they at once conceive new hopes and so fill up the void. With them alone to hope is to have, for they lose not a moment in the execution of an idea. This is the lifelong task, full of danger and toil, which they are always imposing upon themselves. None enjoy their good things less, because they are always seeking for more. To do their duty is their only holiday, and they deem the quiet of inaction to be as disagreeable as the most tiresome business. If a man should say of them, in a word, that they were born neither to have peace themselves nor to allow peace to others, he would simply speak the truth. (1.70)

The Corinthians' sharply depicted contrast between the Athenians and Spartans is confirmed in other speeches, including the one delivered at the same conference by the Spartan King Archidamus, which argued against immediate war (1.80–85), and in some of Pericles' remarks in his funeral oration in 431 (2.35–46). It throws a flood of light on the actions of both sides in the war that was soon to come, and was endorsed by Thucydides in the eighth book when, commenting on the failure of the Spartans to take advantage of an opportunity that might have ended the war after Athens's loss of Euboea in 411, he declares,

> But on this as on so many other occasions the Lacedaemonians proved themselves to be the most convenient enemies the Athenians could possibly have had. For the two people were of very different tempers; the one quick, the other slow; the one adventurous, the other timorous; and the Lacedaemonian character was of great service to the Athenians (8.96)

I choose the second example from the account in the third book of the revolution in Corcyra in 427, in which the historian proceeds to offer a number of thoughts on the causes and consequences of the savage revolutionary conflicts between democracy and oligarchy that swept over the Greek cities during the war. There he notes that

> revolution brought upon the cities of Hellas many terrible calamities, such as have been and always will be while human nature remains the

same, but which are more or less aggravated and differ in character with every new combination of circumstances. In peace and prosperity both states and individuals are actuated by higher motives, because they do not fall under the dominion of imperious necessities; but war which takes away the comfortable provision of daily life is a violent teacher and tends to assimilate men's characters to their conditions. (3.82)

This statement, which serves as a generic model for similar situations, puts before us in universal terms an incisive insight on the deterioration of moral standards that is caused by war and civil war. Its wisdom strikes home in clarifying many of the events the *History* relates.

REALISM

One of the terms that has been widely and accurately used to characterize Thucydides' philosophy is realism. His history has been called "a classic of realist analysis."[6] This characteristic of his historical thought was singled out for praise by two eminent European philosophers, Thomas Hobbes and Friedrich Nietzsche. Hobbes, who published the first complete English translation of Thucydides' *History* directly from the Greek original in 1628, said of him: "Thucydides is one, who, though he never digress to read a lecture, moral or political, upon his own text, nor enter into men's hearts further than the acts themselves evidently guide him, is yet accounted the most politic historiographer that ever writ."[7] The word "politic" in this statement refers to the mature judgment and penetration that Thucydides brought to his understanding of politics and human action. Nietzsche, who had been a professor of Greek literature, saw Thucydides as a thinker distinguished for "his courage in the face of reality," with an "unconditional will not to fool oneself," and hence as a cure against Plato, "a coward before reality," who fled for refuge to the realm of the ideal. While his charge of intellectual cowardice against Plato was grossly prejudiced and mistaken, Nietzsche was absolutely correct in describing Thucydides as the exponent of "a strong, severe, hard factuality" identical with realism.[8]

What realism signifies in the case of Thucydides is his disposition to see men, human affairs, and the world as they are, without

143

illusion or self-deception, and with no attempt to disguise the harsh truth of things by "fine and noble words," *onomaton kalon*, as the Athenians accused the Melians of doing in their famous dialogue (5.89). The realism attributed to him includes his conception of human nature, of politics and empire, and of the enormous significance of superior power in shaping the course of history. Realism is manifest in many of the speeches in the *History*. Although it need not lead speakers to the same conclusion, it permeates much of their reasoning and consists mostly of the estimation of power and interest.

In a sort of variation on the theme of Thucydides' realism, Paul Shorey, a leading classical scholar at the end of the nineteenth century, maintained that his philosophy was based on ethical positivism and intellectualism. By the first, he meant that Thucydides conceived man's nature and actions as strictly determined by the physical and social environment and a few basic desires; by the second, that he was constantly preoccupied with the part played in life by the conscious calculating reason. Assuming the primacy of these modes of thought, Shorey concluded that Thucydides was a cynic devoid of moral sensibility.[9] While this analysis may contain a grain of truth, it ignores other aspects of Thucydides' outlook and is therefore very partial, for the historian who lamented the suffering and moral disintegration that the plague brought upon Athens, and the effects of revolution in Greece, which "gave birth to every form of wickedness" and did away with "the simplicity that is so large an element in a noble nature" (3.83), could not have been indifferent to morality or lacking in compassion.[10]

It has also been said that Thucydides thought only of power,[11] and it is undeniable that his *History* demonstrates the domination of the weak by the strong and the ascendancy of power over morality and justice in the relations between states. This is why well-known modern historians and political theorists like E. H. Carr, Hans Morgenthau, and numerous others who belong to the influential so-called "realist" school in the study of international politics hold him in such high esteem. They regard him as the founder of political realism and the first analyst to have a clear grasp of the amorality of an anarchic international system of sovereign states like that of classical Greece and to understand that states are predominantly motivated in their actions by power and self-interest.[12]

It is part of Thucydides' realism that on various occasions he depicts Athens's spokesmen as not hesitating to admit that their empire is a tyranny. Pericles, in urging the Athenian people to pursue the war energetically and self-sacrificingly, states that "your empire has become a tyranny which in the opinion of mankind may have been unjustly gained, but which cannot be safely surrendered" (2.63). A similar thought is expressed before the war in the speech by the Athenian envoys at the Peloponnesian conference (1.75). Likewise, during the debate in the Athenian assembly in 427 over the punishment of Mytilene for its rebellion, Cleon, who advocated the most extreme penalties, reminds the citizens that "your empire is a despotism exercised over unwilling subjects, who are always conspiring against you" (3.37). The Athenians are equally frank in stating that their policy is determined by the interests of empire. Alcibiades invokes these interests in 415 when he argues in support of the Sicilian expedition and that the conquest of Sicily will likely make the Athenians "the masters of Hellas" (6.18). Later in Sicily, the Athenian representative Euphemus, seeking to enlist the support of the Camarinaeans, declares that "to a tyrant or to an imperial city nothing is inconsistent which is expedient" and that Athens acts upon the principle "of managing our allies as our interests requires in their several cases" (6.85).

Although it may be thought to possess a permanent validity, Thucydides' political realism was rooted in the conditions of his age. Classical Greece knew nothing of the concept of human rights and was unacquainted with any fundamental principles that condemned war and its atrocities or set limits to aggression and the operation of power in the international arena. In the internal affairs of the Greek city-states also, even though Athenian democracy at times approached the rule of law, dissension between democratic and oligarchic factions could easily give rise to violence and civil war. The realism that permeates Thucydides' *History* was thus a reflection of the practice of his time, a theorization derived from his own observation of war and politics in the contemporary Hellenic world.

It is striking and significant, however, that Thucydides' realism, profound as it was, did not lead him to form a conception of the presence of evil as an active force in history. He knows of moral transgression and deterioration, of wickedness, hatred, and

145

oppression, of violence, suffering, and slaughter, but not of the power of evil in human affairs. When he tells of the horrible massacre by Thracian mercenaries of the men, women, and children of Mycalessus, he deplores the atrocity (7.29–30). But he does not think of the event as a manifestation of evil.[13] For comparison, we may cite an American historian's account of her reaction after she first visited the memorial site of the German death camps at Auschwitz-Birkenau, in which the Nazis gassed and murdered over a million Jews and seventy thousand mostly Catholic Poles during the Second World War. On leaving the place at night while the moon shone clear in the sky, she peered through the fences. "I did not know what I was looking at," she recorded,

> but it frightened me to my depths—a young American girl standing with a friend in Poland in the deserted countryside, at Birkenau, I felt an overwhelming sense of evil—not horror, as in the Auschwitz warehouses, but evil. God, it was awful. I stood with my eyes wide and my mouth open, speechless. I had no idea what it was, but I felt evil, and that moment, that time, has never left me.[14]

There is, of course, a vast disproportion between the Holocaust— the attempt to destroy the entire Jewish population of Europe— and the scale of suffering and killing Thucydides reported in the Peloponnesian War. It is possible that he would have been unable even to conceive of the act of genocide, just as today many people who know that it happened still fail to comprehend it. Greek moral philosophy did not prepare him for the idea of evil, which lay beyond its range, and nothing in his experience seems to have prompted him to reflect on the reality of evil as an innate part of human life.[15]

NATURALISM

Beside being a realist, Thucydides was also a naturalist in his outlook. This means that he tended to regard events, men's actions, and the physical world itself as all part of the natural order and subject to some extent to its regularities and natural laws. His naturalism is especially noticeable in his attitude to religion and divinity. In contrast to some of the greatest works of Greek literature, the gods are absent and play no role in his *History*. He never

expresses any belief in divine agency or oracles. When telling of
the terrible plague that struck Athens in 430, he notes that "sup-
plications in temples, inquiries of oracles, and the like . . . were
utterly useless" to deal with the disease (2.47). Insisting that the
war between Athens and Sparta was a single conflict that lasted for
twenty-seven years despite the peace that concluded its first ten
years, he mentions a popular saying that the war would go on for
thrice nine years and then adds, "this was the solitary instance
in which those who put their faith in oracles were justified by
the event" (5.26). He seems to have disdained superstition and
credulity. He says of Nicias's fear of an eclipse of the moon, which
caused him to delay with grave consequences the removal of
the Athenian army from Sicily, that he "was too much under
the influence of divination and omens" (7.50). His view of the
phenomena of nature was generally factual, empirical, and non-
anthropomorphic, possibly owing to the influence of philosophers
like Anaxagoras and Democritus and to his knowledge of some of
the corpus of Hippocratic medical writings.[16] His objective description of the symptoms of the plague in the second book (2.49) reads
like a physician's clinical report. It is not dissimilar in its naturalism
from the well-known Hippocratic treatise, *The Sacred Disease*,
dealing with epilepsy, in which the unknown author states that

> this disease is not, in my opinion, any more divine or more sacred
> than other diseases, but has a natural cause, and its supposed divine
> origin is due to men's inexperience, and to their wonder at its peculiar
> character. . . . But if it is to be considered divine just because it is won-
> derful, there will not be one sacred disease but many, for I will show
> that other diseases are no less wonderful . . . and yet nobody consid-
> ers them sacred.[17]

Thucydides' broadly naturalistic attitude is likewise apparent in
his mention of several earthquakes and tidal waves in the summer
of 426, followed by the observation that "where the force of the
earthquake was greatest, the sea was driven back, and the sudden-
ness of the recoil made the inundation more violent; and I am of
opinion that this was the cause of the phenomenon, which would
never have taken place if there had been no earthquake" (3.89).
The same spirit appears in his notice of an eruption of Mount
Etna in 426, where he states that it had been fifty years since the
last eruption and that three such eruptions were recorded since

the Greeks first settled in Sicily (3.116). In his claim that the Peloponnesian War was the greatest of all wars, he cites the fact that it was accompanied by unprecedented natural occurrences: "earthquakes unparalleled in their extent and fury . . . eclipses of the sun more numerous than are recorded . . . in any former age . . . great droughts causing famines, and . . . the plague which did immense harm and destroyed numbers of people" (1.23). His intention in this statement may have been to point to these manifestations of nature as symbolic correlatives of the magnitude of the war itself; or perhaps, as his editor Gomme suggested, he may have meant that popular opinion regarded all such events as inevitable concomitants of human disaster.[18]

Thucydides' naturalism included his conception of human nature, which he regarded as subject to natural desires and appetites that spring partly from man's egocentricity. It was the sameness of human nature, he also believed, that explained why events similar to those which had happened in the past were likely to occur in the future. This does not mean that he thought human actions could be predicted. He was plainly very conscious of the variety of circumstances that acted upon men and influenced their behavior in different ways. His view of human nature in no way implies that it is inherently wicked or evil. He appears to look at human character objectively as endowed with certain proclivities. While individuals may be predisposed to be either good or bad, what he mainly stresses is that their moral qualities and actions will be strongly affected by the conditions in which they find themselves.

The characteristics of human nature are cited in the first book by the Athenian speakers at the conference of the Peloponnesian allies in 432. In justifying Athens's position, they maintain that its possession of empire was due both to historical circumstances in the years after the Persian invasion and to three successive motives: first of all, fear (*deos*); next, honor or ambition (*times*); and finally, self-interest (*ophelia*). Sparta, they point out, exercises its supremacy over its allies in its own interest, and there is accordingly nothing strange if the Athenians, "acting as human nature always will," acquired and refused to give up their empire, "constrained by the all-powerful motives, ambition, fear, interest." Nor are they the first "who have aspired to rule," they declare, "the world has ever held that the weaker must be kept down by the stronger" (1.75–76).

There is no reason to doubt that these were likewise Thucydides' opinions. He alludes earlier to the self-serving motives of interest and ambition in his account of the growth of wealth and sea power in Greece before the Trojan War, when he observes that "the love of gain made the weaker willing to serve the stronger, and the command of wealth enabled the more powerful to subjugate the lesser cities" (1.8). In his speeches, Pericles, who was for Thucydides an exemplar of great statesmanship, always invokes Athens's glory as one of the reasons to maintain its empire. Fear comes into the picture in his third speech, which warns the Athenians of the danger of surrendering their empire because of the hatred they have incurred by their imperial rule (2.63). Thucydides also stresses the importance of greed or wanting more (*pleonexia*) in relation to these other self-serving motives.

Thucydides' interpretation of the tendencies of human nature is not mechanistic or reductive. His presentation of character in speeches and narrative distinguishes personal traits and makes adequate allowance for the differences between individuals who may nevertheless be influenced by similar motives. Cleon and Diodotus oppose each other in the Athenian debate concerning the punishment of the revolt of Mytilene; Cleon, "the most violent of the citizens" (3.36), strives to persuade the assembly that the men should be killed and the women and children enslaved, while Diodotus condemns these measures as mistaken and proposes a more lenient treatment. In spite of their disagreement, however, both men base their arguments on interest and expediency, although Cleon also maintains that justice demands severity because of the injury Mytilene has done Athens (3.37–48). Thucydides knows very well, moreover, that some men and communities are more moderate than others. In a picture of immoderation mixed with self-delusion, he records of the Athenians in the aftermath of their victory over the Spartans at Pylos in 425, that "in their present prosperity . . . they expected to accomplish everything, possible or impossible, with any force great or small" (4.65). A few years later, guilty of *pleonexia* or greed in wanting to expand their empire even further, they attempted the conquest of Sicily with calamitous consequences. In contrast, he points out about both the Chians, who revolted against Athens's rule in 412, and the Lacedaemonians, that "no people, as far as I know," except for these two, "(but the Chians not equally with the Lacedaemonians), have preserved moderation in prosperity, and in proportion as their city has gained in power have gained also in the stability of their government" (8.24).

Thucydides' discussion of the nature of revolution, which follows his narrative of the civil strife in Corcyra, is the most extended passage of personal commentary in the *History*. It presents an acute analysis of the murderous passions, the loss of moderation, the party hatreds, the excesses of revenge, and the breakdown of common meaning in moral and political discourse that revolution begot. Thucydides sees these evils as the product of innate tendencies in human nature acted upon by the conditions of war. His diagnosis of their cause "was the love of power, originating in avarice [*pleonexian*] and ambition, and the party spirit which is engendered by them." His perception of the consequences is dispassionate yet infused with moral judgment because the condition he describes represents a profound violation of his feelings of humanity: "Thus revolution gave birth to every form of wickedness in Hellas" and "the simplicity which is so large an element in a noble nature was laughed to scorn and disappeared" (3.82–83).

Thucydides imputes the same naturalistic conception of human nature to the Athenian speakers in the Melian dialogue. What they say on this subject corresponds to his own position as stated elsewhere in the *History*. They counter the Melians' appeals to justice and religion with the famous reply that, "Of the gods we believe, and of men we know, that by a law of their nature wherever they can rule they will. This law was not made by us, and we are not the first who have acted upon it; we did but inherit it . . . and we know that you and all mankind, if you were as strong as we are, would do as we do" (5.105).

Throughout the *History*, the triad of fear, honor (ambition), and interest is at work. Fear of the growth of Athenian power, according to Thucydides, is the true cause that compelled the Lacedaemonians to go to war against Athens. Fear of their loss of independence and domination by others, ambition to rule, and self-interest in the preservation of their empire are what compelled the Athenians to continue the war and to crush the revolts of their subject cities. Although this triad is dominant, it need not exclude justice altogether. In their speech at the Peloponnesian conference of 432, the Athenians contend that in indulging its natural ambition for empire, Athens deserved credit for being more careful of justice and more moderate in its treatment of its subjects than it needed to be (1.76).

Generally, Thucydides accepts the uses and consequences of power as an inevitable part of the natural order of things. He deplored power's irrational excesses, however, as in the cases of Corcyra and of the cruelty of the barbaric Thracians in their wild massacre of the population of Mycalessus, of which he says that "no greater calamity . . . ever affected a whole city" and "never was anything so sudden or so terrible" (7.29). Pity is also apparent in his depiction of the suffering and fate of the Athenian army in Sicily. In most instances, though, he remains neutral and unperturbed when he records the exercise of power by the victors in their deliberate, premeditated slaughter and enslavement of the defeated, no matter whether these victors are the Athenians or the Lacedaemonians. In spite of the predatory character of the Athenian empire and the tyranny it became, he was proud of its achievements and greatness. It is difficult to draw any other conclusion from the admiration he expresses for Pericles' leadership and the latter's own exaltation of Athenian imperialism in his speeches. His funeral oration contains an eloquent idealization of the empire and its sea power, whose subjects, he says, considered Athens worthy to rule them, and which has compelled "every land and every sea to open a path for our valor, and . . . everywhere planted eternal memorials of our friendship and enmity" (2.41). In his last speech Pericles boasts that Athens's glory would be eternal because "of all Hellenes, we ruled over the greatest number of Hellenic subjects" (2.64). Thucydides presumably endorses these sentiments. In his criticism of the democratic politicians who governed Athens after Pericles' death and catered to the whims of the people in their competition for power, he notes that their greatest error was the Sicilian expedition. The regret he expresses at Athens's subsequent defeat in Sicily (2.65) is a further indication of his approval of Athenian imperialism.[19]

THINKING ABOUT HISTORY

Thucydides' character as a philosophic historian is seen also in both his historical practice and statements about it, and in his ideas about human history itself. It is apparent that in the gathering of information and the writing of his history, he devoted a considerable amount of thought to the proper method of investigating the past. His primary goal as a historian was "to give a true picture of the events which have happened" so that it would be of use to those who wished to understand what may happen in the future. If he succeeded in achieving this end, he said, "I shall be satisfied" (1.22).[20] In keeping with this aim, he strove to maintain a consistently critical approach with regard to the facts that went into his narrative. The Archaeologia, his reconstruction in the first book of developments in the early history of Greece, dealt with a remote time encrusted with legend. In connection with this subject he commented that "men accept from one another hearsay reports of former events, neglecting to test them . . . even though these events belong to the history of their own country" (1.20).[21] He dismissed the fancies and exaggerated stories of poets and chroniclers who sought to please rather than to ascertain the truth and whose statements could not be tested. Most of the facts, he said, were no longer accessible because of the lapse of ages and one had "to be satisfied with conclusions resting upon the clearest evidence that could be had" (1.21). Based on a variety of sources and inferences, his account of this period was a tour de force of historical thinking. He endeavored to apply the same critical spirit to the investigation of the Peloponnesian War, "the greatest movement" in Greek history (1.1), of which he was a contemporary. Concerning its events, he avowed that he reports nothing but what he saw himself or learned from others after "the most careful and particular inquiry" and by sifting the testimony of different witnesses of the same occurrences (1.22). Of the speeches, since he wrote them himself, he did not claim the same degree of accuracy, of course. But unless his critical spirit completely deserted him, it is reasonable to suppose that he tried, as he said, to include in them the true gist or purport of what each speaker said, even if formulated and elaborated in own thoughts and words.

While Thucydides may conceivably have been affected by some of the skeptical ideas concerning justice and morality that were propounded by Sophist teachers of rhetoric, he never doubted that truth is possible in history. As H.-P. Stahl has rightly said, he "made the struggle for unadulterated truth his life's work, a task of whose difficulty he was well aware."[22] Not only did he take great pains to ascertain the truth, as he tells the reader, but it is also undeniable that historical truth both with respect to the facts of the war and the understanding of their import and meaning was the supreme purpose of his work.[23] He was almost never tentative in his conclusions and very rarely uncertain. He corrected the gaps and errors of previous writers (e.g., 1.97) and popular misconceptions of the period in the latter part of the sixth century when Athens was ruled by the tyrant Peisistratus and his sons (1.20; 6.54–59). He possessed the rationalist's confidence that the right method of studying history based on the critical use of evidence would yield genuine knowledge of what had happened. I imagine he was also convinced that the knowledge and understanding he acquired through his researches as a historian were much wider and deeper than that of the other human actors who took part in the events of the Peloponnesian War. For unlike those actors, whose view was limited, he as the war's historian had investigated the true causes and reasons of events; he knew not only why they happened but how they turned out; he was able to relate particular facts to truths and generalizations that gave them a wider intelligibility; and he could discern in the sequence of events a relatedness, patterns, and meanings which were beyond the sight of the historical actors.

Notwithstanding all that has been said above, I believe that a common view that sees Thucydides as a scientific historian and the founder of scientific history should be discarded as an anachronism and cause of misunderstanding.[24] Despite his naturalism, Thucydides had no idea of a science; and while history is a rigorous discipline with demanding standards of evidence, it has never been a science in the sense in which the word applies to the modern natural sciences.

During the past four decades, the image of Thucydides as a detached scientific inquirer after historical truth has been challenged by a number of scholars who depict him instead as a literary artist with a deep personal and emotional involvement in his work. The latter conception of him has been most strongly expressed in the important study of the historian by W. Robert Connor, a work of valuable insights but also of some questionable claims. Connor associates his position with the emergence of what he calls "a post-modern Thucydides."[25] He maintains—what is hardly controversial—that Thucydides cared profoundly about the events he described and stresses the *History*'s emotional power, its intensity and internal tensions, and its ability to recreate the *pathos* or experience of events so as to lead its readers to participate vicariously in the sufferings of the war. On the basis of these characteristics, he refuses to credit Thucydides with the objectivity that has usually been ascribed to him in his practice as a historian. Convinced in any case that objectivity is impossible and unattainable because every historian has his own personal values that unavoidably color his work, Connor contends that for Thucydides objectivity was "not a principle or goal, but an authorial stance, a device . . . by which the author presented himself to his reader" and "a relationship between reader and author, not one between author and his subject matter."[26]

This radical judgment, which treats the principle of objectivity as merely a rhetorical ploy of the historian in addressing the reader, does no justice to Thucydides and reflects a considerable misconception of the meaning of objectivity in the process of inquiry. It is also self-refuting; for if Connor really believed that objectivity is impossible and did not intend to write an objective study about Thucydides, why should we place any trust in it? I am reminded of the very interesting and well-known work on American historiography by Peter Novick, *That Noble Dream* (1988), a survey, critique, and rejection of the idea of objectivity in history, which was nevertheless praised by some of its reviewers for its objectivity. Objectivity does not mandate an attitude of cool impersonality and emotional noninvolvement or disengagement, nor does it entail a stance of neutrality, noncommitment, and absence or suppression of values (the truth itself can be a commitment and a value). It is rather an indispensable requirement and necessary regulatory principle in the conduct of inquiry, whose conceptually implied aim, irrespective of the subject or problem under investigation, is always to find out and determine what is true or best qualifies as valid knowledge. It does not call for a passionless observer, but for an inquirer whose primary allegiance and interest is to know what is true and who therefore strenuously tries to avoid falsehood, error, credulity, unexamined assumptions, and preconceived conclusions. The opposite of objectivity is not passion or emotional involvement, but prejudice, bias, and the uncritical projection of one's own wishes, desires, and beliefs in disregard or violation of the evidence.[27] As the American philosopher Donald

Davidson has very clearly shown, objectivity is logically and intrinsically linked to the concept of truth itself; for "to have the concept of truth is to have the concept of objectivity, the notion of a proposition being true or false independent of one's beliefs or interests."[28]

Thucydides, of course, had no word for objectivity, which did not exist in the Greek language. But he must have had some concept of it that he strove to implement, as we can infer from his insistence on the centrality of accuracy (*akribeia*) and truth (*aletheia*); his criticism of superstition, popular credulity, and the fables of poets and romancers; and his correction of historical errors. He does not hide his own values in such matters as his praise and admiration for Pericles, his dislike of the demagogue Cleon, and his criticisms of the Athenian democracy in the absence of a wise and incorruptible leader. But he maintains a high standard in attempting to avoid prejudice, and this is especially noticeable in his relative impartiality between Athens and Sparta, a point remarked on by Stahl, who notes that "his courage in recording the vices of his own country is equaled by his generosity in recognizing the virtues of his country's enemies."[29]

Thucydides' perception of the effect of the human condition in the realm of history, as it was mirrored in the events of the Peloponnesian War, constitutes perhaps the most personal aspect of his vision as a thinker. Some scholars believe that a sense of the tragic dominates his conception of history, that his work is constructed on a tragic pattern, and that, as in tragedy, its theme is suffering and loss on a grand scale.[30] But while it is true that his *History* includes profoundly tragic episodes like the plague in Athens, the destruction of Plataea, and the Sicilian expedition, it is questionable whether it should be considered a work of tragedy. The modern reader, of course, knowing the height to which fifth-century Athens soared in its cultural achievements and political greatness, is very likely to regard its defeat by Sparta as a tragic reversal of fortune. Tragedy, however, consists of a series of events that appear to unfold with a certain inevitability and fatality; it cannot be due to avoidable error, but must result from a fundamental flaw that leads ineluctably to a tragic conclusion. This was not, however, the manner in which Thucydides pictured Athens's history or fall. Since he left his work unfinished, he did not record his final thoughts on the end of the war and Sparta's victory. But in the passage in book 2, obviously composed after the war, in which, gazing over the future, he speaks of Athens's eventual defeat and places the blame on the politicians who led the city after Pericles' death, he does not write in a tragic vein. On the contrary, he emphasizes Athens's resilience and continued resistance in the last years of the war. Not only does he endorse Pericles' opinion that Athens could have won an easy victory, but he concludes that the Athenians "were at last overthrown, not by their enemies, but by themselves and their own internal dissensions" (2.65). This is less a tragic vision than an indictment of mistakes that might have been prevented.

In contemplating the actions of men in the historical process, Thucydides seems to have been especially preoccupied with the relationship between human intelligence and judgment and the actuality it seeks to mold and master. This is one of the major themes of his *History*. Men think, plan, and devise policies; sometimes they succeed, at other times they are defeated by their own mistakes or by forces beyond their control, and this is something that can happen often in war, in which the stakes are very high. The interaction between the mind and the conditions and resistance of the world, and the mind's failure, for whatever reason, to realize its projects, is a basic feature of the human condition that had a deep interest for Thucydides. A word that occurs frequently in the *History* is *gnome*, whose meanings include mind, intelligence, reason, judgment, sagacity, thought, foresight, will, resolution, and firmness of purpose.[31] It is associated with *xunesis*, another but narrower term for intelligence and foresight that Thucydides also uses. He held the faculty of intelligence, judgment, and foresight in the highest regard and considered these qualities to be indispensable in a leader and statesman.[32] It was on this account that he expressed such great admiration for Themistocles, Athens's foremost leader during the Persian invasion, who, he said, exceeded all other men as "the ablest judge of the course to be pursued in a sudden emergency" and whose "natural power of mind" enabled him "to foresee with equal clearness the good or evil event which was hidden in the future" (1.138). Pericles, whom Thucydides ranked as by far the greatest statesman of the war, was a supreme example of *gnome*. It was this faculty, together with his integrity and incorruptibility, that gave him his authority over the citizens of Athens and his ability to control them "with a free spirit," as well as to oppose them when necessary (2.65). Mind is also a characteristic attributed to the Athenians by the Corinthians, who said of them that "their true self is their mind" (1.70). Pericles likewise brings out this essential trait in his praise of the Athenians in his funeral oration. "The great impediment to action," he says, "is, in our opinion, not discussion, but the want of that knowledge which is gained by discussion preparatory to action. For we have a peculiar power of thinking before we act, and of acting too" (2.40).

But mind, or intelligence in this broad sense, is not the only power in the world. It must contend with two other forces that occupy a large place in human history. These forces are chance or fortune (*tuche*) and necessity (*ananke*), of whose role Thucydides was very conscious. Chance could prevent an enterprise from turning out as planned, and it could sometimes bring unexpected victory. Pericles confronts intelligence and judgment with chance at the beginning of his first speech in the *History*, which urges the Athenians not to yield to Spartan demands. In advising this course, he mentions the possibility of failure instead of success, because "the movement of events is often . . . wayward and incomprehensible . . . and this is why we ascribe to chance whatever belies our calculation" (1.140). Chance is thus the unexpected, the unforeseen, the incalculable. As a modern historian of the Peloponnesian War has pointed out, Thucydides "stresses above all, and makes his characters stress, that to enter upon a war, as men do, from a calculation that it will provide some advantage is dangerous in the extreme, because it is precisely in war that the unforeseen, the incalculable, the unexpected is most likely to happen."[33]

Both Thucydides and the speakers in the *History* make numerous references to chance.[34] In his last speech Pericles disparages it when he invokes the superiority of intelligence because it relies "on that surer foresight which is given by reason and observation of facts" (2.62). The Plataeans, pleading with the Spartans for their lives, beg them "to think of the uncertainty of fortune, which may strike anyone however innocent" (3.59). Diodotus asserts in the debate on the punishment of Mytilene that "fortune often presents herself unexpectedly, and induces states as well as individuals to run into peril" (3.45). In 432 the Athenian envoys cite the power of chance in advising the Spartans not to go to war with Athens, urging them to consider "the inscrutable nature of war, and how when protracted it generally ends in becoming a mere matter of chance, over which neither of us can have any control, the event being equally unknown and equally hazardous to both"(1.78). The Spartans elevate chance over foresight in proposing peace after their defeat at Pylos. They tell the Athenians not to suppose "because your city and your empire are powerful at this moment, that you will always have fortune on your side. The wise . . . know that war will go on its way wherever chance may lead, and will not be bound by the rules which he who begins to meddle with it would . . . prescribe" (4.18). Thucydides himself allots chance and good fortune a decisive role in his narrative of the unexpected Athenian success at Pylos (4.14), and states that fortune was against the Spartans in the reverses they suffered (4.55). In another passage on the miscalculation of the Chians in revolting against Athens, he speaks generally about being deceived by "those incalculable factors which beset the life of man" (8.24).[35]

Necessity is another force that operates in human life and history. As Thucydides conceived it, necessity seems to be a compulsion springing from men's nature and passions in appraising situations, a compulsion that forces them to act in a certain way and gives rise to a necessary result. It is not an impersonal force but is rooted in the perception of the human agents themselves as to what is necessary. Nonetheless, it seems to act with an objective power as if it left no choice.[36] The greatest significance of the concept of necessity in the *History* is Thucydides' contention that it was the cause of the war itself. For Thucydides declares that the true and real cause of the latter is the Spartans' fear of growing Athenian power, "which forced them into war" (1.23). Here it is fear, a psychological factor, which acts as a form of necessity with a compulsive effect that leads to war. Later he comments that the Spartans were never of a temper "prompt to make war unless they were compelled" (1.118). Pericles likewise saw the war as due to necessity. He tells the Athenians before it began that "war will come, and the more ready we are to accept the situation, the less ready will our enemies be to lay hands upon us" (1.144). Thucydides seems also to present the Athenian empire as the product of necessity. The speakers who defend the empire at the Peloponnesian conference in 432 mention a law of human nature to explain the Athenians' aspiration to rule and claim that the all-powerful motives of fear, ambition, and interest forced them to become an imperial power (1.76). Similarly, in their dialogue with the Melians, the Athenians invoke necessity when they insist that a law of human nature compels men to rule wherever they can (5.105). In the case of the revolutions in Corcyra and other Greek cities, it is the "imperious necessities" of war, according to Thucydides, that caused the degeneration of character and the reckless release of human passions which led to such monstrous crimes (3.82).

The combat between Athenian intelligence and the forces arrayed against it from within and without may be seen as perhaps the deepest meaning of Thucydides' *History*. A recent work on Thucydides has remarked that although the historian's argument that Athens could win "was grounded on a rational assessment of Athenian resources," his narrative of the war's development "thrusts before our eyes the limitations of human foresight that thwart the exercise of reason."[37] This is very true, and it points to an overarching theme in Thucydides' work and its perception of the human condition. It is possible to read his picture of Athens under Pericles' leadership as the collective embodiment of *gnome*. Pericles' funeral oration contains the fullest description of the superior qualities of intelligence that the city represents. His speech praises not only its power and political system, but its stature as a high civilization, which is manifest in the value it places on thinking and discussion prior to action, its citizens' refined style of life, and their power of adaptation to the most varied forms of action with versatility and grace. These and other exceptional qualities he mentions, giving the impression of a society alive with intelligence, allow him to make the unforgettable claim that Athens is the school and education of Hellas (2.41). His portrait is an idealized one, no doubt, but it brings out the distinctive and unsurpassed character of Athenian achievement. While Pericles lived, the Athenian democracy functioned well, according to Thucydides, because he was its leader, and the city was fully provided with money, ships, and men in case of war. The historian agreed with Pericles' advice to the Athenians before the war that they would conquer their enemies if they maintained their sea supremacy, avoided large land battles with the Spartans, and refrained from trying to extend their empire while at war. Pericles also tells the Athenians prophetically that he is "more afraid of our own mistakes than of our enemies' designs" (1.143–44).

His successors deviated from his policy and were responsible, in Thucydides' view, for many errors. Superior Athenian intelligence was defeated by both chance and necessity: by miscalculation and the unforeseen contingencies of war like the eclipse of the moon that prevented the Athenian army's withdrawal from Sicily, and by the internal dissensions and unreason in Athens which sprang from the passions and ambitions of rival politicians. Necessity was also intimated by Pericles in his last speech before his death, in which he forebodingly states that the memory of Athens's glory would live "even if we should be compelled at last to abate somewhat of our greatness (for all things have their times of growth and decay)" (2.64). These words express a tragic presentiment and insight that envisages necessity as an immanent power which makes all outstanding human achievement in history, including that of Athens, transitory and destined to decline.

Thucydides wanted his work to be useful, believing it could help its readers, given the human condition, to understand similar events that might be expected to occur in the future. We must presume, of course, that the kind of events he had in mind were those on which his *History* concentrated, that is, events connected with politics and war within and between states. In thinking of the utility of a work of history, he was not implying that the past simply repeats itself. He understood that the circumstances in which men live and act are too varied and too much affected by chance, the irrational, and the incalculable for the movement of history to be either a repetition or subject to prediction.[38] Nevertheless, he held that ambition; the desire for power, domination, and honor; political rivalry; conflict; and war were common to men and enduring factors in mankind's history. He could therefore conclude that the events of the future would resemble those of the past by exhibiting recognizable similar patterns.

To some scholars, however, Thucydides' work demonstrates that irrational forces, the deranging effect of emotion on judgment, the illusions of unfounded hope, and human error always have the upper hand and are so prevalent and powerful in human history that they repeatedly defeat all rational planning and expectations. The lesson for the reader, as H.-P. Stahl interprets it, is that "present and future will be as unsteerable and unpredictable as was the historical past." Connor similarly maintains that Thucydides' narrative progressively undermines the belief in the possibility of the rational prediction and control of events and hence in the utility of historical knowledge.[39] These conclusions seem to me much too one-sided and to represent Thucydides as considerably more of a pessimist than he really was. If they were correct, there would be no point to his deeply held belief that the highest type of statesmanship includes the ability to foresee possible future eventualities.

I do not think Thucydides ever despaired of political intelligence and what it can achieve at various times or doubted that a gifted statesman like Themistocles or Pericles can sometimes guide and direct events. In referring to the usefulness of history, however, he did not suppose that the future can be predicted. The knowledge he strove to impart to those readers whose concern was to discover what actually happened was not that of a prophet who pretends to foretell the vicissitudes of the future. It consisted, rather, of the insight and wisdom of a philosophic historian who has reflected deeply on the course of events he has reconstructed and studied and has seen a certain meaning in them based on the operation of some constant factors in human affairs. By giving the reader an understanding of these factors and the role they played, his work makes it possible to understand particular kinds of situations that are likely to recur in the future in politics, war, and international relations.[40] What the distinguished nineteenth-century historian Jacob Burckhardt said about the purpose of history in general can be applied to Thucydides' *History of the Peloponnesian War*: "Historical knowledge does not make us shrewder for the next time, but wiser forever."[41] Connor's moving observation is also appropriate: "From our heightened awareness derives the true utility of [Thucydides'] work. We learn from it not how to predict the future or to control events, but their complexity and the consequent vulnerability of civilization and order."[42]

Notes

Introduction

1. Thomas Babington Macauley, *The Letters of Thomas Babington Macaulay*, ed. Thomas Pinney, 6 vols. (Cambridge: Cambridge University Press, 1976–), vol. 3, p. 138 (letter to T. F. Ellis, 11 Feb. 1835).

2. Gilbert Murray, *Our Great War and the Great War of the Ancient Greeks* (New York: Thomas Seltzer, 1920).

3. Quoted from Gen. Marshall and from L. J. Halle, "A Message from Thucydides," *Foreign Service Journal*, August 1952, in W. Robert Connor, *Thucydides* (Princeton: Princeton University Press, 1984), p. 3.

4. Richard Ned Lebow and Barry S. Strauss, eds. *Hegemonic Rivalry from Thucydides to the Nuclear Age* (Boulder, Colo.: Westview Press, 1991).

5. Jacob Burckhardt, *The Greeks and Greek Civilization*, ed. Oswyn Murray (New York: St. Martin's Press, 1998), p. 3.

6. Ibid., p. 10.

Chapter 1
Thucydides' *History* and Its Background

1. On the continuations of Thucydides' *History*, see below, chap. 7.

2. Gomme has reviewed the sources for this period other than Thucydides in HCT, vol. 1, pp. 29–84. They include a few minor historians who were contemporaries of Thucydides, official and unofficial documents, and a number of later authors such as Diodorus Siculus in the first century BCE, who composed a narrative of the years between the Persian and Peloponnesian Wars, and the famous Greek biographer Plutarch (c. CE 46–150), who wrote lives of Pericles, Alcibiades, and several other leading figures of the fifth century who appear in Thucydides' *History*.

3. George Grote, *A History of Greece from the Time of Solon to 403 B.C.*, condensed and ed. J. M. Mitchell and M.O.B. Caspari (London: Routledge, 2001), p. 875, n. 9; this work first appeared in 12 vols., 1846–56.

4. Many studies of Thucydides contain accounts of his life; see Simon Hornblower, *Thucydides* (Baltimore: Johns Hopkins University Press, 2000), pp. 1–4.

5. For a convenient brief survey of the institutions of the Athenian democracy, see OCD, s. v. "Democracy, Athenian"; for democracy and

economy in Athens, see Hammond, pp. 324–29; population figures derive from Josiah Ober, *Mass and Elite in Democratic Athens* (Princeton: Princeton University Press, 1989), pp. 127–28. There are excellent discussions of democracy in Athens and Greece in G.E.M. de Ste. Croix, *The Class Struggle in the Ancient Greek World* (Ithaca: Cornell University Press, 1981), chap. 5; A.H.M. Jones, *Athenian Democracy* (Oxford: Blackwell, 1957); Ober, *Mass and Elite in Democratic Athens* and his *The Athenian Revolution* (Princeton: Princeton University Press, 1996 and 1998).

6. On the history of Sparta and the nature of its society and culture, see the lively, learned account by Paul Cartledge, *The Spartans* (Woodstock, N.Y.: Overlook Press, 2003).

7. On the origin and character of the Spartan alliance or Peloponnesian League, see the accounts in Hammond, pp. 166–68, 195–96; and in Donald Kagan, *The Outbreak of the Peloponnesian War* (Ithaca: Cornell University Press, 1969), chap. 1, "The Spartan Alliance."

8. On the Delian League and the development of Athens's empire, see Kagan, chap. 2, and the basic account by Russsell Meiggs, *The Athenian Empire* (Oxford: Clarendon Press, 1972), chaps. 1–14. I have taken the number of Athens's subject cities from Hammond, p. 327.

9. On the Athenian democracy and imperialism, see the comments in G.E.M. de Ste. Croix, *The Origins of the Peloponnesian War* (London: Duckworth, 1972), pp. 34–44; Hammond, pp. 326, 328; Meiggs, chap. 14, "The Balance-Sheet of Empire."

10. Standard histories of ancient Greece give an account of the period I have briefly sketched between the end of the Persian and beginning of the Peloponnesian War; see the surveys in Hammond, bk. 4, chaps. 1–2, and by J. K. Davies, P. J. Rhodes, and D. M. Lewis in CAH, chaps. 2–6. Kagan, pts. 2–3, contains a detailed treatment.

11. I have used the translation of Herodotus's *History* by George Rawlinson in *The Greek Historians*, ed. Francis R. B. Godolphin, 2 vols. (New York: Random House, 1942), vol. 1. For some discussions of his work, see the excellent article by John P. A. Gould in OCD, s.v. "Herodotus," and the same author's *Herodotus* (London: Duckworth, 2000), as well as his essay, "Herodotus and Religion," in *Greek Historiography*, ed. Simon Hornblower (Oxford: Clarendon Press, 1994); J. B. Bury, *The Ancient Greek Historians* (London: Macmillan, 1909), chap. 2; J. L. Myres, *Herodotus: Father of History* (Oxford: Clarendon Press, 1953); Albin Lesky, *A History of Greek Literature*, 2nd ed. (New York: Thomas Y. Crowell, 1966), pp. 306–28; Donald Lateiner, *The Historical Method of Herodotus* (Toronto: University of Toronto Press, 1989); Hornblower, *Thucydides*, chap. 1; A. D. Momigliano, *The Classical Foundations of Modern Historiography* (Berkeley: University of California

Press, 1990), chap. 2; Donald R. Kelley, *Faces of History: Historical Inquiry from Herodotus to Herder* (New Haven: Yale University Press, 1998), pp. 19–28.

12. Gould, *Herodotus*, p. 58; also see the entire chapter on "The Logic of Narrative."

13. See Lateiner's interesting discussion in chap. 9, which distinguishes five kinds of causal argument and explanation of events used by Herodotus, some of which are interrelated. Among them are divine jealousy; fate or destiny; and divine action and interference. Human action is only one of the five.

14. Although the Greek term *hubris* has commonly been taken to signify overweening pride as its core meaning, recent research has shown that it refers generally to intentionally dishonoring behavior and gratuitous acts and statements that inflict shame and humiliation on the victim; see OCD, s.v. "hubris," by N.R.E. Fisher, which is based on the same author's book, *Hybris: A Study of the Values of Honor and Shame in Ancient Greece* (Warminster: Aris & Phillips, 1992). Kenneth J. Dover gives a similar definition but adds that in a wider context "hubris is overconfident violation of universal or divine laws, and so characteristic of successful kings and conquerors." *Greek Homosexuality* (New York: Vintage Books, 1980), pp. 34, 35 n.

15. On this point, see the further discussion in chaps. 2 and 8.

16. See the discussion below, chap. 8.

17. For Thucydides' view of Herodotus's *History* and his correction of several of its errors, see Sir Richard Jebb, "The Speeches of Thucydides," *Hellenica* (1880), reprinted in H. F. Harding, *The Speeches of Thucydides* (Lawrence, Kans.: Coronado Press, 1973), pp. 232–35. Like Jebb, Hornblower, CT, vol. 1, p. 61, suggests that Thucydides was referring primarily to Herodotus's work in his phrase about a "prize composition . . . heard and forgotten"; for Thucydides' use of Herodotus, see ibid., vol. 2, pp. 122–34.

18. See Lesky, pp. 340–41.

19. Plato, *Theaetetus*, 160d.

20. For several discussions of intellectual developments and the Greek enlightenment in fifth-century Athens and their influence upon Thucydides, see Martin Ostwald, CAH, chap. 8b, "Athens as A Cultural Center"; John H. Finley Jr., *Thucydides* (Cambridge, Mass.: Harvard University Press, 1947), chap. 2 and passim, and "Euripides and Thucydides," in *Three Essays on Thucydides* (Cambridge, Mass.: Harvard University Press, 1967), which stress the historian's relationship to Euripides and the Sophist movement; Lesky, chap. 5, pts. A–B; Friedrich Solmsen, *Intellectual Experiments of the Greek Enlightenment* (Princeton: Princeton University Press, 1975); Hornblower, *Thucydides*, chap. 5. The influence

of the Hippocratic medical writings on Thucydides' history was the subject of C. N. Cochrane's well-known study, *Thucydides and the Science
of History* (Oxford: Clarendon Press, 1929), which viewed the historian
as a dispassionate scientist; on the question of the relation of the medical
writings to his account of the plague, see Gomme's remarks, HCT, vol. 1,
pp. 149–50; Hornblower, CT, vol. 1, pp. 316–17; Adam M. Parry,
"Thucydides' Description of the Plague," in *The Language of Achilles
and Other Papers* (Oxford: Clarendon Press, 1989).

CHAPTER 2
THE SUBJECT, METHOD, AND STRUCTURE
OF THUCYDIDES' *HISTORY*

1. See Hornblower, *Thucydides*, pp. 7–9. What Thucydides says literally in 1.1 is that he wrote or composed (*xunegrapse*) the war between
the Peloponnesians and Athenians.

2. James T. Shotwell, *An Introduction to the History of History* (New
York: Columbia University Press, 1936), pp. 165, 171.

3. The Greek city-states of this period probably didn't preserve many
documents and kept their records in the form of inscriptions on stone
tablets.

4. Hornblower, *Thucydides*, chap. 4, contains an excellent discussion
with many details concerning the types of evidence Thucydides used; Solmsen, *Intellectual Experiments of the Greek Enlightenment*, chap. 6, presents an interesting analysis of Thucydides' use of rational reconstruction
in the Archaeologia and throughout the *History*.

5. See Gomme, HCT, vol. 1, pp. 92, 135, and Hornblower, *Thucydides*, pp. 100–101, on Thucydides' use of the term *tekmerion*.

6. On the subject of books at this period, see B.M.W. Knox in *The Cambridge History of Classical Literature*, vol. 1, *Greek Literature*, ed. P. E.
Easterling and B.M.W. Knox (Cambridge: Cambridge University Press,
1994), pp. 1–16, and the article "Books, Greek and Roman" in OCD.

7. HCT, vol. 1, p. 29.

8. In the Archaeologia and elsewhere in the *History*, Thucydides sees
wealth and money as an essential element of power and stresses its importance in war and naval power. On the role of money in his work, see
Lisa Kallet, *Money, Expense and Naval Power in Thucydides'* History
1–5.24 (Berkeley: University of California Press, 1993), and *Money and
the Corrosion of Power in Thucydides* (Berkeley: University of California Press, 2001).

9. Jowett omits the word "most."

10. In my transcription of this sentence, I have departed from
Jowett's version by translating the critical term *to muthodes* as "anything

mythical," in the modern sense of the English word in which, according to *Merriam Webster's Collegiate Dictionary*, 10th ed., "mythical" means anything fictional or imaginary. Jowett renders the passage as "the strictly historical character of my narrative"; Crawley translates it as "the absence of romance in my history"; Smith's version is "the absence of the fabulous from my narrative"; Gomme's is "the absence of the story-telling element" (HCT, vol. 1, p. 149), and Hornblower's is "the unromantic character of my narrative" (CT, vol. 1, p. 61). In 1.22, Thucydides uses *to muthodes* in the same way as he did previously in 1.21, to contrast his own aim of telling the truth with the chroniclers' aim of pleasing hearers by telling incredible stories that belong to the realm of the mythical or fabulous.

11. English translations offer different readings of Thucydides' striking phrase *kata to anthropinon* in 1.22. Jowett's version gives it as "in the order of human things;" Crawley's is "in the course of human things;" C. F. Smith's is "in all human probability"; Warner's is "human nature being what it is"; a recent translation by Walter Blanco in *Thucydides: The Peloponnesian War*, ed. Walter Blanco and Jennifer Tolbert Roberts (New York: W. W. Norton & Co., 1998), renders it as "given human nature." I think "given the human condition" is a reasonably close transcription of Thucydides' meaning.

12. The essay by Jebb, "The Speeches of Thucydides" (1880), contains a table of all the speeches, pp. 307–9.

13. On his aim and use of the term accuracy or *akribeia*, see Hornblower, *Thucydides*, pp. 34, 36–37.

14. Dionysius of Halicarnassus, *On Thucydides*, trans. and ed. from the Greek text by W. K. Pritchett (Berkeley: University of California Press, 1975), chap. 8.

15. H. T. Wade-Gery, "Thucydides," OCD.

16. On this point, see Jebb, pp. 249–50, who gives some examples, and the discussion by Hornblower, *Thucydides*, pp. 59–60.

17. K. J. Dover, one of Thucydides' editors, refers to but rejects the implausible hypothesis that while the historian at first intended to abide by the rule concerning the speeches that he stated in 1.22, and actually composed many of the speeches in accord with it, he then departed from it at a late stage in the composition of his work and was not able before his death to reformulate the rule in order to take account of his change of method; see HCT, vol. 5, pp. 396–97.

18. See A. W. Gomme, "The Speeches in Thucydides," in *Essays In Greek History and Literature* (Oxford: Blackwell, 1937).

19. HCT, vol. 5, p. 398. Among the works I have consulted in discussing the speeches in Thucydides' *History* are F. E. Adcock, *Thucydides and His History* (Cambridge: Cambridge University Press, 1963), chap. 3; Ste. Croix, *The Origins of the Peloponnesian War*, pp. 7–16;

K. J. Dover, HCT, vol. 5, pp. 393–99, and the same author's *Thucydides* (Oxford: Clarendon Press, 1973), chap. 6; John H. Finley Jr., *Thucydides* (Cambridge, Mass.: Harvard University Press, 1947), pp. 94–104; Gomme, "The Speeches in Thucydides"; Hornblower, *Thucydides*, chap. 3; Jebb, "The Speeches of Thucydides"; Kagan, *The Outbreak of the Peloponnesian War*, preface; Clifford Orwin, *The Humanity of Thucydides* (Princeton: Princeton University Press, 1994), app. 1; Wade-Gery, "Thucydides." Kagan, who accepts that Thucydides' speeches are close to what was actually said, has emphasized that if the speeches are regarded as pure inventions, there would then be no reason to give credence to any of the historian's statements.

20. See Daniel P. Tompkins, "Archidamus and the Question of Characterization in Thucydides," in *Nomodeiiktes: Greek Studies in Honor of Martin Ostwald*, ed. R. M. Rosen and J. Farrell (Ann Arbor: University of Michigan Press, 1993).

21. Many scholars have criticized Thucydides for his omissions and slighting of various subjects; for some recent comments on this point, see George Cawkwell, *Thucydides and the Peloponnesian War* (London: Routledge, 1997), pp. 13–16.

22. See below, chap. 8.

23. Beside reckoning dates according to the successive terms of particular officials, Athens and other Greek cities of this period also kept track of the years and months by means of a lunar calendar. They dated the new year differently and named the months after one of the gods or the festivals held in the god's honor; see OCD, s. v. "Calendar."

24. Andrewes, HCT, vol. 5, pp. 365–66, contains a discussion of Thucydides' system of dating events; see also Thomas R. Martin, "Calendars and Dating Systems in Thucydides," in *The Landmark Thucydides*, ed. Robert B. Strassler (New York: Free Press, 1990), app. K.

25. Finley, p. 77; Adcock, p. 110. In his comments on Pericles' funeral oration, Gomme, HCT, vol. 2, pp. 129–30, notes the difference between those who believe Thucydides composed it after 404 and those who hold that he wrote it close to the time the speech was delivered. Gomme argues for the latter view, and Adcock, p. 37, says that "it was written in 431 while the voice of Pericles still sounded in the historian's ears." For a recent statement of the view that it was written after the war ended, see P. A. Brunt, *Studies in Greek History and Thought* (Oxford: Clarendon Press, 1993), pp. 159–80.

26. It has recently been suggested that an inscription from Thasos published in 1983 may show that Thucydides died as late as 397; see Hornblower, *Thucydides*, pp. 151–52. For some discussions of the order of composition of Thucydides' *History*, see Adcock, chaps. 10, 12; Dover, *Thucydides*, chap. 5; Finley, chap. 3; the comments on 5.25–26, HCT,

vol. 4, pp. 16–17; Hornblower, *Thucydides*, chap. 6; Henry R. Immer-wahr, "Thucydides," in *The Cambridge History of Classical Literature*, vol. 1, *Greek Literature*, pp. 442–44; Wade-Gery, "Thucydides"; Dover, HCT, vol. 5, provides a lengthy analysis of the "Strata of Composition" in app. 2; Andrewes, HCT, app. 1, discusses the indications of incompleteness in various passages of the *History* which suggest that Thucydides might have revised them had he lived to finish his work.

CHAPTER 3
THUCYDIDES ON THE CAUSES OF THE WAR

1. Polybius, *History*, 3.31; 22.18.

2. See Gomme, HCT, vol. 1, p. 153, and Lionel Pearson, "*Prophasis* and *Aitia*," *Transactions of the American Philological Association*, vol. 83 (1952), pp. 205–23. Kagan, *The Outbreak of the Peloponnesian War*, pp. 360–66, discusses these terms and the meaning of Thucydides' statement in light of the question of whether the war was inevitable; Orwin, *The Humanity of Thucydides*, pp. 33–39, deals with them in relation to the question of who Thucydides believed was to blame for the war.

3. F. M. Cornford, *Thucydides Mythistoricus*, 1st ed. (1907; repr., Philadelphia: University of Pennsylvania Press, 1971), pp. 53, 57–59.

4. CT, vol. 1, p. 65, and Hornblower, *Thucydides*, p. 191.

5. Kagan, p. 345.

6. Werner Jaeger, *Paideia: The Ideals of Greek Culture*, vol. 1 (New York: Oxford University Press, 1939), p. 389. Jaeger suggests that Thucydides borrowed his idea of cause from the language of Greek medical science, which first distinguished between the real causes of an illness and its symptoms; ibid., p. 390.

7. Finley, *Thucydides*, p. 111.

8. Jacqueline de Romilly, *Thucydides and Athenian Imperialism* (Oxford: Basil Blackwell, 1963), p. 18 (orig. French ed., 1947).

9. Lesky, *A History of Greek Literature*, p. 459.

10. Ste. Croix, *The Origins of the Peloponnesian War*, pp. 52–58.

11. On necessity as a force in history, see the discussion below, chap. 8.

12. See Kagan's discussion of the causes of the war and the question of its inevitability, chaps. 19–20.

13. Gomme, HCT, vol. 1, pp. 361–413; cf. also Meiggs's pointed comments on the shortcomings of the Pentecontaetia, in *The Athenian Empire*, app. 1.

14. See Hornblower's comment on this subject, CT, vol. 1, pp. 179–81, and D. M. Lewis, "The Thirty Years' Peace," CAH, p. 121. The Athenian politician Callias is supposed to have negotiated a peace with Persia around 450; whether there actually was such a peace and its date has

been a controversial topic among Greek historians, although it is not doubted that hostilities between Athens and Persia ceased about this time and did not revive until the last phase of the Peloponnesian War; on the Peace of Callias, see Lewis, CAH, pp. 121–27.

15. See Hornblower's comment on the Pentecontaetia, CT, vol. 1, p. 133.

16. The dominant place of Athenian imperialism in Thucydides' *History* is the theme of Romilly's important book.

17. The Greek text speaks of *ananke* or necessity. Jowett translates the passage as "we must be aware, however, that war will come." Smith translates it as "we must realize that war is inevitable."

18. P. A. Brunt, "Introduction to Thucydides," in *Studies in Greek History and Thought*, p. 141; see also Meiggs, chap. 14, on "The Balance-Sheet of Empire."

19. Gomme notes that the sacred land lay on the border between Megarian territory and Attica and was sacred to the goddesses of Eleusis worshipped in the Eleusinian mysteries; HCT, vol. 1, p. 449.

20. See Gomme's remarks in ibid., pp. 447–48.

21. Cornford, chaps. 3–4, proposed the possibility that the Megarian decree was the policy of the Athenian mercantile class and associated it with the commercial rivalry between Athens and Corinth. Like Cornford, G. B. Grundy, *Thucydides and the History of His Age*, 2nd ed., 2 vols. (Oxford: Blackwell, 1948), vol. 1, chap. 15, is critical of Thucydides for ignoring the economic causes of the war and sees the Megarian decree as an act of economic warfare. Ste. Croix, *The Origins of the Peloponnesian War*, pp. 214–36, deals critically with the commercial rivalry hypothesis, and presents a lengthy discussion of the Megarian decree in chap. 7. See also on this subject the comments by Lewis, "The Causes of The War," CAH, pp. 376–78, and Brunt, "The Megarian Decree," in *Studies in Greek History and Thought*.

22. See Tim Rood, *Thucydides: Narrative and Explanation* (Oxford: Clarendon Press. 1998), who observes, p. 214, that Thucydides' neglect of Megara was a sign that he did not consider it of importance in explaining the war.

23. Many readers are likely to agree with Rood's discussion of the question of war-guilt, pp. 222–23, which holds that "Thucydides did not put the blame for the war on either side in his overt formulations."

24. In his striking essay, "Thucydides and the Outbreak of The Peloponnesian War," in *From Plataea to Potidaea* (Baltimore: Johns Hopkins University Press, 1993), E. Badian, a distinguished ancient historian, has charged that Thucydides was an apologist for Athens who resorted to deliberate distortion, misinformation, and suppression of facts in order to show that Sparta started the war in a spirit of ruthless realpolitik as

the culmination of a long series of unscrupulous and even treacherous attempts to repress Athenian power. He also believes that Spartan policy consistently aimed at preserving peace. I have not been convinced by his argument and the evidence he cites to support the claim of Thucydides' misrepresentations. For criticisms of Badian's view, see George Cawkwell, *Thucydides and the Peloponnesian War*, pp. 34–37; Elizabeth Meyer, "The Outbreak of the Peloponnesian War after 25 Years," in *Polis and Polemos* (Festschrift in Honor of Donald Kagan), ed. Charles D. Hamilton and Peter Krentz (Claremont, Calif.: Regina Books, 1997), pp. 35–39; Rood, pp. 215–19, 221–22.

CHAPTER 4
THUCYDIDES AND PERICLES

1. See Brunt's well-taken comment on this dictum of Pericles that it comes ill from the man who was Aspasia's lover; P. A. Brunt, "Thucydides' Funeral Speech," in *Studies in Greek History and Thought*, p. 159. An anonymous expert reader of this book has commented that while Pericles may have been expressing an ideological norm, the sum of Athenian attitudes to women was much more complex.

2. For Thucydides' portrayal of individual character, see H. D. Westlake, *Individuals in Thucydides* (Cambridge: Cambridge University Press, 1958), a study of his treatment of twelve of the more prominent men who appear in his work, and Daniel P. Tompkins, "Stylistic Characterization in Thucydides: Nicias and Alcibiades," *Yale Classical Studies*, vol. 22 (1972), pp. 181–214.

3. For Pericles' biography and career, see OCD, s.v. "Pericles"; A. R. Burn, *Pericles and Athens* (London: Hodder and Stoughton, 1948); Donald Kagan, *Pericles of Athens and the Birth of Democracy* (New York: Free Press, 1991).

4. The hoplite, so-called because of the *hoplon* or shield that he carried, was a heavily armed infantry soldier; on the character of hoplite warfare, see chap. 5.

5. I have here adopted Gomme's rendering of the passage in 2.37; see his comment, HCT, vol. 2, p. 114.

6. Brunt, for example, whose analysis of the funeral oration is worth reading, denies its authenticity and thinks (p. 160), that it is "too redolent of Thucydides' own ideas." He believes it was composed at the end of the war and is not based for the most part on what Pericles actually said. Adcock, on the other hand, holds that it was written by Thucydides in 431 soon after it was delivered and at a time that reflects the confidence in Athens's power that then prevailed among the Athenians; Adcock, *Thucydides and His History*, pp. 37–38.

7. See Hornblower's comment on this passage, CT, vol. 1, p. 308.

8. Leo Strauss finds it significant that Thucydides follows Pericles's funeral oration with a description of the plague and interprets this sequence as "a comprehensive instruction"; *The City and Man* (Chicago: Rand McNally, 1964), p. 153.

9. On the authenticity of this speech, which has been doubted, see the comments by Donald Kagan, *The Archidamian War* (Ithaca: Cornell Universty Press, 1974), app. B, "Pericles' Last Speech."

10. Hornblower is surely mistaken when he calls this thought, which I have condensed in my summary, "a frank, even brutal statement of a totalitarian philosophy"; CT, vol. 1, p. 332. Pericles does not conceive the individual as subordinate to or living for the state. What he says is that the interests and benefit of individuals are tied up with the state's flourishing: "states can bear the misfortunes of individuals, but individuals cannot bear the misfortunes of the state" (2.60).

11. See the comments by Romilly, *Thucydides and Athenian Imperialism*, pp. 140–41.

12. See the excellent review and discussion of this subject in Kagan, *The Archidamian War*, chap. 1 and "Conclusions"; Kagan praises Pericles' strategic insight but also criticizes his defensive strategy as incapable of winning the war if the Spartans were willing to hold out.

13. Josiah Ober, *Political Dissent in Democratic Athens: Intellectual Critics of Popular Rule* (Princeton: Princeton University Press, 1998), chap. 2, analyzes Thucydides' political attitude in a lengthy discussion that also includes some comments on his historical concepts and method. Ober observes (pp. 71–72) that while to the ordinary Athenian the term democracy (*demokratia*) meant that the whole of the citizenry held a monopoly of legitimate public authority, to Thucydides it meant that the lower classes had the power to constrain everyone in the state. The historian envisaged the Athenian democracy as "an unstable system likely to promote the spread of destructive, narrowly defined self-interest" and as tending to act selfishly in the narrow interest of "the many" and to make decisions "on the basis of highly misleading speeches delivered by personally selfish and self-interested parties."

CHAPTER 5
SCENES FROM THE ARCHIDAMIAN WAR:
MYTILENE, PLATAEA, CORCYRA, PYLOS

1. See the discussion of the dual beginning of the war in CT, vol. 1, pp. 236–37.

2. The trireme and its role in Greek warfare is described in OCD, s. v. "trireme," and very fully with a great deal of historical and technical

information, illustrations, and plans in J. S. Morrison, J. E. Coates, and N. B. Rankov, *The Athenian Trireme*, 2nd ed. (Cambridge: Cambridge University Press, 2000), which includes an account of the modern reconstruction of an ancient trireme, the *Olympias*, launched by the Hellenic navy in 1987. On hoplite infantry and its manner of warfare, see the account by Victor Davis Hanson, *The Western Way of War: Infantry Battle in Classical Greece*, 2nd ed. (Berkeley: University of California Press, 2000), which contains many illuminating details; see his comments (pp. 112–15) on the high mortality rate of the battlefield commanders on both the defeated and the victorious side. The knowledge that their own generals would be among the first to face the spears of the enemy was an important factor in the high morale and willingness to fight of hoplite armies.

3. See Ober, "Rules of War in Classical Greece," in *The Athenian Revolution*; cf. Gomme's comment that "it was not the ordinary Greek view that prisoners of war were to be killed, frequent as such cruelty was"; HCT, vol. 2, p. 344.

4. See the analysis and discussion of Athenian and Peloponnesian strategy by D. M. Lewis in "The Archidamian War," CAH, chap. 9, and Brunt, "Spartan Policy and Strategy in the Archidamian War," in *Studies in Greek History and Thought*. Kagan, *The Archidamian War*, contains a full and careful narrative of the war that includes an examination of the strategy of the two sides. Hanson, pp. 5, 34–35, shows that it was difficult for invaders to do great damage when they ravaged fields and tried to burn down crops and vines; he believes that agricultural devastation usually produced few long-term effects.

5. Apropos of Cleon, George Grote observed that "Thucydides has forgotten his usual impartiality in criticizing this personal enemy"; *A History of Greece from the Time of Solon to 403* B.C., p. 643; see Grote's excellent discussion of Cleon's personality and reputation, pp. 535–37, 643–47. On Thucydides' treatment of Cleon, see also Westlake, *Individuals in Thucydides*, chap. 5; and Hornblower, *Thucydides*, pp. 166–67.

6. Diodotus's reference to deceit is interesting in light of the fact that the Athenian assembly was said to open all its meetings with a solemn curse upon deceitful speakers; see Orwin, *The Humanity of Thucydides*, p. 146 n.

7. Connor, *Thucydides*, pp. 88–89, says that Diodotus misrepresented the facts in claiming that the common people of Mytilene did not support the revolt against Athens. The question is discussed in detail by Ste. Croix, *The Class Struggle in the Ancient Greek World*, pp. 603–4 n. 28, who argues convincingly that the populace of the city opposed the oligarchy and were in favor of the alliance with Athens.

8. Among the materials I have found helpful in discussing the Mytilene debate are Finley, *Thucydides*, pp. 170–78; Romilly, *Thucydides*

and Athenian Imperialism, pp. 156–67; Westlake, chap. 5; Marc Cogan, *The Human Thing: The Speeches and Principles of Thucydides'* History (Chicago: University of Chicago Press, 1981), pp. 50–65; Connor, pp. 79–91; Orwin, pp. 64–70. Hornblower's commentary on the speeches of Cleon and Diodotus, CT, vol. 1, pp. 410–28, contains many interesting observations.

9. Grote, p. 537.

10. Gomme comments, HCT, vol. 2, p. 206, that "Thucydides himself did not believe in the honesty" of Archidamus's proposals. Westlake states that "Archidamus uses spurious reasoning to justify decisions already taken on grounds of self-interest, and his air of moderation and piety is sheer hypocrisy" (p. 133).

11. Colin Macleod's article, "Thucydides' Plataean Debate," in *Collected Essays* (Oxford: Clarendon Press, 1983), contains a close analysis of the arguments on both sides in relation to the rhetorical strategies used by contemporary speakers in forensic oratory. Cogan, pp. 65–73; Connor, pp. 91–95; and Orwin, pp. 70–75, are among the authors who discuss the events and speeches at Plataea. See also some of the observations on the episode by Thucydides' editors: Gomme declares that the Athenian Cleon was the equal of the Spartan judges at Plataea "in ruthlessness . . . but not in deceit and dishonesty" (HCT, vol. 2, p. 356); Hornblower, CT, vol. 1, pp. 444–46, 462–63, offers interesting general comments and says that "the message of the Plataian Debate is that it would have made no difference if there had been no debate at all" (p. 462).

12. Some decades after Thucydides' death, Aristotle's *Politics* gave a penetrating account of the different forms of government and the nature and causes of revolution in the Greek city-states. Ste. Croix, *Class Struggle in the Ancient Greek World,* pp. 71–73, 283–85, contains a good concise discussion of oligarchy, democracy, and the conflict between them in classical Greece, which includes a summary of Aristotle's views.

13. In quoting from these two chapters, I have as usual followed Jowett's translation, but with some modifications. Because of their great importance, Gomme, who comments that Thucydides "was deeply moved when he wrote this analysis," offers his own translation of both chapters (HCT, vol. 2, pp. 383–85). Finley translates these chapters, pp. 184–87, which he describes as an instance of Thucydides' "desire and ability to rest his work on the lasting truths of men's social experience." See also the translation by Jonathan Price, *Thucydides and Internal War* (Cambridge: Cambridge University Press, 2001), pp. 8–11.

14. CT, vol. 1, p. 478.

15. I omit consideration of a further chapter on revolution in 3.84, which is printed in the text of Thucydides but which modern editors of the *History* regard as spurious and a later interpolation.

16. The present writer has discussed a number of theories of revolution in "Theories of Revolution in Contemporary Historiography" and "Prolegomena to the Comparative History of Revolution in Early Modern Europe," both reprinted in *Revolution: Critical Concepts in Political Science*, ed. Rosemary H. T. O'Kane, 4 vols. (London: Routledge, 2000), vols. 1–2; see also my *Rebels and Rulers, 1500–1660*, 2 vols. (Cambridge: Cambridge University Press, 1982), vol. 1, chap. 1.

17. Gomme, HCT, vol. 2, p. 374.

18. This is Hornblower's view, CT, vol. 1, p. 478.

19. In place of "noble," Crawley translates the passage as "the ancient simplicity into which *honor* so largely entered," as does Gomme: "that simplicity in which *a sense of honor* has so large a part," HCT, vol. 2, p. 380.

20. On Thucydides' analysis of revolution and its pathology in the events at Corcyra, see Cogan, pp. 149–54; Connor, pp. 95–105, who notes (p. 101) that "Revolutionary Newspeak" makes violence "seem simple and appropriate"; Orwin, pp. 175–82; Hornblower, CT, vol. 1, pp. 477–79; Price, chap. 1. Price's book seeks to show that Thucydides' model of *stasis* in dealing with the Corcyran revolution is applicable to the entire Peloponnesian War as a species of internal war. I have not been convinced by this argument, as it seems to me that Thucydides quite clearly distinguishes *stasis* or internal civil conflict from *polemos* or a conflict between states. .

21. See Kagan, *The Archidamian War*, p. 230, and Lewis, CAH, "The Archidamian War," p. 415.

22. See Kagan, *The Archidamian War*, p. 232, who also notes the general opinion of most modern scholars that the Athenians should have accepted the Spartan offer and that Pericles would have done so. Gomme comments, however, that the Spartans' peace offer was "nothing but a sermon" and lacked any quid pro quo (HCT, vol. 3, p. 454); cf. ibid., p. 459.

23. For discussions of the outcome of the Archidamian War and the peace of Nicias, see Kagan, *The Archidamian War*, pp. 345–48, and the comments and references in CT, vol. 2, pp. 470–71. Lewis, "The Archidamian War," states flatly that "Athens . . . won the war" (p. 432).

24. Meiggs, *The Athenian Empire*, p. 343.

CHAPTER 6
DIALOGUE AT MELOS, THE SICILIAN EXPEDITION

1. See Hammond, p. 383.

2. The third volume of Donald Kagan's history of the Peloponnesian War, *The Peace of Nicias and the Sicilian Expedition* (Ithaca: Cornell University Press, 1981), describes "The Unraveling of The Peace" in pt. 1,

which covers the course of events from 421 though the battle of Mantinea and its aftermath.

3. Romilly, *Thucydides and Athenian Imperialism*, p. 274.

4. This device of rapid one-line exchange between the characters in Greek tragedy was known as stichomythia; see OCD, s. v. "stichomythia"; on its use by Thucydides, see Hornblower, *Thucydides*, p. 117.

5. See the editorial comment by Anthony Andrewes, HCT, vol. 4, p. 182. Andrewes further suggests the possibility that since Thucydides tidied up his speeches and imposed his own style upon them, he might have imposed "some alien thoughts on his Athenian speakers" (p. 183).

6. Grote, *A History of Greece from the Time of Solon to 403* B.C., p. 702.

7. Ibid., pp. 702–3.

8. Andrewes reports Gomme's opinion, which was given to him personally, and his own dissent from it, in HCT, vol. 4, p. 187. He also notes that "theories of its [the dialogue's] meaning are at least as various as general theories about the historian himself" (p. 182).

9. Among the works I have found helpful in studying the Melian dialogue are Andrewes' wide editorial discussion in HCT, vol. 4, pp. 182–88, which stresses the importance of the dialogue "for any general estimates of [Thucydides'] attitude and purposes" (p. 182); Finley, *Thucydides*, pp. 208–12; Meiggs, *The Athenian Empire*, pp. 382–89; Romilly, pt. 3, chap. 2, which offers some penetrating observations; Cogan, *The Human Thing*, pp. 87–93; Colin Macleod's insightful treatment, "Form and Meaning in The Melian Dialogue," in *Collected Essays*; Connor, *Thucydides*, pp. 147–57; Orwin, *The Humanity of Thucydides*, chap. 5.

10. As a useful supplement and background to Thucydides' narrative of the Sicilian expedition, see Kagan, *The Peace of Nicias and the Sicilian Expedition*, pt. 2, and the concise survey by Anthony Andrewes in CAH, chap. 10. Connor's analysis, pp. 185–209, of Thucydides' account is also very interesting. The fullest modern treatment of the Sicilian expedition in English is Peter Green's *Armada from Athens* (Garden City, N.Y.: Doubleday, 1970), a vivid recounting of the events by a distinguished classical scholar who maintains that economic interests and motives, especially Athens' need for wheat and other natural resources, was the main reason for its attempt to conquer Sicily.

11. Macaulay, vol. 3, p. 154 (letter to Thomas Flower Ellis, 25 August 1835).

12. Westlake presents an analysis of the characters and conduct of Nicias and Alcibiades in *Individuals in Thucydides*, chaps. 6, 11, 12.

13. See Brunt, "Thucydides and Alcibiades," in *Studies in Greek History and Thought*.

14. On the mutilation of the Hermae and profanation of the mysteries, see Dover's detailed editorial commentary, HCT, vol. 4, pp. 264–86. Regarding the connection between these impieties and political conspiracy, he points out that Alcibiades was a notorious example of "those who conduct themselves as though they were above the law"; and that such irreligious acts "prompted in the Athenians the thought that a whole section of their society demonstrated that it had the will to do as it pleased" and would also demonstrate "the power to do so" if not resisted (p. 285).

15. For several examples of historians who have blamed Athens' defeat in Sicily on Nicias's weak and indecisive leadership, see Grote, pp. 806–7; Kagan, *The Peace of Nicias and the Sicilian Expedition*, pp. 354–72; Connor, pp. 200–201. Dover's editorial comments, HCT, vol. 4, pp. 419–21, point out the critical view which Thucydides took of Nicias's generalship.

CHAPTER 7
ENDINGS

1. The period covered in Thucydides' unfinished eighth book is dealt with in the modern accounts by Donald Kagan, *The Fall of the Athenian Empire* (Ithaca: Cornell University Press, 1987), the fourth and concluding volume of his history of the Peloponnesian War, chaps. 1–9, and Anthony Andrewes, CAH, chap. 11, "The Spartan Resurgence," pts. 1–4.

2. On the unfinished character of book 8, see Andrewes' editorial comments, HCT, vol. 5, pp. 4, 369–75.

3. See D. M. Lewis, CAH, chap. 9, "The Archidamian War," p. 422.

4. Thucydides also speaks of another high Persian official, the satrap Pharnabazus, whom he first mentions in 8.6, and who was likewise involved in negotiations with the Spartans against Athens, but whose role in this matter was much less prominent than that of Tissaphernes.

5. For the probable explanation of Persia's abandonment of its peace treaty with Athens, see Kagan, *Fall of the Athenian Empire*, p. 29.

6. Thucydides states that Lichas, a Spartan official, took exception to the two previous treaties with Persia because they allowed the Persian king to claim power over all the countries his ancestors had ruled. He protested that this sgreement would reduce large parts of Hellas to slavery "and so instead of giving the Hellenes freedom, the Lacedaemonians would be imposing upon them the yoke of Persia" (8.43). Yet the third treaty with Persia, of which Lichas was probably one of the negotiators, conceded Asia, including Greek cities to the king; see Kagan's comments on the treaties (*Fall of the Athenian Empire*, pp. 90–91).

7. The main ancient source for the report of adultery between Alcibiades and Agis's wife was Plutarch's life of Alcibiades; see the comment and references in HCT, vol. 5, p. 26.

8. On these Athenian clubs or associations and their diverse character, see Andrewes's editorial note, ibid., pp. 128–30.

9. Antiphon, a distinguished orator in Athens, has sometimes been identified with a sophist of the same name who wrote on such subjects as truth and the relationship between law or convention and nature; see OCD, s. v. "Antiphon (1)." Andrewes discusses Thucydides' attitude to Antiphon, whom he probably knew personally and whose pupil he may even have been, and explains his praise of the latter despite disapproving of his political extremism (HCT, vol. 5, pp. 170–72).

10. There has been considerable discussion of Thucydides' praise of the Five Thousand in this passage and in particular whether it refers to the constitution or to the way in which government was conducted; see Andrewes's references and comments; he argues in HCT, vol. 5, pp. 331–39, and in "The Spartan Resurgence," CAH, p. 480, that Thucydides had little interest in constitutional forms and that what he singled out for praise was the Five Thousand's conduct of affairs; Kagan, *Fall of the Athenian Empire*, p. 205 n, takes the opposite position that Thucydides' praise referred both to the constitution and to political matters and gave primacy to the former.

11. For the following very concise summary of the events of this period I have drawn mainly on Andrewes, "The Spartan Resurgence," pts. 5–6; Kagan, *Fall of the Athenian Empire*, chaps. 11–16; Hammond, chap. 5, pt. 5.

12. There was also a third continuation of Thucydides' *History* by the fourth-century historian Theopompus of Chios of which some fragments remain. On the work of these writers as continuers of Thucydides, see Lewis, chap. 1, "Sources, Chronology, Method," CAH, pp. 8–9; Andrewes, "The Spartan Resurgence," pp. 481–82; A. W. Gomme, "Thucydides and Fourth-Century Political Thought," in *More Essays in Greek History and Literature* (Oxford: Blackwell, 1962), pp. 126–28.

13. Xenophon, *Hellenica*, quoted in Andrewes, "The Spartan Resurgence," p. 496.

CHAPTER 8
THUCYDIDES AS A PHILOSOPHIC HISTORIAN

1. Aristotle, *Poetics*, 1451b5.

2. Jacqueline de Romilly's writings on Thucydides include valuable discussions of his rigorous objectivity, impartiality, and the place of generalization in his work; see her *Thucydides and Athenian Imperialism*, passim, and the essays in *Histoire et raison chez Thucydides* (Paris: Société d'Edition "Les Belles Lettres," 1956), and *La Construction de la verité chez Thucydides* (Paris: Julliard, 1990); see also Lowell Edmunds' perceptive

analysis of Thucydides' conception of the relation between the particular and the general and his concern with *to saphes*, "a clear, general view," in *Chance and Intelligence in Thucydides* (Cambridge, Mass.: Harvard University Press, 1975), pp. 155–63, and Adam Parry's remarks about the general and theoretical conceptions that inform Thucydides' work, in "The Language of Thucydides' Description of the Plague," in *The Language of Achilles and Other Papers*, p. 156. Leo Strauss has commented that Thucydides "lets us see the universal in the individual event" in *The City and Man*, p. 143. Thucydides' penchant for generalization is linked to his use of abstract concepts and his coinage of new abstract terms, on which see June Allison, *Word and Concept in Thucydides* (Atlanta: Scholars Press, 1997).

3. Many of the writings on Thucydides give some attention to his ideas. In thinking about his character as a philosophic historian, among the works I have found suggestive are Romilly, *Thucydides and Athenian Imperialism, Histoire et raison,* and *La Construction de la verité;* Adcock, *Thucydides and His History,* chap. 5; David Grene, *Greek Political Theory: The Image of Man in Thucydides and Plato* (Chicago: Phoenix Books, 1965), chaps. 6–8; Strauss; H.-P. Stahl, *Thucydides: Man's Place in History* (Swansea: Classical Press of Wales, 2000) [orig. pub. in German, 1966]; Connor, *Thucydides;* Brunt, "Introduction to Thucydides," in *Studies in Greek History and Thought;* Edmunds; Adam Parry, *Logos and Ergon in Thucydides* (New York: Arno Press, 1954), and "Thucydides' Historical Perspective," in *The Language of Achilles;* Hornblower, *Thucydides,* chaps. 5, 7, and passim.

4. On the Greek Enlightenment, see the discussion in chap. 1.

5. Solmsen, *Intellectual Experiments of the Greek Enlightenment,* pp. 4, 5.

6. Gregory Crane, *Thucydides and the Ancient Simplicity: The Limits of Political Realism* (Berkeley: University of California Press, 1998), p. 4; see also the analysis of Thucydides' realism in. chap. 2.

7. Thomas Hobbes, *The History of the Grecian War by Thucydides,* in *English Works,* 11 vols., ed. Sir William Molesworth (London, 1843), vol. 8, "To The Readers," p. viii.

8. Friedrich Nietzsche, *Twilight of the Idols* in *The Portable Nietzsche,* ed. Walter Kaufmann (New York: Viking Press, 1954), pp. 558–59. Nietzsche's hatred of Plato was part of his hatred of Christianity, of which he considered Plato's philosophy to be a forerunner; see ibid., pp. 557–58.

9. Paul Shorey, "On the Implicit Ethics and Psychology of Thucydides," *Transactions of the American Philological Association,* vol. 24 (1893), pp. 66–88.

10. See Grene's comments on Shorey's essay in *Greek Political Theory,* pp. 224–27.

11. Jaeger, *Paideia: The Ideals of Greek Culture*, p. 386. See also A. Geoffrey Woodhead, *Thucydides and the Nature of Power* (Cambridge, Mass.: Harvard University Press, 1970), which contains an interesting treatment of Thucydides' conception of power.

12. For the relationship of Thucydides to the modern and contemporary "realist" conception of international politics, see Robert Gilpin, "Peloponnesian War and Cold War," and the other essays in *Hegemonic Rivalry from Thucydides to the Nuclear Age*, ed. Lebow and Strauss; the introduction and the essays by various authors in *Thucydides' Theory of International Relations*, ed. Lowell S. Gustafson (Baton Rouge: Louisiana State University Press, 2000), in particular Laurie M. Johnson Bagby, "Fathers of International Relations? Thucydides as a Model for the Twenty-First Century," and Stephen Forde, "Power and Morality in Thucydides." In *Thucydides, Hobbes, and the Interpretation of Realism* (DeKalb: Northern Illinois University Press, 1993), Laurie M. Johnson examines the realist position in contemporary political science and its conception of Thucydides, and argues that it is reductive and fails to do justice to the historian's point of view.

13. In his relation of the massacre at Mycalessus, Thucydides also tells how the Thebans, when they heard the news, hastened to the rescue. They pursued and attacked the Thracians, cutting off many of the latter in Mycalessus itself and killing 250 of them out of about 1,300 (7.30). So there was some retribution for the Thracians' actions.

14. Konnilyn G. Feig, *Hitler's Death Camps: The Sanity of Madness* (New York: Holmes and Meier, 1981), p. 337, quoted in Robert Jan van Pelt, "Of Shells and Shadows: A Memoir on Auschwitz," *Transactions of the Royal Historical Society*, 6th ser., vol. 13 (2003), pp. 378–79.

15. Although the myth of Pandora relates how the jar she opened released all kinds of evils upon the earth, Greek moral philosophy seems to have had no generalized conception of evil. This is one of the conclusions I draw from A.W.H. Adkins's excellent study of Greek moral thought and values, *Merit and Responsibility* (Chicago: University of Chicago Press, 1975); see chap. 9 on "*Agathos* and *Kakos*." The Old Testament's Book of Job first broached the question of why God permitted the existence of undeserved suffering, and, by implication, of evil. The conception of evil in the sense in which I refer to it above appeared in Western thought only after the emergence and establishment of Christianity. Christianity traced the origin of evil in mankind to the sin of Adam and Eve in their disobedience to God, and personified evil in the figure of Satan and his diabolical actions in the world. It was Christianity that compelled theologians, philosophers, and historians to grapple with the problem, which remained insoluble, of how evil could exist in a world created by an omniscient, omnipotent, just, good, and compassionate God.

Thucydides, whose religion, if any, is unknown to us, would probably not have been able to conceive of this problem.

16. See above, chap. 1.

17. Quoted in George Sarton, *A History of Science: Ancient Science through the Golden Age of Greece* (Cambridge, Mass.: Harvard University Press, 1952), p. 355.

18. HCT, vol. 1, p. 151.

19. Andrewes, who discusses Thucydides' attitude to empire in connection with his editorial comments on the Melian dialogue, believes that the historian's "feeling that the power of Athens was somehow admirable seems ... beyond question" (HCT, vol. 4, p. 186), and see also p. 184. Hornblower, *Thucydides*, pp. 176–77, argues for a more qualified view.

20. It is worth noting that this statement by Thucydides was the source of the famous and much quoted declaration by the famous nineteenth-century German historian Leopold von Ranke that his sole aim as a historian was "to show what actually happened"; quoted from his *Histories of the Latin and Germanic Nations 1494–1514* (1824), in *The Varieties of History*, ed. Fritz Stern (Cleveland: Meridian Books, 1956), p. 57.

21. Jowett's rendering of this passage is unsatisfactory and I have here adopted Smith's version in the Loeb Classics edition of Thucydides.

22. Stahl, p. 19; see also Stahl's comments on Thucydides' historical practice in chap. 2.

23. June Allison, *Word and Concept in Thucydides*, pp. 206–37, discusses Thucydides' use of the word *aletheia*, truth, which occurs eleven times in his work. She points out that in most instances he means by it, "what is the case," "what has happened," or "reality" (p. 211). She also notes its relationship to the concept *saphes*, meaning clear or true, which characterizes *logoi*, words or thoughts, only when Thucydides determines that they are true (p. 192).

24. This was the thesis of Cochrane's *Thucydides and the Science of History*, which associated Thucydides' approach to history with the influence of Hippocratic medicine.

25. See W. R. Connor, "A Postmodernist Thucydides?" *Classical Journal*, vol. 72, no. 4 (1977), pp. 289–98, and the literature there cited.

26. Connor, *Thucydides*, p. 6, and see also pp. 7–8. I am unable to see the coherence of the proposition endorsed by Connor that "objectivity is an impossible goal for the historian but a legitimate means by which the reader can be helped to an understanding of the events narrated" (p. 8).

27. I have discussed the concept of objectivity and its history and meaning in an essay on the seventeenth-century philosopher Francis Bacon, one of the first thinkers to reflect on the subject; see my "Francis Bacon's Concept of Objectivity and the Idols of the Mind," *British Journal of the*

History of Science, vol. 34, no. 2 (2001), pp. 374–93. Bacon went to the core of the problem of objectivity when he wrote in his *Novum Organum*: "The human understanding is no dry light, but receives an infusion from the will and affections: whence proceed sciences which may be called 'wishful sciences.' For what a man had rather were true he readily believes"; quoted in Perez Zagorin, *Francis Bacon* (Princeton: Princeton University Press, 1998), pp. v, 83.

28. Donald Davidson, "The Problem of Objectivity," in *Problems of Rationality* (Oxford: Clarendon Press, 2004), p. 10.

29. Stahl, p. 21, who is here quoting G. F. Abbott, *Thucydides: A Study in Historical Reality* (1925).

30. On the tragic aspects and tragic character of Thucydides' *History*, see., e.g., the discussion in Colin Macleod, "Thucydides and Tragedy," in *Collected Essays*; Adam M. Parry, "Thucydides' Historical Perspective"; Henry R. Immerwahr, "Historiography," in *The Cambridge History of Classical Literature*, vol. 1, *Greek Literature*, ed. Easterling and Knox, pp. 447–48; Hornblower, *Thucydides*, p. 175.

31. On the importance of this word for Thucydides, see Edmunds. Dennis Proctor, in *The Experience of Thucydides* (Warminster: Aris and Philips, 1980), p. 5, cites Pierre Huart, *Le Vocabulaire de l'analyse psychologique dans l'oeuvre de Thucydides* (1968), and Gnome *chez Thucydides et ses contemporains* (1973), who states that *gnome* is the key word in Thucydides' thought and occurs 174 times in the *History*.

32. See the remarks of Ronald Syme, "Thucydides," in *Roman Papers*, vol. 6 (Oxford: Clarendon Press, 1991), p. 86. This essay by a great ancient historian, which originated as a British Academy lecture on a master mind, is an excellent appreciation of Thucydides.

33. Ste. Croix, *The Origins of the Peloponnesian War*, p. 25; see also the excellent comments on this subject on p. 31.

34. See ibid., p. 31 and n. 57, and Edmunds, pp. 176–88.

35. I have here adopted Ste. Croix's translation, p. 31.

36. On Thucydides' conception of necessity, see the discussion in Grene, chap. 6; Martin Ostwald, Ananke *in Thucydides* (Atlanta: Scholars Press, 1988); Brunt, pp. 156–57; Rood, *Thucydides: Narrative and Explanation*, p. 212; Strauss's treatment of the subject, pp. 182–92, is not much to the point.

37. Rood, p. 283.

38. See Parry, *Logos and Ergon*, pp. 109–11.

39. Stahl, p. 218; Connor, *Thucydides*, p. 246.

40. Note Rawlings's comment on Thucydides' view of the utility of his *History*: "A careful study of the past will not allow one to predict the future, but it will enable one to interpret the future more wisely"; Hunter

R. Rawlings III, *The Structure of Thucydides'* History (Princeton: Princeton University Press, 1981), p. 255.

41. Jacob Burckhardt, *Weltgeschichtliche Betrachtungen* (Leipzig, 1935), p. 10, quoted in P. O. Kristeller, *The Classics and Renaissance Thought* (Cambridge, Mass.: Harvard University Press. 1955), p. 90.

42. Connor, *Thucydides*, p. 247.

Further Reading

The following is a short list of some general studies of Thucydides which present different views and perspectives on his work as a historian and thinker.

Adcock, F. E. *Thucydides and His History*. Cambridge: Cambridge University Press, 1963.

Cochrane, C. N. *Thucydides and the Science of History*. London: Humphrey Milford, 1929.

Connor, W. Robert. *Thucydides*. Princeton: Princeton University Press, 1984.

Cornford, F. M. *Thucydides Mythistoricus*. London: Edward Arnold, 1907.

Dover, K. J. *Thucydides*. Oxford: Clarendon Press, 1973.

Hornblower, Simon. *Thucydides*. Baltimore: Johns Hopkins University Press, 2000.

Orwin, Clifford. *The Humanity of Thucydides*. Princeton: Princeton University Press, 1994.

Romilly, Jacqueline de. *Thucydides and Athenian Imperialism*. Oxford: Basil Blackwell, 1963.

Stahl, H.-P. *Thucydides: Man's Place in History*. Swansea: Classical Press of Wales, 2003.

Index

Adcock, F. E., 38
Aegina, 12
Aegospotami, battle of, 138
Aeschylus, 20
Agamemnon, 28
Agis, 101, 116, 129, 135, 138
Alcibiades, 34, 38, 59, 100, 109, 110, 111, 112, 113, 122, 127, 128–129, 130, 131, 132–33
Amphipolis, 59, 80, 98, 99
Anaxagoras, 20, 60, 147
Andrewes, A., 107
Antiphon, 132, 135
arbitration, 49, 54, 56
Archaeologia, 26, 28–29, 30, 152
Archidamian War, 36, 100, 102
Archidamus, 34, 36, 51, 58, 63, 75, 85–86
Arginusae Islands, battle of, 137
Argos, 34, 77, 100, 101
Aristotle, 42, 93, 139
Aspasia, 61
Athena, 14
Athenagoras, 112
Athens: characteristic traits of its people, 14; citizens of, 11; compared with Sparta, 141–142; democracy in, 10, 52; empire of, 13–14, 46, 47, 48, 49–50, 51, 52, 54; equality before the law in, 11; government of, 11; intellectual developments in, 19–20; liberty in, 11; population of, 11; revolution in, 129–130, 131–135, 136; as sea power, 12
Auschwitz-Birkenau, 146

Badian, E., 170 n.24
Brasidas, 59, 98
Brunt, P. A., 4, 52
Burckhardt, Jacob, 3, 4, 161
Burke, Edmund, 93
Byzantium, 136

calendar, 35–36
Callias, 48
Callicles, 106
Camarina, 114
Carr, E. H., 144
Catana, 113, 119, 121, 122
causality, 41–42
chance, 157–58
Chios, 13, 29, 128–29, 149
Cimon, 60
class conflict, 9
Clausewitz, Carl von, 24
Cleisthenes, 10
Cleon, 58, 59, 80–83, 87, 96, 97, 98, 145, 149
clubs, political, 130, 131
Connor, W. Robert, 153–54, 160–61
Conon, 137
Corcyra, 36, 41, 44, 45, 54, 55, 78, 89–95
Corinth, 12, 41, 44, 45, 49, 51, 53, 54, 55, 89, 98, 100, 138, 140
Cornford, F. M., 42
Crawley, Richard, 4, 30, 41, 46
Croesus, 16, 17
Cynossema, battle of, 127, 135
Cyprus, 48
Cyrus, 17, 136, 137
Cyzicus, battle of, 136

Darius, 127, 128, 136
Davidson, Donald, 155
Decelea, 113, 116, 135, 138
Delian League, 13
Delium, 77
Democritus, 17, 20, 47
Demosthenes, 59, 95, 116, 117, 118, 120, 121, 122
Diodotus, 82–83, 149, 157
Dionysius of Halicarnassus, 31
Dover, K. J., 33